BrainStormer

Dealing logically, ethically, and efficiently with the mentally vulnerable and those with addictive tendencies

What is wrong with the criminal justice system and how to fix it

By Cindy Stormer J.D.

William Collins Publishing
8 Park Street,
Market Bosworth,
Nuneaton,
Warwickshire,
CV13 0LL
United Kingdom

Rev. 1, 1/16

For anyone finding themselves in the criminal justice system or wanting to stay out of it, keep a loved one out of it, or make their community a better place to live, this is a one-source, go-to guide and toolkit. "All rise" is the mantra of the drug courts. A rising tide raises all ships. The rising tide of using best practices in the criminal justice system in all cases will eventually improve our world, communities, and families.

Fresh out of law school and having been a police officer and in police work for ten years, I was once (possibly) the most hard-core, hard-nosed prosecutor in the Tarrant County District Attorney's office in Fort Worth, Texas (in the four years there, never dismissing a single case). I now consider that to be irresponsible (but those were different times). As a police officer I had seen so many criminals get away with their crimes, I wasn't about to let one slip through my prosecutorial fingers. There was that "you may beat the rap but you won't beat the ride" mentality. With all the safeguards that were in place, how could someone be wrongfully convicted? Coming to work for the Dallas District Attorney's Office and have an opportunity to work on exonerations and being involved in the science of DNA changed my opinion about what we can do in the criminal justice system to improve it.

After studying the science-based and evidence based procedures and protocols for years I have become one of the biggest "hug a thug", "Kumbaya Court" prosecutors - possibly in the State. I have come to realize and have great empathy for those who suffer from addiction and mental illness

I now realize that they could no more stop drinking or stop using drugs than many of us could stop breathing. In fact, withdrawal from a drug can result in death in some cases. While they may have voluntarily taken that first drug or drank those first drinks, many times the drug will hijack the person's brain and they're not able to stop. It takes over their prefrontal cortex: judgment and reasoning.

Drug addiction is like the creature from the movie Alien, or a really bad ex-spouse-a parasitic host that will not let go of its prey. It seems so harmless and seductive in the beginning, but it can take over your life (your job, your finances, your joy . . .), changes that can kill you. Addiction is not simply a matter of willpower, it includes an element of brain damage.

Forty years experience working in every aspect of the criminal justice field from police dispatcher, to patrol officer, to prosecutor, to defense attorney, and an educator along the way hopefully gives me a perspective to share with others.

Herein is science and evidence based practices that should be followed by professionals in the criminal justice system that truly seek justice and a guide for those outside the system. While mental illness is not an excuse for crime, it is a management opportunity to reduce recidivism (prevent crime), help families, and improve our world. Each chapter is self-contained. If you sense that a chapter does not pertain to you, feel free to skip it.

FORWARD

Cindy Stormer

"BrainStormer is a needed book that has a blueprint to change the failed 100 year war on drugs. Our nation has spent one trillion dollars on this war. The result is prisons are full, left behind destroyed families, and no cures for addicts. Judges, prosecutors, defense lawyers, police officers, citizens, drug rehab centers, can benefit from this book. We must start doing the right thing by understanding that drug addiction for the most part is a medical problem versus being a total law enforcement responsibility. Cindy Stormer the author of Brainstormer has given the nation a new highway to take to finally solve our drug addiction problem."

Bob Massey,
Minister and Christian Book author.

"Finally someone has put all the basic information needed to improve the criminal justice system (as it pertains to the mentally ill and those suffering from substance abuse) in one convenient, well drafted resource. Every parent, judge, prosecutor, attorney, service provider, counselor, doctor, probation officer, teacher, family member, clergy, and concerned citizen should have this book."

Judge Dominique Collins
Criminal District Court Number Four
Dallas, Texas

"Stormer has accumulated multi-perspective first hand experiences, enabling her to write a detailed reference for professionals, a reassuring guide for the rest of us."

Larry Mayfield,
Author/composer A Whisper's Shadow Apart

ABOUT THE AUTHOR

Cindy Stormer is the author of *Texas Small Firm Practice Tools*, a best-selling law book by James Publishing. Stormer previously served as the Chief of the Mental Health Division of the Dallas District Attorney's Office (where for many years she handled thousands of cases involving mentally ill defendants). She also served as DNA Attorney for Dallas County's internationally famous Conviction Integrity Unit---responsible for exonerating more than thirty wrongfully convicted men. A documentary in real time chronicles the efforts there in 2009 and can be seen on the Discovery Channel (among other places) – *Dallas DNA*. She was formerly the Elected District Attorney, Cooke County, Texas. She was an attorney in private practice for fifteen years, the former Chief Attorney for the Dallas Police Department, a former Assistant District Attorney in Fort Worth, Texas.

Stormer is a former police officer with ten years experience in police work. She was selected as Attorney Ad Litem of the Year, by CASA (Court Appointed Special Advocates) of North Texas, Inc. for her representation of abused and neglected children in court. She has made presentations at the Advanced Criminal Law course for the State Bar of Texas; the Center for American and International Law regarding Conviction Integrity; the American Bar Committee for Indigent Defense. She taught Legal Ethics for the first legal delegation from the United States allowed into Lhasa, Tibet. She has taught for the Texas District and County Attorney's Association; and numerous police academies.

She has had numerous publications. Her appellate experience includes the United States Supreme Court; United States District Courts; Courts of Appeals in Texas: Second (Fort Worth); Fourth (San Antonio); Fifth (Dallas); Sixth (Texarkana); Seventh (Amarillo); Eighth (El Paso); Ninth (Beaumont); Tenth (Waco); and Eleventh (Eastland).

She was the Founder and Former Director of the Texas Association for Women Police; State Coordinator International Association of Women Police.

She has been an Adjunct Professor, North Central Texas

College in Gainesville, Texas, and Tarrant County Junior College (where she received the Distinguished Alumni award) teaching: United States Government; American State and Local Government; Family Law; Probate, Trusts and Estates; Torts; Civil Litigation-Texas Trial Practices; English as a Second Language, Legal Research; Legal Writing; Criminal Procedure and Evidence.

She currently the Chief of the Administrative Division (which includes supervision of several divisions including the Mental Health Division, over one-hundred and fifty employees, and a budget of over forty-five million dollars) of the Dallas District Attorney's Office.

DEDICATION

To my beautiful daughter Stacy.
And to all those hard working, courageous professionals in
specialty courts and elsewhere saving one life at a time.

TABLE OF CONTENTS

CHAPTER ONE
INTRODUCTION-JAILS HAVE BECOME THE NEW MENTAL INSTITUTIONS

"Injustice anywhere is a threat to justice everywhere"
Martin Luther King

Breaking habits by original thinking and creativity can solve about any problem. We can reduce crime, reduce homelessness, save money, improve public safety, and downsize prisons by applying science to the criminal justice system.

Imagine a future world where persons who commit offenses are instantly incapacitated after their crime by the police with no harm to anyone. The perpetrators are immediately brought before an individual in the role of the prosecutor/Judge/defender - let's call them a "Tribuanlist." This is a highly skilled professional who examines the perpetrator. A SPECT scan (brain scan) is conducted, and the criminal and medical history is reviewed (available instantaneously and in precise form). An analysis is made; DNA[1] is tweaked; restitution is determined; and after a scan of the perpetrators retina funds are transferred from the perpetrator's account into that of the complaining witness.

Instead of prosecutors trying to make a name for themselves with big verdicts (a direct cause of some wrongful convictions), they would make a name for themselves by recidivism success rates.

No incarceration, no drama, just swift justice. They are evaluated by professionals, treated for their defective behaviors,

---

[1] DNA (deoxyribonucleic acid) is an organic molecule that is found in all living cells. See *Kelly v. State*, 824 S.W.2d 568, 569 n.1 (Tex.Crim.App. 1992)

7

"fixed," and released back into the community as better, more productive individuals (as opposed to being warehoused, at tremendous financial drain on society, with violent offenders where they are abused and learn how to commit more crimes, and then released as hardened criminals).

And look even further into the future where we are able to prevent crime before it happens by DNA manipulation. Science has already advanced to the point of taking genetic abnormalities that result in some diseases out of the DNA of embryos before they are born. Leaving our free will, personalities, and everything that makes us who we are intact, but tweaking out those sociopathic, psychotic, schizophrenic, bipolar, etc. tendencies. TomorrowLand.

If this sounds unattainable, think of how far we have come since 1692 where twenty women were executed by the State in Massachusetts for being witches. Brutally tortured, hanged, pressed to death right here in America four hundred years ago. Or consider the Great Hangings at Gainesville, Texas where forty suspected Unionists were hanged by the State in 1862 during the American Civil War. Two additional suspects (doctors who saw the results of the hasty executions) were shot while trying to escape. It was alleged to be the largest mass hanging in the history of the United States.[2] Just one-hundred and fifty years ago, martial law was imposed, a grand jury was convened, no real trials were held, and indictments were handed out for executions to appease the masses. Between 1941 and 1945, six million people were targeted and methodically murdered by the State in the largest genocide of the 20th century – the Holocaust. Those deaths included horrific tortures by the State including medical experiments. Yes, we have indeed come a long way, but we have so much further to go.

There have been dramatic improvements in the criminal justice system in recent years. With the DNA exonerations we had

---

[2] McCaslin, Richard B., *Tainted Breeze, The Great Hangings of Gainesville, Texas* (1997).

a unique, good fortune to look through a rapidly closing window of opportunity, information and knowledge. This window is rapidly closing because in all cases in the future where there is DNA to test - it should be tested. Those cases in the past where DNA was not tested and we learned years later that the wrong person was convicted, gave us a unique learning opportunity. Those exonerees did not suffer wrongful imprisonment in vain. From those exonerations we learned that eye-witness identification was not the gold standard that we once thought it was. We learned why and how false confessions can be coerced. We learned how sloppy police work and tunnel vision can lead to disastrous results. We learned that there were some bad prosecutors that withheld exculpatory evidence. We learned that a judge was capable of withholding exculpatory evidence from a jury. The State destroyed these men and women's lives, locking them up for decades then releasing them to a world in which they had no connections. The State (we taxpayers) must now pay for those mistakes. In Texas, each exoneree receives eighty thousand dollars for each year they were in prison and eighty thousand per year for the rest of their life with free health care. Wow – is right – and yet it is such a small price to pay for the damage caused.

The issues are complex and the only way to solve the problems and arrive where we need to be is through collaboration, coordination, brainstorming. We learned this with the exonerations. No one person was ever responsible for the outcomes; it required many people from different disciplines and professions (defense attorneys, prosecutors, judges, scientists, students, law enforcement, nutritionists, psychiatrists, medical doctors, pharmacists, family members, loved ones, witnesses, social workers, etc.) all working in unison for a common goal.

There are risk alleles (a portion of a gene that is located at a specific position on a specific chromosome, useful in DNA codings) associated with schizophrenia, bipolar disorder, depression, and autism spectrum.[3] Epigenesis is the process by which plants, animals and fungi develop from a seed, spore or egg through a sequence of steps in which cells differentiate and organs form. Aristotle was the originator of this theory in his book *On the Generation of Animals*. Epigenesists believe that what our ancestors were subjected to affects their descendants DNA. What a woman is subject to during pregnancy, e.g. stress can affect the development of her offspring and descendants.

Texas leads the world in death penalty cases and exonerations. Sounds like a conflict. And we are now leading the world on dealing intelligently with the mentally ill and drug addicts in the criminal justice system, at least in the urban areas, but we all have a very long way to go.

Today, science is regularly used to solve crimes. Increasingly precise forensic evidence, including but not limited to DNA, is used to solve cases that have turned cold and exonerate the innocent in wrongful convictions.

It is often said that it costs more to send a person to the penitentiary than it costs to send them to Harvard. It costs three times as much to send the mentally ill to prison. One in twelve adults in America suffers from alcohol abuse and an estimated forty-eight million people, aged twelve and older, used an illegal drug or were involved in non-medical use or abuse of prescription drugs in the past thirty days. It is probable that someone you love has been affected by substance abuse. Eighty percent of adult offenders have some level of substance involvement.[4] And those are the ones most likely to continue committing criminal acts.

Invariably when giving a talk of substance abuse to

---

[3] The American Psychiatric Association Diagnostic and Statistical Manual of Mental Disorders, Fifth Edition (2013) p 103.

[4] Such offenders may have been charged with a drug or alcohol offense, intoxicated at the time of offense, reported commiting their offense to support a drug habit or had a significant history of substance abuse treatment. *The Drug Court Judicial Benchbook* National Association of Drug Court Professionals (2011) P. 65.

citizens, prosecutors, defense attorneys, law enforcement, etc. and starting the talk with a request that everyone stand that has a mental illness or knows someone who has one, approximately ninety-nine percent of the people in the room stand. Mental illness affects us all.

Millions of Americans are in long term substance abuse recovery. Two thirds of all American families are affected by addiction. It is our black plague. Five hundred and fifty billion dollars was the cost to the United States in 2013. Texas, on the other hand, has closed prisons due to the work of drug courts and implementation of evidence based, scientifically backed protocols. Many methods that have been used in the past have been proven ineffective and caused more damage to individuals. For example, consequences must be immediate and not unduly harsh.

We spend eighty-three billion dollars each year on corrections in the United States (federal, State, local governments in 2013). One half of all Federal inmates are incarcerated for drug crimes (it was estimated as high as eighty percent in the 1980s). The Federal prison population has doubled since 1994. We spend fifteen billion per year keeping the mentally ill in jail in the United States, seventy percent are non-violent. Ninety-eight percent of people with a mental illness in society are not violent. A day in jail or prison can cost between five and twenty times more than a day on probation or in community-based treatment.[5]

New York has implemented a drug court in every county in the State. In a three year study, the New York State Court System estimates that $254 million in incarceration costs were saved by diverting 18,000 drug offenders into drug court. Texas is following suit, with Texas' Governor bragging on talk shows that we have closed down prisons with these methods saying "nothing is more conservative than that."

---

[5] Belenko, S. Patapis, N., & French, M.T., *Economic benefits of drug treatment: A critical review of the evidence for policy makers.* Philadelphia: Treatment Research Institute (2005).

The United States ranks number one in the world in the number of persons suffering from mental illness. The United States also ranks number one with the largest number of untreated cases of mental illness.[6] The United States mental health system fails to reach and/or adequately treat the millions of Americans suffering from mental illness and substance abuse. Jails have become the de facto mental institutions. One half of all youth in justice system have a diagnosable mental illness or substance use disorder with the majority experiencing both.

Each of us is just a car crash, an elevator fall, or a slip away from being a different person. Freud said we are all mentally ill to some degree.[7]

In the criminal justice system we seem to be suffering from a Common Sense Deficit Disorder[8] when it comes to dealing with substance abusers and the mentally ill.

In Texas, a mentally ill person is eight times more likely to be incarcerated than to find help in a psychiatric hospital.[9] Outside of the criminal justice system, civil commitments require that a mentally ill person must be a danger to themselves or others before there can be any intervention, and many times that is too late. Mental illness alone cannot justify confinement. It is unconstitutional to confine a mentally ill person when there is no danger to others and that mentally ill person can live safely in freedom. As long as the mentally ill person is a non-dangerous individual "who is capable of surviving safely in freedom by himself or with the help of willing and responsible family members

------

[6] Final Report Of The Miami-Dade County Grand Jury, In The Circuit Court Of The Eleventh Judicial Circuit Of Florida In And For The County Of Miami-Dade Spring Term A.D. 2004.
[7] Nassir Ghaemi, *A First Rate Madness* (2011) p. 257.
[8] A term coined by Psychologist/Attorney David Bunger.
[9] Mentally ill prisoners outnumber the mentally ill in psychiatric institutions seven to one. Dallas Observer 1/13/11, Eight times more in Dallas per Dallas Sheriff Lupe Valdez at the *Mental Illness and the Search for Solutions Symposium* held in Dallas 2/5/13.

or friends", a State cannot constitutionally confine that individual.[10] To receive court-ordered treatment, the person must be experiencing some sort of behavioral crisis that presents an acute danger. This is the balance between the State's right to protect the people and the mentally ill person's constitutional right to liberty.

One in five Americans has some type of mental disorder in any given year, and 16-20% of the jail and prison population has a significant mental illness[11]. According to the National Institute of Health, forty-nine percent of the United States' population will suffer from a psychiatric illness at some point in their lives. Two-thirds of admissions to juvenile detention or corrections meet diagnostic criteria for one or more mental disorders.[12] [13]

The best thing that can be done regarding mental illness is to build a healthy family; the best way we can help with that is to build a healthy community. The best way to build a health community is to not destroy the most fragile citizens among us that are doing the best they can with what they have.

Mental illness can be its own punishment. Being mentally ill carries its own life sentence. Jail is devastating for the mentally ill. Prison should be to punish and deter, not to warehouse sick people. We do not blame someone with high blood pressure or asthma for the biological malfunction happening in their bodies. We certainly don't shame them when they have acute flare-ups of their illness. Why is it different for the meth addict? What is

---

[10] *O'Connor v. Donaldson*, 422 US 563, 575 (1975).
[11] *Mental Illness, Your Client and the Criminal Law*, Texas Tech University School of Law (2005).
[12] Teplin, L., Abram, K., McClelland, G., Dulcan, M., & Mericle, A., (2002) *Psychiatric disorders in youth in juvenile detention. Archives of General Psychiatry,* 59, 1133-1143.
[13] Wasserman, G., McReynolds, L., Lucas, C., Fisher, P., & Santos, L. (2002). The Voice DISC-IV with incarcerated male youths: Prevalence of disorder. *Journal of the American Academy of Child and Adolescent Psychiatry,* 41, 314-321.

relapse but an acute flare-up of an addiction/illness?

Mental illness is a medical illness like any other physical illness. "Mental illness is not like being pregnant - you either are or you are not- it's more like hypertension, or diabetes or heart disease, all of which involve gradations of abnormality leading, in extreme cases, to specific events like a stroke, coma, or heart attack."[14] Proper treatment is necessary to achieve recovery. Likewise with substance abuse (which is a mental illness listed in the Diagnostic and Statistical Manual of Mental Disorders, hereinafter referred to as the DSM5[15]), if you or a loved one were diagnosed with cancer, you would go to any lengths to get the appropriate treatment. Addiction can be no less toxic or life threatening to a family. Just like cancer, one needs medication, counseling, therapy, exercise, proper nutrition, etc. to overcome the disease.

Drug cases should be on a different track than other criminal offenses. Treat the sick, incarcerate the criminal. An alcoholic or addict cannot be punished out of their dependence.

Reduction in Services

The cause of the burgeoning number of prison inmates with mental illness in recent decades appears to be linked to the falling number of state funded psychiatric beds (90%) since the 1960's. Treatment before that time was barbaric and archaic and included isolation, insulin-induced comas, cold baths with ice, shock therapy, lobotomies, and other atrocities. Such beds were supposed to be replaced with a more humane system of community mental health centers, which never materialized due to lack of funding. Prisons are now the largest mental health providers in the United States. According to a 2013 article in *USA Today*, psychiatric beds

---

[14] Nassir Ghaemi, *A First Rate Madness* (2011) p.258.
[15] The American Psychiatric Association Diagnostic and Statistical Manual of Mental Disorders, Fifth Edition (2013).

in the United States have dwindled back to the per-capita level of 1850, and those services have not been replaced with sufficient community-based treatment services. At Terrell (State Hospital for the mentally ill), in 1900, 2300 individuals were housed there; in 1960, 3000 were housed there; as of February 2013 a mere 316 mentally ill persons were housed there. Of that number only thirty beds are dedicated to forensic i.e. restoration of competency in criminal cases. There are several large empty buildings on the campus that are boarded up and no longer used.

The three largest de facto psychiatric hospitals in the United States are the Cook County Jail (Chicago), the Los Angeles County Jail in California and the Rikers Island Jail in New York City. The Miami-Dade Florida prison, however, has a higher percentage of mentally ill due to the influx of mentally ill from Castro's Cuba in the 1960's. Pete Earley's Pulitzer Prize winning book, *Crazy A Father's Search through America's Mental Health Madness* (2006) has an excellent summary of the history of the treatment of the mentally ill in asylums and prisons.

The brain is where violence, war, and terrorism originates. A better understanding of neuroscience is critical to improving the criminal justice system and society.

Today we use science/DNA to prove that people were wrongfully convicted (i.e. did not commit the crimes for which they spent decades in prison). Many mentally ill are also wrongfully charged, i.e. neighbors don't want them in the neighborhood and make false accusations, step-parents don't want the children in the home and make false accusations, health care workers are accused of abuse and make false claims against these mentally vulnerable people. We can start with the easier, non-violent cases e.g. low level drug cases, prostitution cases, etc. and see what we discovered about changing behavior. And then we can move on to the more serious crimes.

CHAPTER TWO

THE SOLUTIONS-STARTING WITH THE CRIMINAL JUSTICE SYSTEM

"Liberty lies in the hearts of men and women, when it dies there, no Constitution, no law can save it."
Judge Learned Hand

We must separate those we are just mad at from those of whom we are afraid. An alcoholic or addict cannot be punished out of their dependence.

As with any problem we must first identify the source. Research suggests that four key factors are associated with criminal offending and recidivism:

- An established history of benefitting from criminal activity;
- A social environment that encourages and tolerates crime and criminals;
- Personal attitudes and values supportive of criminal behavior; and
- A personality style that finds impulsive, high risk behavior rewarding.[16]

Addiction is the #1 most diagnosed mental illness in children in the United States today. Brain science will improve the legal system, not impede its function. The emphasis must shift

---

[16] Alison MacPhail and Simon Verdun-Jones, *Mental Illness and the Criminal Justice System* International Centre for Criminal law Reform and Criminal Justice Policy (2013) and studies cited therein.

from punishment toward recognizing problems and meaningfully addressing them. Rather than continuing to send more Texans to prison, we must take action to institute evidence based responses that combine accountability and extensive treatment. As a result, drug courts abound throughout Texas, changing lives, cutting crime and saving money. Tens of thousands of lives have been saved, families have been restored, and taxpayers have been spared the burden of building new prisons.

Evidence based practices means that there is a definable outcome; it is measurable and it is defined according to practical realities (recidivism, victim satisfaction, etc.) The interventions are effective as they reduce offender risk and subsequent recidivism, therefore making a positive long-term contribution to public safety.

Holistic[17] solutions provide better outcomes of the defendant and society.

Win/win situations occur when the persons involved focus on each person's needs (not the solutions). Creative thinkers generate more alternatives, challenge assumptions, make analogies, see things as their opposite, find the dominant ideal, brainstorm, and suspend judgment.[18] To get different results we must put information together differently. New and better ideas are always at the heart of progress. We keep digging the hole deeper when we should be digging the hole in a different place. Answers, like life, are not black and white, but gray like the soft gray matter within the skull.

In Malcolm Gladwell's book *The Tipping Point*,[19] he gives example after example of how small acts can be the catalyst for big change, like cleaning up the subways in New York resulted in a decrease in crime. We can each be a catalyst for change.

---

[17] Holistic health (or holistic medicine) is a diverse field of alternative medicine in which the whole person (body, mind, spirit, emotions, etc.) is focused on, not just the malady itself

[18] Edward de Bono, *Lateral Thinking: Creativity Step-by-Step* (1970).

[19] Malcolm Gladwell, *The Tipping Point: How Little Things can make a Big Difference* (2000).

A problem well-defined is a problem half-solved. All stakeholders must brainstorm together, share data and information, technology, so that we can create this more perfect future world together. We must come together in a synergistic movement, the sum of all our parts being many times over more effective than we are individually, as this is a monumental task that will require all our efforts. Brainstorming allows a group or individual to bring creativity and find a conclusion for a specific problem by gathering a list of ideas. Brainstorming is essential as the solution is multidisciplinary. Confronting stigma and promoting the understanding of addiction as a biologically based, relapsing chronic illness is a paramount task for all stakeholders.

Stanley Milgram's famous experiment showed that, given the right conditions, human beings exhibit a frightening willingness to inflict pain on others in order to be seen kindly by those in authority.[20] Two-thirds of the participants administered what they thought was four hundred and fifty volts of electricity to a screaming stranger solely because a person of apparent authority told them to do so. This is why it is so important that leaders in the criminal justice system train those coming into the field that empathy is not weakness and servant-leadership is desired. Man is a communal animal. The fear of being isolated is greater than the fear of harming others. The desire to please the person in authority takes precedence over the desire to help those in need. Prosecutors must understand that mentally ill defendants are their charges, their responsibility and should not become collateral damage. The prosecutor is just as responsible to ensure that a violent offender is kept from the public as they are to ensure that no one spends a day longer incarcerated than is right and just.

Liability

In 2007 in Florida, the head of the state's social services

---

[20] Stanley Milgram Obedience to Authority: An Experimental View (1974).

department resigned abruptly, after having been fined $80,000 and was charged criminally for failing to transfer severely mentally ill jail inmates to state hospitals. Gregg County, Texas was ordered to pay a $1.9 million settlement to relatives of a drug-recovering inmate who died in custody. The inmate died after being denied her prescription drugs from a methadone clinic while she was in jail. Two jailers were indicted based on their actions stemming from the incident.[21] High risk of death for heroin addicts without methadone treatment has been so well proven that courts now have an ethical obligation to get treatment for people with that addiction.

Jail Space

We cannot arrest and incarcerate our way out of this drug-addiction epidemic. Jail space is a resource paid for by the citizens. It is the single biggest budget item for Dallas and other jurisdictions in the United States. We have to be accountable and use that resource wisely. It costs about ten times more to take care of a mentally ill person in the jail than it does outside the jail.

Since the early 1990s, crime rates have been steadily declining in Texas. Despite recent reforms[22], Texas has one of the highest incarceration rates in the country and the world, with approximately 150,000 people incarcerated in Texas state prisons and 69,000 people in county jails.[23]

Nearly sixty percent of individuals sitting in Texas county jails haven't been convicted of a crime; they're just awaiting trial - on the taxpayer dime.[24] Some individuals could be released until trial but they can't afford the bond payment.

---

[21] Dallas Morning News 2/13/13.
[22] U.S. Department of Justice, *Uniform Crime Reporting Statistics* (2014).
[23] Texas Commission on Jail Standards. *Abbreviated Population Report* (2014). www.tinyurl.com/lkg92mx
[24] Texas Criminal Justice Coalition http://www.texascjc.org.

All Dallas jailers are trained in Mental Illness. It is estimated that for every dollar spent on mental health and substance abuse disorders, Texas would see a return of twenty-three dollars. There is no better way to be *smart on crime* than investing in the evidence based, best practices demonstrated in mental health divisions. Texas has a national reputation for being tough on crime and being smart on crime. Improper resolutions of cases are costing everyone significantly more at all levels.

The good news is Texas is reducing its prison population through common sense reforms after years of unrestrained prison growth.

Mentally ill defendant's decompensate in jail compared to the mental hospitals for many reasons, some of which are: because there is not as much support, not as much individual treatment, not as much freedom, it is a more confined space, some hospitals, e.g. Terrell are even co-ed, the jail is noisy 24/7, and they can go outside at the hospitals.[25]

It is estimated that twenty percent of males are sexually victimized during incarceration. Twenty-five percent of females are sexually victimized while incarcerated. And one in ten youths are raped by staff during incarceration. Inmates with mental illness are at increased risk of sexual victimization. Also the weak and elderly and those that cannot defend or advocate for themselves for whatever reason are more likely to be the victims of sexual abuse. Often sexual victimization occurs within the first forty-eight hours of incarceration. Severe physical and psychological effects hinder their ability to integrate into the community and maintain stable employment upon their release from prison: PTSD, depression, suicide, and the exacerbation of existing mental illness. This sexual abuse among defendants fosters an epidemic of HIV and other sexually transmitted diseases. The Prison Rape Elimination Act

---

[25] Texans in prison are four times more likely to have a serious mental illness than Texans in the general population. One in three Texans with serious mental illness will be re-incarcerated within three years.

(PREA) is bringing much of this to light.

Recidivism

Sixty percent of defendants reoffend.

With mentally ill defendants that receive outpatient treatment the recidivism rate is fifty percent less. The mentally ill defendant is no more likely to reoffend than the non-mentally ill. An exception is those with a chemical dependency – untreated, they are 25 times more likely to reoffend.

Ninety-eight percent of people with a mental illness are not violent

We should not be locking up mentally ill individuals with hardened criminals.

Jails do not have sufficient manpower, training or resources to effectively deal with all those suffering from mental illness.

There are many individuals who have found themselves at the brink of death, and fought their way back to a productive, successful life (most of whom were parents of small children); those who bring you to tears when they tell of what nightmares their lives had become and how they have their families and jobs back now. And when a small child stands up in front of the thousands of professionals that attend the National Drug Court Professionals Association Annual Conference (also the largest training conference for mental health professionals in the criminal justice system) and poignantly states "thank you for giving me back my mom" there is not a dry eye in the house on the faces of many who have had careers as tough, no nonsense, hard-nosed prosecutors and law enforcement officers.

We cannot continue to not allow our criminal justice system to become a substitute for a public health approach to addressing the disease of addiction.

CHAPTER THREE

THE REALITY

Johnnie Lindsey, an exoneree, pauses and sighs. "It's sad that I see so many people living in a prison out here. It's unbelievable, if they just knew what I've been through. If they could just go in there and experience a fraction of what I have, then life wouldn't be so bitter out here. Some people are free, but they're still locked up. We can create prisons for ourselves out here. Just live your life!"[26]

The businessman, S.D., was placed in a 10 foot by 13 foot detox cell in the county jail. His only crime was possession of a controlled substance. The eight men in the cell were forced to sleep on the cement floor. This was not the appropriate Multiple Occupancy Cell or Individual Cell for someone serving ten days of weekend time as a condition of probation yet it does not violate the law or the regulations of the Texas Jail Standards Commission. One man had to sleep under the toilet due to lack of space. The temperature was kept at about sixty degrees. They were only given one blanket that was so thin you could see through it. The men spent their time with the blankets over their heads because of the cold. They were given a very thin mat. The matt that the businessman was provided with on his first night there was smeared with fecal matter. The only source of water in the cell was a vomit covered faucet; needless to say it was not used all weekend. He was kept there for three days. They were only given

---

[26] Dorothy Budd, *Tested: How Twelve Wrongfully Convicted Men Held on to Hope* (2010).

approximately twelve ounces of liquid per day to drink, and that was served in filthy, used, unwashed cups with the previous user's lip prints still on the cup. When one of the men used the toilet, i.e. had a bowel movement, that experience was shared with the other seven men in the cell. This jail cell had no bunks and only two small metal benches. Some of the men had recently been arrested and were intoxicated. No one in the cell was given anything to read or pass the time, they were not even allowed a bible, there was no television, not even a toothbrush. S.D. was not given toilet paper though he asked for it. There were cockroaches in the cell. S.D. had severe health conditions, and was no threat to public safety as is evidenced by letters (from a medical doctor and a psychiatrist) that were presented to the DA and the court. S.D. was not a criminal; he had a brain disease for which he should have been receiving treatment. S.D. was suffering from a major depressive episode brought on by this impending incarceration and is not capable of advocating for or defending himself. S.D. had recently tried to kill himself to avoid jail.

When his lawyer made a complaint to the Commission on Jail Standards about the man's treatment, conditions got worse. Upon arrival at the jail for the next three weekends he was stripped of all his clothing, including his socks and shoes. He was only given a rubber vest to wear. While this was supposedly for suicide prevention, the jail had the information about his attempt to commit suicide to avoid jail, in writing, before his incarceration on both prior incarcerations and they did not take these drastic actions. Before the complaint they attempted to justify this treatment saying it was necessary to protect them in the event he did attempt suicide in their jail.[27] S.D. was given hard plastic trays and plastic cups with which a person could injure themselves if they wished, he was still denied access to his bible (or any book)

---

[27] Inmates in suicide cells are given no sheets, mattresses, toiletries, clothing, books, pens, papers or recreational activities. There is absolutely nothing for these inmates to do as they are confined to their cells.

though he, several family members and his lawyer requested that he be allowed to have it. The officials at the jail managed to make the reality of incarceration even worse than the poor man who had tried to kill himself to avoid it could have imagined. The actions could not be more calculated to induce a relapse.

Suicidal inmates, if they are lucky, wear rubber suits. They are kept in cold rooms with no blankets. In some jails they are kept naked and even strapped down to beds with no covers.

Sounds like something from a third world country? No this is happening here in America. But you say – no way – we have standards. This violates the Texas Administrative Code which contains the Jail Commission Standards. Many jails, especially in rural areas routinely operate out of the bounds of the law. Even when complaints are made, they go for years out of compliance.

In addition to sexual assaults in jails and prisons, basic necessities and visitations are denied. Jails are a breeding ground for contamination and the spread of disease and assaultive behavior.

S.D. had recently completed almost four months of successful intensive outpatient treatment for his illness and was still in treatment. Instead of being rewarded for his efforts (as is the best practice and supported by science and evidence based treatments) he was tortured for testing positive seven months prior to his incarceration.

These actions are exposing local governments to unnecessary liability. While jail is not meant to be pleasant, it is also not meant to be an instrument of torture for the sick and the mentally ill.

Imagine when we look back from the future and ask "what were we thinking" when we put mentally ill people in jail cells with hardened criminals, where more than twenty percent of them are sexually assaulted while they are waiting weeks for a bed to open up at a hospital. And far too many are mentally ill, I watched a young client hurl himself against a plate glass window of a conference room during a break in court proceedings in a failed attempt to commit suicide. I have seen a defendant who cut off her own bottom lip, defendants slitting their own throats, and many in restraint chairs in their book-in photos and so much more.

Texas keeps approximately 7,000 prisoners in isolation

with an average stay of 3.7 years according to a report from the ACLU of Texas and the Texas Civil Rights Project. It damages prisoners, wastes taxpayer money and endangers public safety by disgorging offenders who are significantly more prone to recidivism. This is 4.4 percent of the Texas prison population at a cost of $19.17 more per day. Attacks on Mississippi corrections officers dropped by 70 percent when the State dropped its solitary population from around 1,000 to around 150.[28]

The thirty plus exonerees from Dallas will tell you that one more night in jail is not worth a million dollars.

---

[28] Eric Nicholson, *Alone at the Bottom,* Dallas Observer, Feb. 12, 2015) p. 6.

CHAPTER FOUR

WHY, WHY

There are two ways to approach life-as a victim or a fighter -you must decide to act or to react, to deal your own cards or play with the stacked deck and if you don't decide which way to play with life it always plays with you.
Author unknown

On a cold, overcast day in 1989, I came home from my work as a Tarrant County prosecutor to find my beautiful, blonde, blue-eyed fifteen year old daughter convulsing in a pool of vomit and blood with a bullet wound through her head. Terror and numbness gripped me as I shoved the gun away from her body and ran to call for an ambulance. She was careflighted to the hospital where I stayed by her side for seven days and seven nights, never resting. She never awoke from the coma. I never learned what had happened. In fact, even though I was more familiar with the evidence at the scene than anyone, I refused to believe she had taken her own life for a very long time and continued making futile demands on the police to investigate tidbits of information that I was sure would lead to her killer.

She was the happiest, smartest, prettiest, most well-adjusted and most all-around perfect person that I have ever known. She had a quick sense of humor and made friends easily. She was very smart and scored in the top 2% in national achievement tests. She had a beautiful voice and wanted to be singer. I thought our lives were near perfect. I did not ever anticipate losing my child.

When your parent dies, you have lost your past. When your child dies, you have lost your future. That tragic event lead me into the world of mental illness myself. Never treated for depression (too numb by the pain to seek help) I was sucked into a world of deep, dark grief which took many months from which to recover. If it were not for my wonderful, loving sister and caring friends who picked me up and carried me through the dark days, I am certain that I would not have survived my grief.

Over four hundred people attended her funeral service. My grief was so great I did not recognize the faces of lifelong friends. I buried myself that cold February day. It was me they lowered into the frigid ground. I wanted to crawl in the coffin with my precious daughter. At the time I felt emotionally lobotomized. It was as if I was inside a bubble. I could feel my brain reprograming, reconstructing the portion that had been damaged and removed as surely as if a physician's scalpel had taken it. One beautiful, curly blonde haired, blue eyed princess wrapped up in such a beautiful package - once the source of all my joy, goals and aspirations now the source of all my pain.

Though I have always been a person who does not cry much, I cried so much after her death that my eyes suffered from subconjunctiva (capillaries or tiny blood vessels in the eye under such pressure that they pop out and bleed into the tissues) and the whites of my eyes became blood red.

After months of blackness I had a profound and brilliantly bright dream where she came to me. I asked her "Why, Stacy, Why", she explained that all was well and I would understand in time. That was a turning point in my own recovery.

A single person is missing and the whole world was empty. My grief was so great, I could not even speak about Stacy without breaking down, and consequently I did not speak of her at all. For decades co-workers and others near me never knew I had a daughter. I was even an elected District Attorney and I am sure that none of the thousands of citizens I served knew of her. Later as the Chief of the Mental Health Division of the Dallas District Attorney's Office I was frequently asked why I had developed such an interest in Mental Health. I would mention my study of legal medicine in law school, psychology classes in college, work at a hospital, work at a nursing home, police work, and many other credentials but never the strongest one – my own personal story.

Ninety-nine percent of my own silence was the pain. Each time a person asks "do you have any children", if you just answer "no" or "I have step-children" that is the end of the inquiry, but if you were to answer "I had a child that died" the next question is "How?" and you have to relive the most painful moment of your life. Stigma derives from pain. We all want to believe mental illness, suicide, substance-abuse etc. couldn't happen to us or someone that we love. Some rationalize "they must have done something wrong to have that illness." The truth is, mental illness is as common as the common cold and everyone can suffer from it in their lifetime. You get treatment for a mental illness, just like any other illness. Anyone who has experienced tremendous grief, as I did, has suffered a mental illness.

In the years after Stacy's death, while practicing as an attorney, I continued to come into contact with many people that suffered from mental illness. I was frequently appointed to represent mentally ill people, more so than other local attorneys as I was told by judges that they appreciated how thorough I was with such cases and those involving children.

I finally came to realize that my sweet, beautiful, perfect Stacy may have suffered from depression and bipolar disorder (a disease that I had never heard of during her life). A child who seemed to have everything in the world – beauty, intelligence, a family that adored her, friends, teachers and fellow students that admired her . . . She had had the lead role in a school play, was a majorette in the school band, made good grades, . . . And no one saw it coming. In retrospect, I remember days shortly before her death when she had difficulty getting out of bed, I remember mood swings, but she was my only child and with nothing to compare it too, at the time, I did not think anything was significant enough to merit special attention. I failed my daughter. If I had known more about mental illness I might have noticed a sign. If I had taken her to a professional there might have been a diagnosis. Perhaps she would have been here today.

My paternal grandfather had taken his own life also. Other close relatives had attempted, almost successfully, to take their lives. My father and a brother were alcoholics. I come from a very large family with a cousin that suffers from schizophrenia and another that suffers from bipolar disorder, and nephews and nieces that suffer from anti-social personality disorder, narcissism, etc. And other relatives that suffer from substance abuse. I grew up with a front row seat to a hands-on education about mental illness in that theater. Many of us have such an exposure to mental illness.

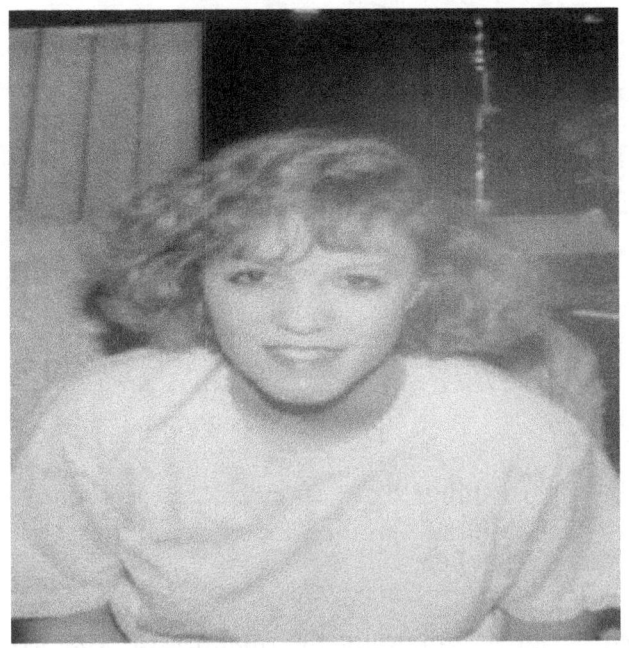

Stacy

CHAPTER FIVE

WHAT CITIZENS CAN DO - TOP 10 THINGS WE CAN DO

"To know even one life has breathed easier because you have lived, this is to have succeeded."
Ralph Waldo Emerson

The top 10 things that you can do as a parent or community to heal children, families and communities:

1. READ!!

It is not so important the quantity of what you know, but the quality.

While talking to your children about drugs should be the number one priority, it is most important that you have something to say when you talk to them. Read quality material. Self-help (*The Book of Proverbs* is the original self-help book); nutrition, health, etc.

Learn about mental illness. Mental illness is as common as the common cold. Get treatment, just like you would with any other illness. Get help: hospitals, local mental health authorities (known as Metrocare in this North Texas area), counselors, . . .

The best thing we can do as a community is to read more. We need to get out from behind our televisions and exercise and read.

2. Have dinner as a family as often as possible.

Families that eat together are much less likely to have children who become addicts. Children who have dinner with their parents at least three times a week are less likely to develop drug or alcohol problems. Every night at the White House, everything stops while the President has dinner with his children at six o'clock. If he can make time, so can we. They play "Roses and

Thorns" (a game where they go around the table with each person taking a turn describing the best and worst thing that happened that day).

3. Talk to your children.
Tell your children regularly and emphatically that you want them to stay away from drugs, including alcohol and prescription medications. Studies show that children who know their parents care whether they use drugs are less likely to use them.

Be involved, limit internet use, report bullying, . . .

For information about talking with children about drugs consider these websites: TheStutmanGroup.com, then click "Links" (Robert Stutman, special agent in charge of several DEA field divisions). For information on how to fight drugs in your community: Drugfreeworld.org

4. Exercise
According to a study done by the Secret Service on thirty-seven school shootings by forty-one perpetrators, besides being male, the one characteristic that all of the shooters shared was that they suffered from a mental illness. The one mental illness that they all shared was depression.[29]

What is one of the best cures for depression . . . better than antidepressants? *Exercise.* This is why sports and even better - aerobic exercises - in our schools are important

5. Lock up your prescription drugs away from children
Purchase a lockbox or gun safe in which to secure your prescription drugs. Maybe you trust your children, but other children can access these when they visit, also babysitters, contractors or anyone in your home could have access.

---

[29] Dr. Daniel Amen, *Change your Brain, Change your Body* P. 112 (2010).

6. Educate yourself about your own health and the health of your family.

Don't expect your doctor to do it. Doctors are not about health care, they are trained in disease management.

The number one cause of death in the United States is substance abuse. It is also the number one cause of death in teenagers specifically (surpassing car accidents).

Addiction is the number one most diagnosed mental illness in children in the United States today.

Today the average starting age for drug abuse is twelve or thirteen.

Start talking with your kids about the dangers of drugs before they set foot in junior high school. By high school, it may be too late.

The biggest problem this country faces is prescription drugs.

The three most accurate predictors of substance abuse are:

1. Age of first use,
2. Tobacco users are twelve to sixteen percent more likely to become drug addicts or alcoholics, and
3. The number of days a week parents have dinner with their children.

Studies also show that spiritual individuals or those that have faith-based beliefs are less likely to have substance abuse problems.

If you combined all other addictions, you would have to multiply by ten to get the number of alcoholics.

Make a fist - that is the size of the prefrontal cortex of your brain: reasoning, judgment, thinking and when drugs are used one will lose control of it.

Many teens suffer from sleep deprivation.

Inform teens that if one of their peers ever passes out from drinking or drug abuse in their presence, they should immediately roll this person onto his/her side (to prevent suffocation if the person vomits), then call 911. Thousands of lives would be saved if every teen knew this.

7. Do not drink to get drunk in front of your child.

This is true even if your child is still too young to fully understand what drinking means. As early as age two, children begin forming lifelong beliefs and behaviors based on what they see their parents doing. Certainly never allow teens to get drunk in your presence. Some parents permit their teens to drink at home because they think this is safer than the teens drinking elsewhere and then driving home. Studies suggest that teens that drink with their parents are slightly more likely to become alcoholics than those who do not.

8. Confront your teen if you smell cigarette smoke on his/her clothes or discover other evidence of tobacco use.

Teens that use tobacco are at greater risk than nontobacco users of becoming drug addicts. If you smoke, quit. Peer pressure is the main reason kids give for using. Tell them - drug dealers will tell you anything to get you hooked. They just want to make money. Some just want to control you.

Be honest with youth. If you only tell them "if you use drugs your're gonna die" they will know it is a lie and won't believe you on other issues.

Research shows that the best way to influence your child to avoid drinking is to develop a strong, trusting relationship. Why? First, when they have that bond, it follows that they feel good about themselves and therefore less likely to fall to peer pressure and drink alcohol. Second, your good relationship fosters the desire for them to try and live up to your expectations because they want to please you and maintain their close tie.

9. Nutrition

Eliminate gluten if depressed, or if you suffer from Attention Deficit Disorder, bipolar or schizophrenia disorders. Avoid highly processed, genetically modified, herbicided, sucrose or fructose corn syrup-filled, hydrogenated (trans) fat, salty, corn-starched, glutenized, radiated foods. This will be covered in further detail in the chapter on nutrition

10. Help others

Recognize mental illness, if someone is struggling or isolated: talk to them, ask if they need help, tell them about Metrocare (or similar services in your area), bring it to others attention: teachers, counselors, nurses, police, etc. Take every effort to end the stigma. Seventy percent of children with parents in prison will wind up in prison. Mentoring of just four hours per month is shown to break the chain. Volunteer at Boys and Girls Clubs, schools, YMCAs, anywhere that children gather. Children that are not given positive reinforcement and are told that they will struggle, even when the negative reinforcement only lasted for a few months in their lives, will continue to have negative outcomes in life many years after the negative influences.[30] Two-hundred and fifty thousand Texas children have an incarcerated parent. Volunteer at reading centers. Eighty-five percent of juveniles who interface with the juvenile court system are functionally illiterate. [31] Seventy-five percent of inmates are illiterate.

---

[30] Philip C. McGraw, PhD, *Self Matters* (2001).
[31] National Assessment of Adult Literacy.

CHAPTER SIX

THE DALLAS MODEL

*The States Attorney's interest "in a criminal prosecution is not that
it shall win a case, but that justice shall be done. As such, he is in a
peculiar and very definite sense the servant of the law, the twofold
aim of which is that guilt shall not escape or innocence suffer. He
may prosecute with earnestness and vigor--indeed, he should do
so. But, while he may strike hard blows, he is not at liberty to
strike foul ones. It is as much his duty to refrain from improper
methods calculated to produce a wrongful conviction as it is to use
every legitimate means to bring about a just one."*
Berger v. United States, 295 U.S. at 88, 55 S.Ct. at 633. (Tex.
Crim. App. 1987).

"If you want to find Justice, come to Dallas."
Barry Scheck

In 2006, Dallas County had 144 lawsuits pending against the
county jail. Approximately 65 were mental health related. In
2014, there were two lawsuits pending.

In Dallas County, between 2004 to 2014, the number of
misdemeanor cases filed by police plummeted 43.2 percent, felony
cases plummeted 24.4 percent. Using evidence based treatments
and protocols to reduce recidivism as is done in Dallas is the future
of criminal justice.

The Dallas County Jail is the 7th largest jail in the nation.
The Dallas jail is the 4th largest "provider" of mental health
services in the state (after the Texas Department of Criminal
Justice [Rusk, Montford, and Sugarland Units], and the State
Hospital [which also houses the mentally ill in different units], and
the Harris County Jail).

The Mental Health caseload has grown (tripled in six years)
since the Mental Health Divisions of the Dallas County District

Attorney's Office and Public Defender's Office were established in 2007.

Approximately one-third of the people in the Dallas County Jail have a diagnosed mental illness. Mentally ill defendants spend more time in jail and cost more to house. The following figures show a percentage reflecting a NorthStar[32] match, i.e. these are the individuals that are receiving treatment (medications) in the jail (and does not necessarily represent the total number of mentally ill in the jail).

    2007 - 7%
    2008 - 8%
    2009 - 11%
    2010 - 14%
    2012 - 20% (tripled in six years)
    2013 - 22%
    2014 - 24%

These figures do not indicate that there is an unprecedented explosion of mental illness in Dallas County, Texas, they merely represent how rapidly expanding our ability to recognize and diagnose those mental illness is becoming. If the mentally ill constitute twenty-four percent of those that are booked in to the jail but they are thirty-one percent of the jail population, this is proof that the mentally ill spend more time in jail. Even in Dallas where we put great emphasis and significant resources on getting the mentally ill out of jail and into services, they are still serving more time incarcerated than those without a mental illness. They are not getting out on bond before trial and/or they are serving longer sentences.

More than 16% of jail inmates have a mental illness,

---

[32] Northstar is the insurance. Metrocare, Lifenet, Adapt, ABC, and an extensive network of over 300 entities are the providers. The NorthSTAR behavioral health program serves Collin, Dallas, Ellis, Hunt, Kaufman, Navarro and Rockwall counties. It is a cost-effective open-access model providing mental health and substance abuse treatment and has not had a waiting list since its inception.

according to the United States Department of Justice. Some studies have that figure as high as 73% of female inmates (female inmates are diagnosed with mental illness more often than males).

One third of youth under the supervision of probation departments in Texas have a confirmed mental illness, and the vast majorities do not receive mental health services.

In 2006, a study of public mental health service delivery systems published by the National Association of State Mental Health Program Directors Medical Directors Council found that in Texas, individuals with severe and persistent mental illness die twenty-nine years earlier than the general population.

There are 4,500 cases handled annually by the Dallas Public Defender's Office and one-half of those defendants have a mental illness.

Metrocare is the mental health provider of medications probably referred to as Mental Health Mental Retardation (MHMR) in your county. Metrocare Services is a Dallas nonprofit providing affordable mental health care to children and adults living with mental illness or special needs.

Dallas County was one of the first to adopt a mental health criminal justice program and was found to have the most successful mental health program in Texas (of the counties studied) according to a 2010 comprehensive, eighteen-month study conducted by a research scientist from Texas A&M University in conjunction with the Texas Task Force on Indigent Defense. Defendants from the mental health caseload in Dallas exhibited the lowest risk of recidivism of the counties studied. Dallas has the broadest and most comprehensive array of diversion-oriented programming of any Texas county studied in that research. The Dallas County Probation Department claims to have a reduction in recidivism of 70% via CATS [Comprehensive Assessment Treatment Services] Evaluation (far better than that of the general population).[33] Many times our success is relative, e.g. "he's not as

---

[33] CATS is a program started in Dallas in 1996 (originally called Treatment

paranoid as he used to be", and "she's buying her food now instead of stealing it at Wal-Mart". These baby-steps can lead to a brighter future for the individuals today and for society as a whole in the future.

In Dallas groups such as the Behavioral Health Steering Committee (BHSC), Behavioral Health Leadership Team (BHLT)[34], and Behavioral Health Housing work group meet regularly to network, collaborate and brainstorm on solving behavioral health issues. The purpose of these groups is to improve patient outcomes and costly repeated hospital admissions and criminal justice involvement. They improve communications and collaboration between and less fragmentation of the diverse array of services provided in the system.

The mission of the Mental Health Division is to coordinate activities related to the diversion of inmates from the jail into the appropriate community-based services. We link inmates with relief services. The office of the Director of Criminal Justice employees twenty-nine staff members and contracts for additional resources (case managers, social workers, peer counselors, and other staff). Defendants with a history of utilization of mental health services are identified with fifteen minutes of book-in to the jail. Assessors identify treatment needs and develop treatment plans. There are peer specialists that follow some defendants upon release. Housing is provided to those with greatest needs. Transportation is provided for treatment and court.

Alternative to Incarceration Program "TAIP"). There are two psychologists and twenty-two master's level clinicians on staff. In 2012, CATS reviewed 2900 cases prior to early intervention and 2900 after early intervention finding that there was a 70% reduction in recidivism in those cases with early intervention. CATS primarily evaluates for drug or alcohol abuse but 80% of the people they evaluate have an overlapping of problems, i.e., mental illness. These evaluations can tell you what the mental illness is, how to deal with it, and services that are available to assist the defendants. They claim to reduce recidivism (70% reduction in those evaluated early).

[34] BHLT is concerned with treatment, care, and housing.

The Dallas County jail has a forty bed Intensive Care Psychiatric Unit, which is the largest in the State (over four hundred beds with forty dedicated to Acuity I - crisis stabilization). All Dallas County jail staff has a minimum of forty hours of Crisis Intervention Training (CIT) for dealing with the mentally ill. The training is presented by the National Alliance for Mental Illness (NAMI).

The Dallas County Jail has twenty-four hour psychiatric services. After release, those populations utilizing those services are in the emergency rooms of local hospitals less. The mentally ill are identified early in the jail via a NorthStar (Local Mental Health Authority) match. This is entered into the computer at the book-in process. Every fifteen minutes the computer of the Mental Health Coordinator for the County is updated with the new information. Persons who have not been in the jail before may be identified as being mentally ill via private attorneys, Grand Jury referrals, family members, etc.

The attorneys in the Mental Health Division save the taxpayers hundreds of thousands of dollars each year. The Competency Attorney in the Mental Health Division of the Dallas District Attorney's Office handles competency matters including monitoring all outpatient competency restoration which is a full time caseload. This attorney's position (Outpatient Competency Restoration Program) alone more than pays for itself. This position was created specifically in response to a lawsuit filed in 2006 regarding defendants being held in the Dallas jail for months before transfer to State Hospitals and after one Dallas inmate nearly died awaiting transfer. In 2009, the pilot program saved the county $300,000 by not housing mentally-ill defendants in the jail. And the program has grown significantly since then, saving more money for Dallas taxpayers. This program allows defendants to be treated in their communities, which is more beneficial than being in a hospital.

These defendants are less frequently charged with new crimes than defendants that are sent to the hospital. This requires weekly staffings (meetings with the Judge, defense attorney, case managers, etc. in court). These individuals are required to come to court at least every two weeks. The attorney monitors the community based programs, whether the defendant is taking medications, attending court ordered doctors' visits, drug testing, etc.

Today, there are an estimated thirty to fifty individuals in this outpatient program at any given time (and hundreds more in the mental health diversion programs over which this attorney monitors check-ins). The work of this prosecutor, the corresponding public defender, and the judge of the OCR court saves taxpayers of Dallas County incarceration costs of approximately $150 per day for each mentally ill defendant.

Courtney Heard, with the Department of State Health Services, who oversees the Outpatient Competency Restoration (OCR) program for the State has stated "Dallas is the gold standard for OCR. Dallas always meets or exceeds standards. The OCR program in Dallas is the best in State. I never worry about Dallas." But this program is probably too complex for most citizens to understand (it's all about getting sick, non-violent offenders out of jail, which we are required by law to do).

Further, the Mental Health Division has:

- Developed a protocol for dealing efficiently with low level drug cases with the mentally ill;
- Developed a protocol for dealing efficiently with prostitution cases with the mentally ill; and
- continue to make presentations to the criminal defense bar, the District Attorneys Office, fire departments, police departments, NAMI, and various citizens groups.

Mental health professionals strive to follow and educate others to follow the scientific, evidence based, research based principles set out by the National Association of Drug Court Professionals (world's largest educator of mental health professionals in the criminal justice field). Staff monitoring phone calls and the front desk at the District Attorney's Office indicate that they receive more phone calls for Mental Health Attorneys and the services of these Mental Health Division attorneys are requested more than any other attorneys in the office. These attorneys frequently work long hours to assist in staying on top of the ever burgeoning case-load. The supervisor says he gets more compliments on the attorneys of that division than anyone else he supervises.

Jail Based Competency Restoration (JBCR)

Incompetency and presumptions of incompetency are defined and outlined in the Texas Code of Criminal Procedure. The mental health and educational services for people found incompetent to stand trial include cognitive remediation classes (which work best in small groups) with patients alternating group social skills sessions with computer lab sessions working on restoring cognitive function through tests and games. Cognitive remediation works well to restore competency to the defendants suffering from traumatic brain injuries, Alzheimer's, and other mental diseases or defects.

Mentally ill people don't belong in jail. Jails by their nature are designed to dehumanize and humiliate. Imprisonment has a negative impact. It is counter to treatment. However, it is more inhumane to have a mentally ill person in a spiral of competency restoration (at the mental hospital) and decompensation (upon return to the jail) then having to wait weeks or months in jail before returning to the hospital.

While jail is generally not a therapeutic environment, another ground breaking, cutting edge program in Dallas is the Jail Based Competency Restoration Program. Dallas was selected to receive the grant for the pilot program that should result in saving even more taxpayer money by restoring mentally ill defendants to competency in the jail instead of waiting in the jail for a State Hospital bed. I had the honor of being selected by the Texas Department of State Health Services, Adult Mental Health Division in Austin to be the only prosecutor in the State on the Workgroup in Austin to develop the law (in conjunction with other stakeholders such as the Dallas Chief Public Defender and Dallas Sheriff and mental health professionals from around the State) in getting the program off the ground. There is no other program like this in Texas and very few in the United States (only two known by the author at this time).

The Dallas jail has thirty-nine physicians and one-hundred

and fifty-four nurses.[35] The eleven pharmacists distribute 400,000 doses of medication per month.

The Dallas District Attorney's Office has a psychologist and a counselor on staff. The attorneys consult with the psychologist on therapies and protocols often. There are three hundred and eighty two officers in the Dallas Sheriff's Office and all have received a minimum of forty hours in mental health training.

Defendants (as we all do) have the right to be free from unnecessary or excessive medication, which includes the right to give or withhold informed consent to treatment with psychoactive medication, unless the right has been limited by court order or in an emergency. They also have the right to confidentiality of records and the right to be informed of the conditions under which information can be disclosed without the participant's consent. The provider shall only disclose participant-identifying information in accordance with the law.[36]

Texas spent thirty-five dollars per day per patient on mental health services when the national average is one hundred and twenty dollars per day.[37] Texas ranks at the bottom of all the states in per-capita spending for mental health. Texas' mental health and substance abuse treatment systems are already at such a breaking point, anything but improved funding would be fiscally irresponsible. This low level of spending is not saving taxpayers

---

[35] Eighty percent of cities in Texas are smaller than the Dallas County jail population. The Dallas County jail has a total of 300 medical staff members for 6,000 to 7,000 inmates. Compared to Chicago, Cook County, Illinois: 550 staff to 9,000 inmates or New York: 1,400 staff to 14,000 inmates, Dallas has a smaller percentage of staff but claims to have better outcomes.

[36] Health Insurance Portability and Accountability Act of 1996, Public Law 104-191; Texas Health and Safety Code §576.005 and §§611.001-611.005; and 42 Code of Federal Regulations, Part 2.

[37] The survey by the Henry J. Kaiser Family Foundation indicates the NorthSTAR program community programs funding has dropped to $25 per Texas in 2012 from $35 in 2003 per the Center for Public Policy Priorities. Dallas Morning News 2/11/13.

money, it's costing us significantly more at all levels. Lack of access to community-based mental health and substance abuse treatment drives up the cost of health care, law enforcement and criminal justice for city, county and state government.

Mentally ill individuals can be placed on probation or promised conditional dismissals with requirements including but not limited to:

- Stay on their medications;
- Not consume illegal drugs, or in some cases alcohol (imperative as this diminishes and conflicts with the effect of prescribed medications);
- See mental health professionals; and
- See case managers who can obtain supportive housing, transportation, etc. for them.

In cases involving mentally ill defendants:

- The cost is an average of three times as much to house – $66 per day for inmates in the general population compared to $150 per day estimated for the mentally ill (doctors, nurses, medications, special procedures [i.e. restraint chairs], etc);
- They tend to "decompensate" (deteriorate) when left languishing in the jail, and
- Their incarceration results in more injury to staff with their unpredictable assaultive behavior in some instances.

Providing housing and positive social supports to mentally ill offenders with a ten year history of contact with the justice system reduced arrests by seventy-five percent and resulted in reduced costs to the criminal justice system and the health and social service systems.[38] Appropriate housing results in less frequent utilization of expensive and sometimes unnecessary inpatient stays, emergency department visits and incarceration. Resources are targeted toward those at high risk for poor outcomes. Homeless recovery and other unmet needs are addressed.

With each mass murder elsewhere committed by a mentally ill individual, there are increased demands for the services of Mental Health Divisions. These Mental Health attorneys now provide continuing legal education to the District Attorney's Office; provide liaison and training to police and firefighters; speak to citizens and families about issues (Apprehension by Police Officer Without Warrant [APOWW], civil commitments, services available, etc.); presentations to the grand jury (briefing each session and presentation of individual cases as needed); holding hearings and monitoring releases of defendants found "not guilty by reason of insanity" when hospitals deem it is appropriate; attendance at meetings of mental health committees; respond to emergency requests from judges (sometimes requiring extensive legal research that includes contacting other jurisdictions for procedures); bond hearings (agreeing to personal bonds, holding bonds insufficient, and overseeing the re-arrest of defendants that are deemed dangerous), etc.. Also, with the reduction in beds at the State Hospital – it is necessary to obtain creative solutions and alternatives for treatment of the mentally ill.

Duties of the Competency Attorney include those duties listed above and the following additional duties: trial work; intake of cases; monitoring those found "not guilty by reason of insanity" monthly after release from the hospital for the duration of the court's jurisdiction of the defendants; providing interface with the F.B.I. and Homeland Security to keep them apprised of threats to

---

[38] Alison MacPhail and Simon Verdun-Jones, *Mental Illness and the Criminal Justice System* International Centre for Criminal law Reform and Criminal Justice Policy (2013).

National Security; community outreach; etc.

Mental health attorneys carry a caseload that is equal to or greater than other prosecutors in the office; however their cases require additional work that other prosecutors do not do:

- Review of voluminous medical and psychiatric records;
- Hearings regarding incompetency and insanity;
- Monitoring the necessity for extensions for hospital and psychiatric commitments (competency and insanity);
- Continued monitoring of cases (insanity and incompetency institutionalizations);
- Knowledge of the DSM-V[39];
- Consultations with judges;
- Education of, consultation with, and advice to prosecutors, other attorneys, police, grand juries, probation officers, firemen, and other professionals, which includes the presentation of Continuing Legal Education;
- Attendance at mental health committee meetings;
- Legal research specific to mental health;
- Keeping informed and being knowledgeable about services available;
- Communications with family members about services available;
- Communications with the mental institutions where defendants are sent;
- Being aware of the rules and peculiarities of the seventeen different felony courts, specialty courts, and the misdemeanor courts, as these attorneys practice in all courts;
- The attorneys of the Mental Health Division are the only

---

[39] The American Psychiatric Association Diagnostic and Statistical Manual of Mental Disorders, Fifth Edition (2013).

attorneys in the District Attorney's office that practice law in every court in the Frank Crowley Courts Building;

- Knowledge of HIPAA (Health Insurance Portability and Accountability Act);
- Outpatient competency restoration;
- Presentations to grand juries regarding mental illness;
- Attendance at committees and meetings regarding mental illness;
- Apprising appropriate authorities regarding security threats; and
- The additional burden of obtaining services, i.e. housing, transportation, etc. for the defendants, etc.

With more support in the Division, there could be more involvement with the families and therefore possibly more civil commitments, resulting in a safer and healthier community. Involuntary civil commitments are very rare and sometimes difficult to obtain with the current law. Intervention in a criminal setting may be the only help these people and their families will ever get.

Therapeutic Justice Courts (problem solving courts) are dramatically reducing the high recidivism rate in criminal cases (especially of drug offenders which is the offense of many of the mentally ill – attempting to self-medicate their illnesses). These courts work—individuals successfully treated do not reoffend, or do so at a much lower rate, thus saving money and public resources. These courts compel individuals to respect the system and participate in the treatment services offered or face swift consequences, which is regarded as a superior form of accountability to traditional sentences. With more personnel in the Mental Health Division, there could be more mentally ill defendants receiving the attention that they should be receiving in those courts. These courts claimed successes are enthusiastically trumpeted by the media, thereby improving the legal system's public image. Dallas has twenty specialty courts.

While the mentally ill commit all types of offenses, the most common offenses in Dallas that the mentally ill defendant commits are:

- Criminal trespass (16% of charged offenses against mentally ill defendants), followed by :
- Assault,
- Possession of a controlled substance,
- Prostitution, then
- Other crimes.

If the most frequent crimes that the mentally ill commit are criminal trespass, assault, possession of a controlled substance, and prostitution that tells you a lot about these mentally vulnerable people. People don't want to be around them, they engage in stupid behavior, they self-medicate, and they are desperate. Illegal drugs interfere with the psychotropic medications they are taking and exacerbate the symptoms of the mental illness.

Many mental illnesses (including the most frequently diagnosed of those in jail i.e. bipolar disorder, schizophrenia, etc.) can be seen on a brain scan and can be treated by medication allowing the individuals to lead normal, productive lives. This is why early detection, intervention and diversion from the criminal justice system are so crucial for these individuals.

Proper funding of mental health prosecutors will result in less exposure to liability.

The events at Newtown, Connecticut in 2012 (deaths of 20 children and 6 adults), and numerous other mass murders (almost all of which were done by a person with a diagnosed mental illness), are a reminder to us that we are on the front lines and in a unique position to recognize mental illness in dangerous individuals. Unlike most prosecutors, Dallas prosecutors can have defendants evaluated by psychologist where they can determine those with mental illness and more importantly, homicidal ideations. Some low-level cases (usually assaults against family members) have had homicidal ideations revealed in the evaluation. To prevent tragedies like those of Newtown; Columbine; Aurora, Colorado; etc. there must be early mental health intervention. Early mental health intervention is equivalent to prevention of more crime and tragedies. With each mass murder consciousness is raised regarding mental illness and there is a corresponding increase in the demands for service on mental health divisions. Currently there are far too many defendants and their families that do not receive services. It is smart public policy to treat the mentally ill. Not only is it the right thing to do, it reduces expenditures in other areas. The only answer to the mental health crisis is increased funding. Call your legislator.

Funding

Successful operation of the Mental Health program in the criminal justice system of Dallas County for six years has resulted in the referral of many more defendants to the program. Funding is critical for these operations and they must be backed up with sufficient psychiatric hospital beds, outpatient community clinic services, caseworkers, and appropriate housing.

Therapeutic jurisprudence is defined as: "The study of the effects of law and the legal system on the behavior, emotions, and mental health of people: especially a multidisciplinary examination of how law and mental health interact. This discipline originated in the late 1980s as an academic approach to mental health law."[40]

The Dallas County Community Supervision and Corrections Department claims to have a reduction in recidivism of seventy percent via the Comprehensive Assessment Treatment Services (hereinafter CATS) evaluations. This is better than that of the general jail population. CATS is an evidence based program started in Dallas, in which psychologists evaluate the defendant and recommend the best course of action for defendants in a comprehensive report.

Evidence based programs are those that have been rigorously tested, have yielded consistent replicable results, and have proven safe, beneficial and effective.

The Mental Health caseload in Dallas has grown since the Mental Health Unit was established in 2007.

---

[40] Black's Law Dictionary (9th ed. 2009).

Approximately one-third of the people in the Dallas County Jail have a diagnosed mental illness.[41] Mentally ill defendants spend more time in jail and cost more to house. Research shows that it costs eleven times more to treat individuals with mental illness in the criminal justice system than in the community. (per Dallas Sheriff Lupe Valdez at the Mental Health Symposium Dallas 2/5/13). Nearly eight times more Texans with serious mental illness are in jails and prisons than in hospitals. Nationally, the ratio is 3 to 1. Defendants in prison in Texas are four times more likely to have a serious mental illness than Texans in the general population. For example, in one case that was brought to my attention after the fact, Caroline (a homeless, mentally ill lady) committed the crime of taking a Kroger grocery cart (which was recovered) and putting it in the Tom Thumb parking lot. She received thirty days in jail. The cost to Dallas taxpayers was $4,500 (thirty days at $150 per day). Perhaps if services, and housing had been provided, future episodes might be prevented.

The most common mental illnesses of defendants in the Dallas County jail are: bipolar, schizophrenia, and schizoaffective disorder, in that order. Other less frequently diagnosed mental illnesses in the Dallas jail are: intellectual disability, major depressive disorder, post traumatic stress disorder (PTSD), traumatic brain injury (TBI), and borderline intellectual functioning, in that order. There are numerous other mental

---

[41] In 2009, the average daily population in the Dallas County Jail was 6,164 persons. Of that total, the average mental health census was 1,201 inmates, or nineteen percent who self-disclosed a mental illness. In September 2010, Sheriff Lupe Valdez stated that of the 7,100 inmates in the jail, 2,200 had a mental illness (31%). The number of persons committed to the Dallas County Jail who have a history of receiving mental health or substance abuse services has increased from seven percent of jail admissions in 2007 (6,501 admissions) to 20% in 2012 (17,012 admissions). Since the jail population at any given time is thirty-one percent mentally ill but admissions of the mentally ill are twenty percent annually, this is evidence that mentally ill defendants spend more time in jail. This is in part due to the fact that there are insufficient resources allocated to assist the mentally ill.

illnesses diagnosed in criminal defendants, but these are the types dealt with most often. Most of these mental illnesses can be seen on a brain scan,[42] can be treated by medication (with the exception of TBI and intellectual disability), and helped with therapy, allowing many of the individuals to lead normal, productive lives. This is why early detection, intervention, and diversion from the criminal justice system, when possible, can be so crucial for these individuals.

Dallas County currently has six full-time mental health public defenders and three full-time felony mental health prosecutors. The Public Defender's Office also has four full-time case managers with doctorate or master's degrees assigned to the Public Defender's Mental Health Division. These case managers are extremely beneficial to the program and provide a plethora of services such as locating housing, transportation, etc. Successful operation of the Mental Health program in the criminal justice system of Dallas County for six years has resulted in the referral of many more defendants to the program. Funding is critical for these operations and they must be supported with sufficient psychiatric hospital beds, outpatient community clinic services, caseworkers, and appropriate housing.

Some of the reasons that defendants decompensate in jail compared to the mental hospitals is because there is not as much support, individual treatment, or freedom as in hospitals. Also, jails are a more confined and restricted space (some hospitals, e.g. Terrell are even co-ed).

One of many specialty courts that focus on mental illness in Dallas is the Achieving True Liberty and Success Program (ATLAS).[43] This is a highly structured program where the

----

[42] To see Single Photon Emission Computerized Tomography (SPECT) scans, by category of illness go to www.amenclinics.com/the-science/spect-gallery/category/images-of-treatment.

[43] ATLAS focuses on probationers on the brink of revocation. Participants are reviewed by a team of professionals and appear in court weekly. Atlas focuses on rewarding positive behavior within a support group environment. Graduates

defendants must report weekly to the court. They must be accepted into this program before the plea. Qualifications for ATLAS are: serving a term of felony probation or deferred adjudication, a pending motion for revocation of their probation, no new cases pending, no prior convictions or deferred adjudications for sex-related offenses, a minimum of two years remaining of their term of supervisions and willing to have it extended, and one of the following: bipolar disorder, major depression, schizophrenia or schizoaffective disorder, and mental retardation along with one of the above disorders. They also must have a GAF score of thirty or better, and live in the target area (Dallas County).

---

of ATLAS achieved major reductions in arrests. Chelsea E. Fiduccia and Richard Rogers, *Criminal Justice and Behavior; Final Stage Diversion: A Safety Net for Offenders with Mental Illness* (2012).

CHAPTER SEVEN

FAMOUS PEOPLE

"The greatest use of the life is to spend it for something that will outlast it."
William James

High functioning individuals can hide addiction. Robert Stutman says he cannot identify a opioid addict by observing them physically. Stutman is a 25-year veteran of the Drug Enforcement Administration (DEA). He served as special agent in charge of several DEA field divisions, including the New York field division, the Nation's largest. In 1990, Stutman founded The Stutman Group, a consulting company that designs and implements substance-abuse prevention programs. He was special consultant on substance abuse for CBS News and speaks to more than 100 groups a year. A movie was made about his work.

Rush Limbaugh was an opioid, OxyContin addict. For three years no one knew he was a an OxyContin addict while he was on the Nation's airways. The Chief Justice on the United States Supreme Court, William Rhenquist, was Vicodin dependent while on the bench.

Benjamin Franklin was addicted to laudanum, a mixture of alcohol and opium (for pain, it was considered as harmless as tobacco in his day). Pope Leo XIII, who had the third-longest pontificate in the history of the church, was a devoted drinker of the powerful Vin Mariani, a Bordeaux treated with coca leaves, i.e. cocaine.

Sigmund Freud was addicted to cocaine. Edgar Allan Poe was an opium addict. Thomas Edison was addicted to cocaine elixirs. Steve Jobs was once addicted to LSD. Carl Sagan, preeminent astrophysicist and cosmologist, was addicted to marijuana.

Many famous people have overcome addition. Oprah

Winfrey used crack cocaine in the 1980s. Eric Clapton once spent $16,000 a week on heroin, giving away three years of his life to the dangerous drug. Elton John suffered from bulimia and substance abuse.

Chevy Chase broke a bone falling impersonating President Ford, got addicted and recovered at a Betty Ford clinic.

Many famous people have suffered from mental illnesses in their lives. Mahatma Ghandi, Martin Luther King Jr., Abraham Lincoln, Leo Tolstoy[44], Winston Churchill[45], Ernest Hemingway[46], Sylvia Plath[47], and Herman Melville[48] all suffered from depression. The depression of Mahatma Ghandi and Martin Luther King was so profound that they attempted suicide when they were young.[49] Issac Newton suffered from a rage disorder, and bipolar disorder.

Ludwig van Beethoven, German composer and pianist, was a child prodigy who suffered from bipolar disorder, as did Adolph Hitler[50], and Sylvia Plath[51]. Howard Hughes had obsessive

---

[44] Leo Tolstoy was the famous Russian author of *War and Peace* and *Anna Karenina*. Tolstoy revealed the depth of his own mental illness in the memoir *Confession*. He suffered from clinical depression, hypochondriasis, alcoholism, and substance abuse.

[45] Winston Churchill suffered depression and bipolar disorder.

[46] Ernest Hemingway, writer, suffered from bipolar disorder, paranoia, and depression.

[47] Plath described her mental illness – clinical depression – in her semi-autobiographical novel *The Bell Jar* (1967). Plath committed suicide one month after its publication.

[48] Herman Melville, writer of one of the greatest American novels– *Moby Dick*, suffered from bipolar disorder, alcoholism, and depression.

[49] A First-Rate Madness: Uncovering the Links Between Leadership and Mental Illness, by Nassir Ghaemi (2012).

[51] Sylvia Plath, poet, writer, suffered from bipolar disorder and depression. The Sylvia Plath effect is a term coined by psychologist James C. Kaufman in 2001 referring to the phenomenon that poets are more susceptible to mental illness than other creative writers.

compulsive disorder (OCD). His career and personal battle with the disorder inspired the 2004 Oscar-winning film *The Aviator*.

King George III had a blood disease, porphyria, an enzymatic disorder that affects the nervous system, resulting in mental disturbances, including hallucinations, depression, anxiety, and paranoia, among other symptoms. It has been suggested that the film *The Madness of King George* underestimates his degree of suffering.

Vincent van Gogh suffered from substance abuse (absinthe, a highly alcoholic beverage), paranoia, and hallucinations. He cut off his ear (after threatening his friend, artist Paul Gauguins with a knife) and gave it to a prostitute, did not even remember the psychotic episode the next day (and later shot himself taking two days to die at age thirty-seven). He painted a self-portrait with the bandage. He was in a mental hospital when he painted many paintings including *Starry Starry Night*. He repeatedly attempted to poison himself with paints while in the mental institution. Based on the 992 letters he wrote, doctors today believe he suffered from bipolar disorder. Other absinthe drinkers were Pablo Picasso, Oscar Wilde (writer), and Ernest Hemingway.

Catherine Zeta-Jones, Carrie Fisher, Mel Gibson, Demi Lovato, and Patty Duke suffer from bipolar disorder. Numerous articles have been written, linking bipolar mood disorder with artistry. In 2008, a study at the Stanford University School of Medicine found that those with the condition expressed enhanced creativity.

Robin Williams had Parkinson's disease, substance and alcohol abuse, depression and anxiety. Brooke Shields suffered postpartum depression and wrote a book about it. [52] Emma Thompson suffers from depression (most recently in the movie *Saving Mr. Banks*). Richard Prior, David Letterman, Roseanne Bar, and John Belushi all suffered from depression.

---

[52] Brooke Shields Down Came the Rain: My Journey Through Postpartum Depression (2006).

Susan Boyle suffers from Asperger's disease (ability to hyper focus). It is speculated that Bill Gates suffers from this same illness. This is the same diagnosis as the Sandy Hook Elementary shooter in 2012 in the Newtown Connecticut mass-murder of twenty elementary students and six teachers.

Margo Kidder (Superman's Lois Lane) suffered from manic depression and paranoia which gripped the actress in a well-publicized nervous breakdown in which she cut her hair to avoid being recognized and went missing for days before being found hiding in a suburban California backyard.

Billy Joel is a six-time Grammy Award-winning rock musician, pianist, and singer-songwriter. The sixth best-selling recording artist in the United States, he was inducted into the Rock and Roll Hall of Fame and the Songwriter's Hall of Fame. Joel battled many years with depression, and in 1970, left a suicide note and attempted to commit suicide by drinking furniture polish, saying later, "I drank furniture polish. It looked tastier than bleach." He received inpatient psychiatric care for depression. His suicide note later became the lyrics to his song, "Tomorrow is Today." Joel later recorded "You're Only Human (Second Wind)" as a message to help prevent teen suicide.

Comedienne Drew Carey attempted suicide.

John Nash suffered from paranoid schizophrenia. He won a Nobel prize. His struggle with the mental disorder also inspired the award-winning film "A Beautiful Mind" in 2001. Mary Todd Lincoln suffered from schizophrenia, and schizoaffective disorder.

Craig Ferguson, talk show host, suffered from alcoholism as did Dick van Dyke who spoke to the United States Congress on the issue. Billy Holliday (singer of music like *Strange Fruit* and *God Bless the Child)*, considered the greatest jazz singer of all time, was arrested for prostitution (starting at age 14). She was an addict, and an alcoholic.

Jeffrey Dahmer (serial killer) had autism. Albert Einstein, Isaac Newton, Thomas Jefferson, Emily Dickinson, Paul Dirac (quantum physicist), Glenn Gould (Canadian pianist), James Joyce (author), Michelangelo, Wolfgang Amadeus Mozart, Nikola Tesla (inventor, electrical engineer, mechanical engineer, physicist, and futurist with eidetic memory) are just a few of the talented people that were believed to have had autism. Temple Grandin, a professor, has autism. Her master's thesis and later work resulted in the (more humane and efficient) design for more than 50% of the slaughter houses in United States today. She states "the world needs different kinds of minds to work together". And "if by some magic, autism had been eradicated from the face of the earth, then men would still be socializing in front of a wood fire at the entrance to a cave."

CHAPTER EIGHT

BEST PRACTICES WITH SUBSTANCE ABUSERS

"I don't want to go to Saint Pete's (SAFPF[53]), I'm not even Catholic."
A Dallas Defendant

Prosecutors should ask if they have done all they can to reduce recidivism before sending a defendant to a Substance Abuse Felony Punishment Facility, SAFPF, which has an estimated cost to taxpayers of a minimum of $20,000 with estimates of up to $50,000[54]. The costs from being in a punishment facility to the defendants who lose their jobs, homes, relationships, etc., is much greater and eventually results in yet more costs to the taxpayers. The Hippocratic Oath for doctors is "first do no harm." The number one rule of surgery is "limit exposure." We must consider those rules when handling drug addicts and those defendants with mental illnesses; as these are diseases of the brain that require treatment, just as physical disease. Neuroscience supports this. Addiction and many mental illnesses can be seen on brain scans. They have biological, sociological and psychological

---

[53] Substance Abuse Felony Punishment Facility
[54] It is difficult to assign an exact cost of SAFPF as each case has different variables that impact the overall cost. SAFPF beds cost approximately $65.00 per day, and it is a 180 day program which equals approximately $11,700. SAFPF aftercare is approximately $45.00 per day and is generally 90 days which equals approximately $4,050. Then there is a continuum of outpatient counseling and supervision (partially funded by the State) equaling approximately $5,000. One must also consider that Special Needs SAFPF is a nine month program. There can be lengthy waits in local jails for a bed, and defendants with mental illness can cost closer to $300 per day.

components. Placing persons in jail for more than six days on non-violent offenses where there is no public safety risk is doing more harm than good–to the defendant and society. If they are in jail more than six days they lose their jobs, longer than that and they lose their homes, relationships, etc. If they are in jail more than thirty days they lose their social security benefits. All of this contributes to homelessness and desperation upon the final, and inevitable release of these defendants. Gone are the days when it was just the prosecutor's job to put someone in jail or prison. We must be smarter than that. Supportive outpatient treatment, intensive outpatient treatment, counseling or other options should be considered first.

Sanctions must be appropriate for the individual. Low risk offenders should not be mixed with high risk offenders. When you put rotten apples with good apples, you never get more good apples. Defendants should be evaluated by mental health providers (who will diagnose illnesses and assess risks) and have conditions of their release or probation that they take prescribed medication, attend a 12-step program, attend classes as appropriate and/or other sanctions. For more resources, see: https://www.dallasda.com/mental-health/

Courts and prosecutors can benefit from the best practices that have been developed by the National Drug Court Institute. These science and evidence based practices and standards are published in the *Drug Court Review, Vol. Viii, Issue 1 (2012)*. One does not have to be in a designated drug court to reap the benefits of this research. Most of these approaches are little or no cost. The second category lists practices that actually save money.

These practices are especially beneficial to defendants with mental illness or co-occurring disorders, i.e. substance abuse and mental illness. Implementation will result in a greater reduction in crime and substance abuse. Those practices to which every court and prosecutor should strive to adhere to in order to improve the system are listed in bold below:

Top Ten Practices for Reducing Recidivism: Ranked by effect size, starting with the largest.

1. "Drug courts with a program caseload (number of active

participants) of less than 125 had more than five times greater reductions in recidivism than programs with more participants.

2. Drug courts where participants were expected to have greater than 90 days clean (negative drug tests) before graduation had 164% greater reductions in recidivism compared with programs that expected less clean time.

3. Drug courts where the judge spent an average of three minutes or greater per participant during court hearings had 153% greater reductions in recidivism compared with programs where the judge spent less time.[55]

4. Drug courts **where treatment providers communicated with the court or team via e-mail had 119% greater reductions in recidivism.**

5. Drug courts where a representative from treatment attended drug court team meetings (staffings) had 105% greater reductions in recidivism.

6. Drug courts where **internal review of the data and program statistics** led to modifications in program operations had 105% greater reductions in recidivism.

7. Drug courts where **a treatment representative attended court hearings** had 100% greater reductions in recidivism than programs where treatment did not attend.

8. Drug courts that **allowed nondrug charges** (e.g., theft or forgery) had 95% greater reductions in recidivism than drug courts that accepted only drug charges.

9. Drug courts that had a **law enforcement representative** on the drug court team had 88% greater reductions in recidivism than programs that did not.

10. Drug courts that had **evaluations conducted by independent evaluators** and used them to make

---

[55] Simply inquiring into how things are going for the defendant, asking if they have been complying with the programs, and showing compassion are very affective in motivating many deprived individuals.

modifications in drug court operations had 85% greater reductions in recidivism than programs that did not use these results."[56]

Drug Court Review, Vol. VIII, Issue 1 (2012) p. 22-27
(emphasis added).

Top Ten Practices for Cost Savings:

"Many of the top ten practices for reducing recidivism are the same ones that also contribute to saving costs. Following are the top ten practices related to increased cost savings ranked by effect sizes, starting with the largest.

1. Drug courts where **internal review of the data and program statistics** led to modifications in program operations had 131% higher cost savings.
2. Drug courts that had **evaluations conducted by independent evaluators** and used them to make modifications in drug court operations had 100% greater cost savings.
3. Drug courts where **sanctions were imposed immediately** after noncompliant behavior had 100% greater cost savings.
4. Drug courts where **the defense attorney attended** drug court team meetings (staffings) had 93% greater cost savings.
5. Drug courts where **participants must have a job or be in school in order to graduate** had 83% greater cost savings.
6. Drug courts where a **treatment representative attended court sessions** had 81% greater cost savings.
7. Drug courts **where team members are given a copy of the guidelines for sanctions** had 72% greater cost savings.

---

[56] The Bureau of Justice Assistance offers free assistance in evaluating programs. Bureau of Justice Assistance/U.S. Dept. of Justice Programs Office, School of Public Affairs, 810 Seventh Street N.W. American University, Washington D.C. 20531 Website: www.american.edu/spa/jpo

8. Drug courts where **drug test results were available in 48 hours or less** had 68% greater cost savings.
9. Drug courts where drug tests were collected at least two times per week in the first phase had 68% greater cost savings.
10. Drug courts where **a law enforcement representative attended** court sessions had 64% greater cost savings than courts where law enforcement did not."
   Drug Court Review, Vol. VIII, Issue 1 (2012) p. 28 – 31
   (emphasis added).

You will see these Best Practices in federal grant applications. "Drug courts are significantly more effective and cost-effective when they use jail sanction sparingly." *Adult Drug Court Best Practice Standards Vol. 1* (National Association of Drug Court Professionals 2013) p. 33. "Use Jail As a Sanction Sparingly—This study assessed the impact of using briefer compared with longer **jail** sanctions. Drug courts that levied longer-term **jail** sanctions had worse outcomes than those using shorter-term jail sanctions." *Drug Court Review, Vol. VIII, Issue 1 (2012)* P. 33 (emphasis added) "Programs that used **sanctions of less than six days** had average reductions in recidivism of 46% compared with 19% for programs that used longer-term jail sanctions. In addition, jail is an extremely expensive resource. Programs relying on jail sanctions longer than two weeks saw 45% less cost savings after program participation." *Drug Court Review, Vol. VIII, Issue 1 (2012) p. 33 (emphasis added)*; see also, *Adult Drug Court Best Practice Standards Vol. 1* (National Association of Drug Court Professionals 2013) p. 33. "Unless a participant poses an immediate risk to public safety, jail sanctions are administered after less severe consequences have been ineffective at deterring infraction. Jail sanctions are definite in duration and typically last no more than three to five days." *Adult Drug Court Best Practice Standards Vol. 1* (National Association of Drug Court Professionals 2013) p. 28. "[J]ail sanctions of longer than one week were associated with increased recidivism and negative cost-benefits." *Adult Drug Court Best Practice Standards Vol. 1* (National Association of Drug Court Professionals 2013) p. 33.

"Some drug courts may place participants in jail as a means

of providing detoxification services or to keep them 'off the streets' when adequate treatment is unavailable in the community. Although this practice may be necessary in rare instances to protect participants from immediate self-harm, it is inconsistent with best practices, unduly costly, and unlikely to produce lasting benefits. As soon as a treatment slot becomes available, the participant should be released immediately from custody and transferred to the appropriate level of care in the community." *Adult Drug Court Best Practice Standards Vol. 1* (National Association of Drug Court Professionals 2013) p. 42.

"Drug Courts that had a policy of terminating participants for positive drug tests or new arrests for drug possession offenses had 50% higher criminal recidivism and 48% lower cost savings than drug courts that responded to new drug use by increasing treatment or applying sanctions of lesser severity." *Adult Drug Court Best Practice Standards Vol. 1* (National Association of Drug Court Professionals 2013) p. 33.

"The best outcomes are achieved when addicted offenders complete a course of treatment extending over approximately nine to twelve months . . . six to ten hours of counseling per week during the first phase of the program . . . and 200 hours of counseling over the course of treatment." *Adult Drug Court Best Practice Standards Vol. 1* (National Association of Drug Court Professionals 2013) p. 42 (*citations omitted*). "Sustained benefits are more likely to be attained if participants engage in recovery-relevant activities such as developing a sober-support social network, . . .engaging in spiritual practices, . . . and learning effective coping skills from fellow group members." *Adult Drug Court Best Practice Standards Vol. 1* (National Association of Drug Court Professionals 2013) p. 45 (*citations omitted*). In relapse prevention therapy or intensive outpatient treatment "participants learn to identify their personal triggers or risk factors for relapse, take measures to avoid coming into contact with those triggers, and rehearse strategies to deal with high-risk situations that arise unavoidably." *Adult Drug Court Best Practice Standards Vol. 1* (National Association of Drug Court Professionals 2013) p. 46. "Contrary to some beliefs, individuals who are court mandated to attend self-help groups perform as well or better than non-mandated individuals." *Adult Drug Court Best Practice Standards*

Vol. 1 (National Association of Drug Court Professionals 2013) p. 45.

Drug courts should be used for offenders with high risks and high needs. Drug courts have been shown to produce the greatest benefits for offenders who have relatively more severe antisocial backgrounds or treatment-resistant histories.[57] The more drug courts meet the needs of these individuals, the healthier they and their families will be. Our communities will be safer. There will be less burdens placed on public dollars.

Other courts should take advantage of this science and implement as many of the policies and protocols as possible of drug courts. All courts and prosecutors should strive to benefit from and implement the research based principles upon which drug courts operate. We have great success with Intensive Outpatient Treatment. It is far better, more successful, and less disruptive than SAFPF.

So the next time you have a defendant's mother saying "I want him in Saint Pete's as much as you do, but you are talking about a year of his life" ask yourself – have you done everything you can to help this sick defendant and his family before you make their situation worse.

When people are incarcerated for an extended period of time they lose everything, their jobs, relationships, homes, cars, etc. In war, you can burn people out of their homes, take their possessions, and they can come back from that, but when you take their history and their experiences; they can't recover from losing that much.

The ten components of successful specialty treatment courts
1. Multi-disciplinary team (i.e. Brainstorming).
2. Judicial supervision. It is unethical to proceed without this

---

[57] Andrews and Bonta, *The Psychology of Criminal Conduct* (5th ed.) (2010).

because they are so beneficial to the cause.

3. Clinical case management. Visit more than once per week.
4. Legal leverage. The more serious the crime, the more leverage you have.
5. Drug testing.
6. Jail sanctions.
7. Staff training. Drug courts are the paradigm of evidence based procedures. There is a 500 % increase in cost benefits when staff receives training provided by the National Association of Drug Court Professionals NADCP (also the world's largest trainer of mental health professionals in the criminal justice system). The reason this training is so essential is because the science changes and evolves.
8. Driving under the influence (DUI) courts. Some increase reduction in recidivism as much as twenty-one percent. Others actually increase recidivism as much as eight percent. That is why the above mentioned training is so essential.
9. Family drug courts.[58] These courts address those cases where the complaining witnesses are at risk for domestic violence. High risk, high need. They have consistently better outcomes especially with co-occurring disorders. These courts address unemployment, lack of education, criminal records, inadequate housing, etc.
10. Best practices. Which include: weekly counseling sessions, fifteen month treatment plans, positive judicial and counselor attributes, home base outreach to teach parenting and other skills, and frequent drug and alcohol testing.

---

[58] Family Drug Courts have achieved higher rates of parental participation in substance abuse treatment; longer stays in substance abuse treatment; higher rates of family reunification; shorter lengths of stay in foster care for children; and less recurrence of maltreatment.

If they say you don't trust them, that you don't believe them - they are right, you do not-and should not. This is a drug court. It is not a treatment program. The goal is to protect the community.

CHAPTER NINE

CAUSES OF MENTAL ILLNESS

*Keep my word positive. Words become my behaviors. Keep my
behaviors positive. Behaviors become my habits. Keep my habits
positive. Habits become my values. Keep my values positive.
Values become my destiny.*
Mahatma Gandhi

The three things that are the most likely source of mental illness are:

1. Genetics influence (biological),
2. Drug use (substance abuse is a mental illness listed in the Diagnostic and Statistical Manual of Mental Disorders), and
3. Environmental (psychological–trauma, abuse, etc.)(social–people, places, community, peer, family, school/work, culture, poverty, economics, social standing, etc.), or a combination of influences.

Three things that influence chemical dependency are:

1. Genetics,
2. Drug use and
3. Environmental influences or a combination of influences.

Since substance abuse is a mental illness, it is not surprising that the sources and influence are the same as with mental illness. Many mentally ill individuals are drawn to substance abuse as a means of self-medicating their illness. This of course is always the wrong course.

Genetics

The most common cause of mental illness is genetics. While Lady Gaga may say one is "born that way" and one may be in fact genetically predisposed and destined for a mental illness, many mental illnesses manifest later in life. Schizophrenia and bipolar disorder usually become apparent after age seventeen; however, there can be very late in life revelations of these disorders. Many conditions once thought to be caused by a person's environment alone are now proven to be genetic, e.g. schizophrenia, depression, and bipolar disorder.[59]

Einstein's brain had large and unusually shaped inferior parietal lobules, which are important in spatial and numbering intelligence. In contrast, studies on the brains of convicted murderers found their brains to have smaller than average prefrontal cortex.[60]

"A piece of your brain the size of a grain of sand would contain 100,000 neurons, two million axons and one billion synapses, all talking to each other."[61]

Telomeres[62] are 50% shorter in people with more stress, resulting in aging faster. [63]

Drug Use

A man asks his son "do you know what the resurrection is?" The son answers "I'm not sure but if it lasts more than eight hours you have to see a doctor."

---

[59] Steven Pinker, *The Blank Slate* (2002).
[60] Steven Pinker, *The Blank Slate* (2002).
[61] V.S. Ramachandran, *Phantoms in the Brain* (1998).
[62] Telomeres are a DNA sequence that appears at the end of each chromosome. Without telomeres, the main part of the chromosome — the part with genes essential for life — would get shorter each time a cell divides.
[63] Michael F. Roizen M. D., Mehmet Oz M. D., *You Staying Young* (2007) Page 19.

More than two thirds of American families have been touched by addiction. It is a disease of the brain. This is irrefutable and supported by decades of research.

Between 1970 to 2010 there has been a reduction in drug use of thirty percent. Unfortunately drug use has increased in young users and this is increasing deaths. With youth age twelve and over drug dependence has quadrupled during that same time period. In 1993 the United States congress allowed direct advertising for pharmaceuticals to the public. The United States is the only country that does this. Think of how we are all bombarded by erectile dysfunction ads in recent years.

Veterinarians get more training on opioids than medical doctors. Lobbyists for pharmaceutical companies have input into medical curriculum. Patients expect a prescription when they visit a doctor. There are quality survey polls on the internet with patients evaluating doctors. Doctors get dinged if a patient is unhappy with the doctor. This affects their income. Bottom line: doctors in America are rewarded for dolling out drugs and penalized for saying "no."

Drug addiction is a brain disease.

The prefrontal cortex of the brain controls reasoning, insight, decision making, personality, concentration, planning, strategy formation, impulsivity, capacity to determine consequences of actions, focus, problem solving, feeling empathy, guilt, etc. It matures until age twenty-six. When considering an action that would affect others, teens are less likely than adults to use the medial prefrontal cortex. Also, adolescent's brains are awash in dopamine. The only people that figured this out before neuroscientists were car insurance salesmen (teens have higher insurance rates because they have so many more accidents than the rest of us).

Frontal lobe damage leaves people living in a permanent present, and they do not bother to make plans. They do not suffer from anxiety.[64]

In families where a parent is abusing substances, violence is more prevalent, and physical and sexual abuse of children is more prevalent. Witnessing violence can have emotionally destructive consequences on children and others. Children from such homes are more likely than their peers to have learning disabilities, failed grades, truancy, and expulsions from school. Children from such homes are more likely to suffer from stress related health disorders such as gastrointestinal disorders, headaches, asthma, migraines, etc.

Brain damage can also be caused by a stroke or a series of strokes. Such damage can manifest in criminal activity and even homicidal ideations. Strokes can be the side effect of illegal drug use or might be genetic in origin or could even be related to one's environment.

Epigenetic changes can be passed along from one generation to the next long after the original exposure to chemicals has passed. Once it is in the great-grandchildren it is permanent.

While generally drug abuse does not cause someone to become mentally ill, many mental illnesses first become apparent after an extremely traumatic event. A bad experience with drug abuse can be an extremely traumatic event.

C.H. had been trying to kick his illegal drug habit for many years, he became sicker and sicker and finally attempted suicide by taking a lethal dose of over the counter drugs. The toxicology tests revealed that he had his wife's illegal drug of choice along with his wife's prescription drugs in his system. He had not voluntarily taken any illegal drugs in months. She had been trying to poison him.

---

[64] Daniel Gilbert, *Stumbling on Happiness* (2006).

Environment

First you get the short end of the stick, and then you get beaten with it.
Me

We dig up a tree from a diseased forest and plant it in good soil and we are amazed when it thrives and does well. We take it back and put it in the same diseased hole and wonder why it dies. . . again. Don't treat the individual trees. Treat the soil. People initiate recovery in treatment but they RECOVER in their communities. The two most important things to consider accomplishing for successful recovery in the community are (1) housing and (2) employment.

Ninety percent of cancers are caused by the environment– what we put in, on and around our bodies. Environmental influences that precipitate mental illness are prescription drug use (many well-meaning parents ensure that their children are addicted to Adderall and Vivanse–treating hyperactivity–before the children even reach their teen years); illegal drug use; post-traumatic stress (from abuse, including sexual abuse, especially as children); trauma; deprivation; bullying; abuse; and traumatic brain injury (the most difficult to treat because there is no medicine for it). Use of illegal drugs, close proximity to and the availability of illegal drugs lead to and exacerbate mental illnesses.

Start young. Horse trainers know that on the first day of a colt's life, if the colt is rubbed all over its body by a human (preferably with the mare standing near), that horse will always be gentler and easier to train. This is called imprinting. Animal behavior teaches us that, like humans, the earlier you start training, the more success you will have. The more challenging tasks are those that come with individuals who have been abused and neglected.

The younger a person is that starts using drugs, the more serious the addiction is generally. A history of head trauma, parental drug abuse during pregnancy, malnutrition, chronic illness or pain all contribute to substance abuse.

Children that live in families with less stable environments, such as parents with multiple partners and harsh or hostile parenting styles, have a higher probability of having shorter telomeres. Telomeres are segments of DNA at the ends of chromosomes. The longer telomere is an indication of: longer life expectancy, less stress, and less depression per studies at Princeton University and in the Netherlands.

We cannot expect individuals to pull themselves up by their own bootstraps if they don't have any boots. A juvenile delinquent in Dallas was named Infant Jones, his father was unknown and his mother did not even care enough to name him. The hospital gave him that moniker. Another had the first name of Lanee because his parents did not care to take the time to correct his birth certificate to Lance. He spent the rest of his life explaining this.

Life experience changes the DNA. Experiences and environment affect the proteins that are made. Some people's genetic makeup makes them more susceptible to addiction.

The brain releases oxytocin (the same chemical that is released in the brains of a mother and a child that causes mothers to bond with their babies), serotonin, dopamine, and endorphins when one focuses on a happy memory. These are the molecules of emotion. The science of using the brain to heal the body is known as nueroimmunology.[65] Nueroplasticity is using the mind to reshape matter, as thoughts trigger new neural growth and rewire the brain.[66] When people are taught to shed bad habits they sleep better, anger slower, will feel more in charge of their lives, and make better choices.

Children must be given positive activities to keep their brains engaged. Boredom can have the same effect as emotional starvation and the same consequences.[67]

---

[65] Rudy Tanzi, PhD, *Super Brain: Unleashing the Explosive Power of Your Mind to Maximize Health, Happiness, and Spiritual Well-Being* (2013).
[66] Rudy Tanzi, PhD, *Super Brain: Unleashing the Explosive Power of Your Mind to Maximize Health, Happiness, and Spiritual Well-Being* (2013).
[67] Dr. Eric Berne, *Games People Play* (1964) p. 8.

We must also protect our brains from the constant stream of violence fed to us via television, movies, video games, etc. If all this just seems like too much (limiting exposure to stress, substance abuse via prescription drugs, and violence) the corporations will supply the demand. If we all expected healthy stress and violence free choices, corporations would stop forcing these negative influences on the American people. It's simple supply and demand. As long as we have an insatiable demand for this garbage and sludge that is being poured into the minds of our children that is what we will receive. Change the channel, or better yet, turn off the television and computer and supply books to your children.

Persons in the field of prostitution, and others who have been placed under tremendous stress or suffered head injuries in beatings, people who were repeatedly sexually abused growing up by their own mentally ill parents or some other relative, or prolonged sexual abuse will result in a variety of mental illnesses: post traumatic stress syndrome, borderline personality disorder, inability to form attachments, social anxiety, etc., living this life will inevitably lead to substance abuse. Soldiers and rape victims frequently suffer from post traumatic stress.

Twenty-five percent of all human trafficking victims in the United States are in Texas. Dallas is a hub with the Interstates 30, 20, 45, and 35 running through it. Persons charged with prostitution are a particularly difficult and challenging group of defendants. Many times they have had such difficult lives they are not able to begin to recall all the crimes of which they have been victimized. They have frequently been raped by other family members on a regular basis starting at a young age.

Among the many cases I have handled, one was forced to live in a shed as a child behind her family's home with no running water and no heat in the winter. One was hit by a semi-truck at age eleven and suffered from traumatic brain injury, had to quit school in grade school, suffered from seizures so bad she ripped out her own ear lobes, was repeatedly raped by her father as a child, and was now living in a vacant house with a pimp who threatened to kill her if she left. One was missing her front teeth, drooling, bald and severely mentally ill, and had been sexually abused by her mother and stepfather. And now they are charged with prostitution.

Mostly because they are too dysfunctional to apply for the social security benefits to which they are undoubtedly entitled. One woman who stepped on an elevator in her office building and it plunged to the ground became addicted to prescription pain killers. All the women are now performing oral sex for as little as five dollars per customer (strangers to the women). It is a vicious cycle that exposes them to mentally ill customers that inflict more damage.

Take the case of C. J., she did well in school, was attractive, and married a successful businessman. They used cocaine. He quit. She couldn't. She began to sell things out of house. They divorced. She ended up with a man that beat her with a baseball bat when she tried to leave him and dumped her at a hospital (ten years ago). She suffered serious brain damage. Months went by before the family knew where she was. She underwent one year of inpatient therapy and then one year of outpatient therapy. Her mother died. She was put in a nursing home. These facts were confirmed by her family. She assaulted a roommate unprovoked, in a boarding home. She is now incompetent and not likely to ever regain competency.

Boarding homes for the mentally ill sprung up after mental institutions were shutdown. They look like any other residence and there could be one in your neighborhood. They are usually located in the lower socio-economic areas of town. They receive federal money. I have been inside many of them while preparing for trials. Mentally ill frequently assault each other in these homes.

Dallas now has recently enacted ordinances to govern boarding homes. One case I prosecuted had one boarding home manager (the defendant) who stabbed another boarding home manager for exposing the fact that the first boarding home manager/defendant was bringing cocaine into the home. Both had lengthy criminal histories.

Brain cells can die with prolonged stress. Managing stress effectively is essential to good brain function. When the basal ganglia (nerve cell clusters) in the brain are overactive, e.g. stress results–people freeze, become anxious, etc. Basal ganglia problems cause anxiety, muscle tension, conflict avoidance, fear of being judged, excessive worry of what others think, shyness, a low threshold of embarrassment. Propranolol is prescribed to musicians to calm tremors.

Kava extract and valerian root have a calming effect on basil ganglia.

There was a study that showed that every time we drink beer we lose a certain number of brain cells. For some reason I can't remember the number of brain cells lost, or who did the study or when . . .What were we talking about?

CHAPTER TEN

SOME HELP – FOR MENTAL ILLNESS

Do not store up for yourselves treasures on earth, where moths and vermin destroy, and where thieves break in and steal. But store up for yourselves treasures in heaven, . . . For where your treasure is, there your heart will be also.
Matthew 6:19-21

We must be the change we wish to see in the world.
Mahatma Ghandi

Mental disorders are varied and complex. A starting place to determine some solutions is the Diagnostic and Statistical Manual of Mental Disorders DSM-V. NAMI.org is an excellent initial resource. Becoming educated about mental illness and bringing relevant individuals together in a community to brainstorm and address the issues is imperative. Educating stakeholders about the many concepts, ideas and resources contained herein is another important step. It would be naïve in the extreme to think that there are simple solutions to the issues facing us; however, there are some concepts of which we should all be aware.

Thoughts create feelings. Feelings become actions. Actions become our reality with which we must live. While some mental illness is hereditary, much mental illness is preventable. Temperament, personality characteristics are very important to mental health.

Fetal Alcohol Syndrome Disorder (FASD) for example, is one-hundred percent preventable. Pre-natal exposure to alcohol is the single biggest cause of preventable intellectual disability (mental retardation). People who were prenatally exposed have a significantly higher likelihood to need special education classes, be involved in the juvenile and justice systems, have alcohol and other drug dependent tendencies, experience foster care, have facial malformations, hyperactivity, inattention, sleeping problems, organ damage, have co-occurring mental health disorders, etc., etc., etc.. Their brains are damaged and smaller. More children are born with FASD than Spina Bifida, Downs Syndrome, childhood cancer, and juvenile diabetes combined.

Mental developmental disability outpaces physical disability in children in the United States.

We must take better care of ourselves and those around us.

PRACTICE TIP:

Change environments for the positive. Induce the positive: dance, music, pleasant movies. Reduce negative: violent movies, violent games, etc. Read. Reduce the number of hours watching television. Consider volunteering for Boys and Girls Clubs or Habitat for Humanity.

Limit exposure to television, especially violent television and video games. Two or more hours of television each day make you twice as likely to develop dementia. Alzheimer's patients will feel the emotions, happy or sad, for hours after they have seen a movie, even though they are unable to recall the movie that they saw.

Change nutrition for the positive.

Low cholesterol levels are associated with severe depression, violence, homicide and suicide.[68] Aspartame is associated with memory problems, mental confusion and a myriad of other maladies.[69]

Foods with Monosodium glutamate (MSG, also known as sodium glutamate) can induce violence.[70]

Omega-3 fatty acids (found in fish, especially wild salmon)

---

[68] Dr. Daniel Amen, *Change your Brain Change Your Body* p. 90, 146 (2010).
[69] Dr. Daniel Amen, *Change your Brain Change Your Body* p. 97 (2010).
[70] Dr. Daniel Amen, *Change your Brain Change your Body* p. 105 (2010).

promotes emotional balance and positive mood.[71] Milk helps your body produce serotonin. Eating regular small meals reduces anxiety.[72]

One can reduce their anxiety by simply drinking water, doing yoga, Tai chi or exercising. Massages, reading positive works like Ghandi, and being in love all elevate one's mood. Valerian root reduces anxiety, and it is as effective as psychotropic medicine. It is known as poor man's valium (don't take it if you have fatigue).

_____

[71] Dr. Daniel Amen, *Change your Brain Change your Body* p. 91 (2010).
[72] Dr. Daniel Amen, *Change your Brain Change your Body* p. 104 (2010).

CHAPTER ELEVEN

LEGAL DRUGS

ALCOHOL

"The gem cannot be polished without friction nor man without trials."
Confucius

Alcohol is the most commonly used addictive substance in the United States. Approximately 17.6 million people, or one in every twelve adults, suffer from alcohol abuse or dependence along with several million more who engage in risky drinking patterns that could lead to alcohol problems.[73] Alcoholism is a disease that kills one-hundred thousand annually, tobacco kills five-hundred thousand.[74]

It is estimated that thirty-five percent of Americans don't drink alcohol at all. About that same amount consider an alcoholic drink as just another beverage. Others consider a beer, a glass of wine or a cocktail a way to relax and unwind after a difficult day, an opportunity to celebrate (about nineteen percent of the United States population. However, nine percent of Americans consider alcoholic beverages as a completely necessary reinforcement to get them through every day. Twenty percent of all drinkers consume

---

[73] National Council on Alcoholism and Drug Dependence https://ncadd.org/for-the-media/alcohol-a-drug-information
[74] Kevin Sabet, PhD *Refer Sanity* page 105 (2013).

eighty percent of the alcohol.

Forty percent of people who start drinking before age fifteen become alcoholics. Children have a fifty percent chance of becoming alcoholics if they are the same sex of an alcoholic parent and a forty percent chance if a different sex from the alcoholic parent.

A study by the Centers for Disease Control and Prevention found that people who practice four healthy behaviors - not smoking, eating healthy, getting enough exercise and limiting alcohol use - were sixty-three percent less likely to die within the eighteen-year study period than those who kept none of those practices.

The most frequently diagnosed diseases are (1) cancer, (2) heart disease, and (3) alcohol addiction. One third of prisoners in state correctional facilities were using alcohol at the time of their offenses.

The frontal lobe does 3 main things:

1. Multi-tasking.
2. Decision making.
3. Insight and judgment.

Alcohol affects the frontal lobe. This is why alcoholics can't see that they have a problem.

Addiction is a preventable and treatable disease of the brain. Four approved medications for alcoholism: Anabuse (can make you sick); Revita (takes away the high, you still stagger); Campral; Vivitrol (same as Revita but it's a shot). Persons with alcoholism are kept on the drugs for 1 to 1 ½ years. Local mental health providers pay for this if the individual is unable to do so (NorthStar in Dallas).

With hypertension high blood pressure sixty percent of doctors know what to prescribe. With asthma fifty-two percent of doctors know what to prescribe. With diabetes forty-five percent of doctors know what to prescribe. But with alcohol addiction only eleven percent of doctors know what to prescribe.

It normally takes five to seven years of regular use to develop an addiction to alcohol. In contrast a person who uses cocaine usually takes a few weeks or months of use to develop an addiction.

Alcohol affects the brain by reducing brain size, diminishing memory, altering brain cell functions, and causing and contributing to depression.

Alcohol affects the body's cardiovascular system by raising blood pressure and triglycerides, risk of strokes (the leading cause of long-term disability), plus damage to the heart muscle. It affects the body's nervous system by brain damage, tremors, dementia and nerve damage, also affecting coordination, self-control, judgment and reaction times.

Alcohol affects the gastrointestinal system by stomach inflammation and bleeding. It affects the liver via cirrhosis, causes cancer, hepatitis, fatty changes, and liver failure. It affects the endocrine system by problems controlling blood sugar, loss of libido and reduced fertility. Alcohol can result in oral cancer – cancer of the oral cavity, pharynx, esophagus, and larynx. Alcohol breaks down muscle and predisposes bones to fracture. Abuse of alcohol can result in immune system disorders, and altered blood sugar levels.

Persons that insist on drinking alcohol should follow these recommendations: no more than seven drinks per week for women and no more than fourteen drinks per week for men.

Injuries and deaths related to alcohol each year include: sixty percent of fatal burn injuries, drownings and homicides; and forty percent of fatal motor vehicle crashes, suicides and fatal falls per year. Driving under the influence is responsible for more injury than domestic violence.

And alcohol is used as the weapon in many sexual assaults, especially on college campuses.

One year of binge drinking results in a ten percent loss of the hippocampus. The hippocampus is the registrar of memory, motivation, and social behaviors (interacting with your family, going to work, etc.).

Here's how the alcohol-related injuries break out:

30% of transportation injuries,
22% of the twelve million home-accident injuries,
59% of fire fatalities have alcohol in their systems,
45% of drowning fatalities,

15.5% of occupational injuries,

56% of assault victims have alcohol in their bodies,

In short, you have a 2.5 times greater risk of a violent death when you drink.

Alcohol reduces one's inhibitions. Many relapses start with that first drink of alcohol, regardless of the drug of addiction. Alcohol is a depressant, can lower one's mood and cause the person to relapse. A person recovering from addiction needs all the good nutrition they can get. Consumption of alcohol is taking up the space of more important nutrition. And many people suffer injuries while drunk, e.g. traumatic brain injury from falling or car accidents that further exacerbate their mental and criminal problems.

If one has experienced any form of brain trauma it is critical that they adopt a brain healthy program to enhance brain function. People who drink more than three times a week have smaller brains than nondrinkers.[75]

If you are on probation, hair provides a three month history of alcohol and drug abuse. Tests for some drugs can be defeated by consuming large quantities of creatin (found in some power drinks). If they're using a small amount of drugs, it will not show on the test.

Treatment, of course, is more effective than prison. In one study regarding re-addiction following prison:

Users of opiates had an 88-91% chance of relapse. Users who mixed drugs had a 70% percent chance of relapse. Alcohol addicts had a 50-70% chance of relapse after treatment.[76]

Anyone can develop a serious alcohol problem, including a teenager. Because the brain is not fully developed until the mid-

---

[75] Dr. Daniel Amen, *Change your Brain Change your Body* (2010) page 189. *Change your Brain Change your Body* is based on 600 different sources.
[76] Joseph Lunievicz, Director, NDRI, National Development Research Institute, Bureau of Justice *Neuroscience of Addiction* (2012) Webinar.

20s, using alcohol during adolescence can cause alterations to the structure, neuron connectivity (wiring) and physiology of the brain, which can affect everything from emerging sexuality to decision-making.

Beer and wine are not "safer" than hard liquor. A 12-ounce can of beer, a 5-ounce glass of wine, and 1.5 ounces of hard liquor all contain the same amount of alcohol and have the same effects on the body and mind.

On average, it takes two to three hours for a single drink to leave a person's system. Nothing can speed up this process, including drinking coffee, taking a cold shower or "walking it off."

Studies show that if a parent drinks alcohol, the children are more likely to do so, but you can lessen the likelihood when you follow these suggestions: Use alcohol moderately, never suggesting that alcohol is a good way to handle problems. For instance, do not come through the door after work saying, "What a horrible day; I need a drink!" Be sure to exhibit healthy ways to cope with stress such as exercise, meditation, talking things over or listening to music.

If there is a history of alcoholism in your family, be upfront and let them know they can be more vulnerable to developing a problem with drinking in the future.

Warning signs of alcohol abuse in teens are: mood changes, rebelling against rules, problems in school, switching friends, sloppy hygiene or appearance, lack of involvement in former activities, low energy, finding alcohol in your child's room or backpack or smelling it on their breath, memory lapses, poor concentration, bloodshot eyes, slurred speech, and lack of coordination.

Withdrawal from alcohol is potentially life threatening.

Health food stores sell red wine pills because they contain resveratrol which is good for the heart. Just another example of how some things are good in moderation. Resveratrol found in red wine, grape skins, chocolate, peanuts, and mulberries fights

Alzheimer's disease and dementia and improves longevity. The concentration of resveratrol in dark grape skins is greater than that of red wine. Resveratrol is actually found in greater amounts in dark grapes than in wine. One to three glasses of wine per day may benefit the heart and brain.[77] Too much alcohol causes mental problems, shortened attention span, confusion, tremors, strokes, depression and eventually alcohol dementia, and more.

---

[77] Dr. Majid Fotuhi M.D., PhD, *Boost Your Brain* (2013) p. 234.

CHAPTER TWELVE

PRESCRIPTION DRUG ABUSE

"If we desire respect for the law, we must first make the law respectable."
Justice Louis Brandeis

The average age of a prescription recipient is sixty. The average age of an emergency room overdose patient on prescription drugs is in the teens.

The number one cause of death in the United States of eighteen to twenty-four year olds is substance abuse. Alcohol and other drugs including a combination of alcohol and drugs are equal. The United States (with only five percent of the world's population) consumes eighty percent of opioids (morphine, hydrocodone, oxycodone, OxyContin, Percocet, codeine, and related drugs) and ninety-five percent of the Vicodin in the world. Almost twenty percent of doctor visits in the United States include a prescription for opioids. Every year we write about 200 million prescriptions for opioids.[78] There were at least 38,329 drug-related fatalities in 2010, according to preliminary data compiled by the United States Centers for Disease Control and Prevention (CDC). For the first time ever non-heroin opiate addiction surpassed heroin or cocaine as the leading cause of drug treatment admission in the United States.[79]

The United States is in the grip of an epidemic of prescription drug overdoses.[80]

---

[78] Archives of Internal Medicine.
[79] Cesar Fax July 30, 2012 Vol. 21.
[80] Centers for Disease Control and Prevention. http://www.cdc.gov/about/grand-

What is an epidemic?[81]

- In the past decade, more than 100,000 people from across the United States died from overdoses involving prescription painkillers. That's enough people to fill Yankee Stadium to capacity - twice.
- For every person who died from a prescription painkiller overdose in 1999, nearly four died in 2009.
- If the painkiller overdose death rate had remained level since 1999, rather than rising so sharply, more than 60,000 people would still be alive today.
- Enough prescription painkillers were prescribed in 2010 to medicate every American adult around-the-clock for a month.

Foster children are fifty-three times more likely to be prescribed psychotropic medications than non-foster children.

At the nursing home where my niece works, seventy-five percent of the residents are under age sixty-five. Many people in their eighties and nineties have worked hard and lived a drug free life. Many tenants at nursing homes today are not elderly but suffer from alcohol or substance abuse related dementia with a sprinkling of traumatic brain injury. This is becoming more common in America.

In the 1940s we used ten percent of the amounts of prescriptions we use now. Almost all prescriptions we use today should be used temporarily. To use them long term has a negative affect.

Adderall (amphetamine, dextroamphetamine mixed salts) is a Schedule II controlled substance. This is the most abused prescription drug in America.

Calling it an "upper" is like calling a hydrogen bomb a

rounds/archives/2011/01-February.htm
[81] Centers for Disease Control, September 28, 2012.

grenade. It is made of pure amphetamine (note: Hitler was taking an injection of amphetamine daily for the last four years of his life, it drove him insane; amphetamine abuse leads to Parkinson's disease, the same thing that Michael J. Fox has). It has already picked up its share of street monikers: Speed, Beans, Black Beauties, Christmas Trees, and Double Trouble, among others

Adderall is used for treating attention deficit hyperactivity disorder (ADHD) and narcolepsy. Adderall should only be used as a temporary medication to help control symptoms and help regulate brain activity. Long-term use of Adderall as a prescription medication treatment for attention-deficit hyperactivity disorder may make symptoms worse and make withdrawal symptoms unbearable.

Side effects of Adderall include nervousness, restlessness, excitability, dizziness, headache, fear, anxiety, psychotic episodes, easy to anger, hallucinations, and tremor. Minor side effects include anxiety, and transient depression. More serious effects include bipolar condition symptoms, heart palpitations, critical cardiovascular problems, elevation of blood pressure, Tourette's syndrome, seizures, stroke, and psychotic episodes or plain old psychosis. Blood pressure and heart rate may increase. Adderall is habit forming and chronic use may lead to dependence. Taking too much Adderall medicine initially, could make attention-deficit hyperactivity disorder symptoms worse. Manifestations of chronic intoxication with amphetamines include severe dermatoses, marked insomnia, irritability, hyperactivity, and personality changes. The most severe manifestation of chronic intoxication is psychosis, often clinically indistinguishable from schizophrenia.

Psychosis is the feeling of detachment from reality that you're not in control, and that's a very frightening feeling for anyone.[82]

Amphetamines have been extensively abused. Tolerance,

---

[82] Leonard Mlodinow Subliminal - How Your Unconscious Mind Rules your Behavior page 17 (2012).

extreme psychological dependence, and severe social disability have occurred. There are reports of patients who have increased the dosage to levels many times higher than recommended. Abrupt cessation following prolonged high dosage administration results in extreme fatigue and mental depression; changes are also noted on the sleep EEG. The attention deficit hyperactivity disorder (ADHD) drug Adderall (an amphetamine) is known to cause serious physical side effects including heart attack, stroke, elevated blood pressure and heart rate, and even sudden death. The United States Food and Drug Administration (FDA) is aware of this and more, but takes no action to prevent people continuing to take the drug anyway.

Adderall is basically a cocktail of various amphetamine stimulants and is often referred to as "prescription speed." And because it is similar in makeup to illegal methamphetamines, it is highly addictive. So in addition to its many side effects, users will have a difficult time functioning without Adderall once they start taking it.

Adderall also comes with a full slate of mental side effects as well as physical ones. Ironically, the drug can actually cause behavior to become worse, leaving one to wonder how or why such a drug was ever approved as a legitimate medicine to treat a disorder that it may actually aggravate.

Taking Adderall can also thwart proper brain function, increase behavioral aggression, and even cause episodes of psychosis in which the patient becomes maniacal and starts hearing voices. In other words, it is absolutely insane for this dangerous drug to be on the market, let alone be touted as a safe medicine for children. And the FDA is aware of the seriously dangerous nature of this drug because it warned the public back in 2009 about its many extreme side effects.

The FDA conducted its own study of Adderall's effects on children and early data pointed to the fact that the drug increases the risk of sudden death in children. But neither the study nor any of the other facts about the drug's dangerous effects prompted the FDA to actually pull the drug from the market. In fact, the FDA made a point of denying the results of its own study and patients continue to take the drug.

Prescriptions can and are sold for a great deal of money.

Never mind the human cost, there is money to be made. Take that prescription to the pharmacy. Or, take your money to a nearby local college or university. You will pay $30 to $40 dollars per pill for a very small amount of Adderall, usually sold to you by a student. Sales are usually student to student although the numbers of genuine drug dealers are growing rapidly, bringing with them all the problems of criminal drug dealers. Dealers recognize good business opportunities.

If one overdoses alone, the chance of survival is slim.

Adderall is very, very addictive. Along with physical and psychological damage, this drug opens the awful Pandora's Box of addiction, with all its' sadness, pain and misery. It is a gateway drug, often leading to other drugs like cocaine, heroin, etc.

Signs of withdrawal include severe depression or dysphoria, irritability, rage, trouble sleeping and an intense craving for the medication. Symptoms of attention-deficit hyperactivity disorder may be more severe during the withdrawal phase. Close supervision from a psychologist is recommended until symptoms are under control with cognitive or behavioral therapy.

Additionally there are concerns regarding the prescription of Adderall to children. For example physicians in the United Kingdom are advised to refrain from prescribing Adderall to children under five in any circumstances and to prescribe it to children over five only if no other viable options are available. In some countries, concerns over Adderall are so strong that it is banned completely, even for prescription use.

People who use Adderall as a recreational drug are at severe risk of further complications if they mix it with alcohol. Due to the fact that Adderall counterbalances some of the common signs of excessive alcohol consumption, it is very easy to succumb to alcohol poisoning without any prior warning. There are further complications possible if Adderall and alcohol are mixed, given that both Adderall and alcohol have dehydrating properties and that alcohol is a depressant, which can aggravate the psychological issues associated with the withdrawal from Adderall.

Due to its stimulating properties, Adderall can cause smokers to crave cigarettes substantially more than they usually do, thereby increasing their risk of smoking-related illnesses.

At the current time, although there are no specific

medications available to assist users with the withdrawal process, it is possible to use antidepressants to help with the psychological effects of the interruption of Adderall use. The physical effects of Adderall withdrawal include fatigue and disorientation. It is strongly recommended that when ceasing Adderall use, the method be undertaken slowly to minimize these effects.

I am personally aware of cases where Adderall abuse led to suicide and homicide in high functioning adults who were perfectly normal before they began taking the drug.

Other drugs can also be prescribed with negative effects. Seroquel and other SSRIs (selective serotonin reuptake inhibitors) have been linked to violence, suicide, and even murder.

CHAPTER THIRTEEN

ILLEGAL DRUGS

"The problem with the rat race is, even if you win, you're still a rat."
Lily Tomlin

The number one cause of death in the United States is substance abuse.

Drug addiction is a brain disease. Substance abuse is listed as a mental disorder in the Diagnostic and Statistical Manual of Mental Disorders DSM-V.[83]

The legal definition of mental illness in Texas is an illness, disease, or condition, other than epilepsy, senility, alcoholism[84], or mental deficiency, that: (A) substantially impairs a person's thought, perception of reality, emotional process, or judgment; or (B) grossly impairs behavior as demonstrated by recent disturbed behavior.[85]

Education about the health dangers is the key to drug treatment. Drug users have far less dopamine activity.

---

[83] The DSM-V sets out the diagnostic criteria for clinicians to diagnose a mental illness. It is used by insurance companies, psychiatrists, psychologists, courts, etc.

[84] However the DSM-V indicates that alcoholism is a mental illness. This is an example of how the legal definition may not always be the same as the legal definition.

[85] Texas Health and Safety Code 571.003.

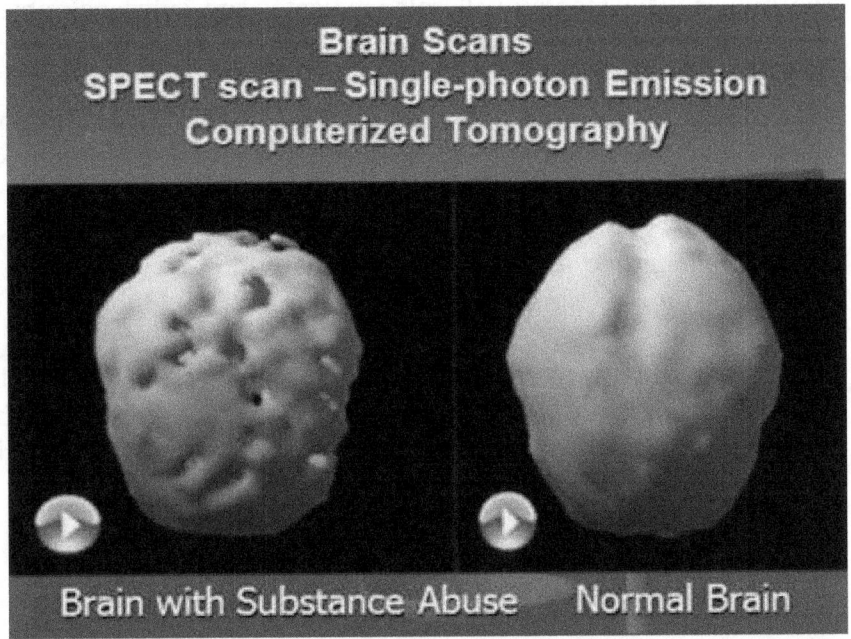

Mental illness and drug abuse not only changes the way your brain looks and functions, it changes your outer appearance. Methamphetamines and alcohol are the most physically toxic of drugs; they damage every organ of the body.

When normal people have a bad day they may feel a little sad. When drug addicts and the mentally ill have a bad day they are suicidal due to damages to the limbic region of the brain. This is why it is so important to be positive with them.

Having read thousands of psychiatric reports and evaluations on mentally ill criminal defendants, I can attest that it is a rare report where the person has never taken an illegal drug or abused prescription drugs. Though it is estimated that seventy percent of the mentally ill suffer from addiction,[86] that figure could

---

[86] Per Robert Stutman, in charge of drug enforcement under President Obama.

be higher. The mentally ill self-medicate, and substance abusers eventually become mentally ill. It is the great spiral downward of the criminal mind.

The relationship between substance abuse and child abuse and neglect is well-documented. Illegal drug users are more likely than non-users to have experienced physical or sexual abuse as children. A recent study found that thirty-three percent of methamphetamine users had been sexually abused before the age of fifteen and a similar percentage reported childhood physical abuse.[87]

Usually peer pressure is the reason people use the first time. Each one thinking they are stronger and smarter than others before them. Each one thinking that they can stop anytime they wish. Each one was wrong.

---

[87] Cathleen Otero, M.S.W., M.P.A. et al, *Methamphetamine Addiction, Treatment, and Outcomes: Implication of Child Welfare Workers* National Center on Substance Abuse and Child Welfare (2006).

CHAPTER FOURTEEN

MARIJUANA

"Good judgment comes from experience, and a lot of that comes from bad judgment."
Will Rogers

Marijuana has been used since 2800 B.C. and probably longer. It is not your grandma's marijuana. While marijuana is basically the same, some varieties are more potent than in the 1970s. The more potent varieties have greater availability today. During the 1970s the first age of use was nineteen on average, today it is age twelve.

Just because it's legal in some places does not mean it is safe.[88] From 1885 to 1929 Coca-Cola (originally marketed as medicine) contained cocaine as an ingredient. It included two "medicinal ingredients": extract of coca leaves and kola nuts. In 1898 Bayer Pharmaceuticals marketed heroin as cough medication. Ecstasy was originally patented as an appetite suppressant and then used for psychotherapy before being designated as having no legitimate medical use. In the 1950s, the medical community used phencyclidine (PCP) as a surgical anesthetic (it causes memory loss among many other detrimental side effects). In 1964, doctors posed for cigarette advertisements indicating that they preferred Camel, but in 1909 scientists had already discovered the link between cigarettes and lung cancer. Doctors were quoted in advertisements as saying that baby formula was better than breast

---

[88] Colorado and Washington State legalized marijuana in 2012. Oregon and Washington D.C. legalized it in 2014.

milk. As recently as 1995, Oxycontin was marketed as non-addictive (it is highly addictive).[89] So just because some states have chosen to legalize marijuana, it does not mean that it is healthy or safe. Today's marijuana is possibly the most genetically modified plant there is.

Alcohol (accidents) and tobacco (pulmonary disease and cancer) are the leading substance abuse causes of death in the United States, and now we are adding a third drug.

According to a recent study, smoking marijuana when young changes DNA and can affect later born children causing them to be more susceptible to addiction, and causing a strong appetite for heroin in particular.

The THC from one joint of marijuana takes seven days to get out of body (forty-two days if used daily). Marijuana withdrawal starts three weeks after the last dose. Symptoms include: Irritability, insomnia, decreased appetite, increased aggression and cravings. Marijuana smoke is four times more carcinogenic than cigarettes. There is a fivefold increase on heart attack risk one hour after use.

Marijuana with someone predisposed to schizophrenia can facilitate the onset of psychosis. At least 25,000 persons suffering from schizophrenia in the United Kingdom could have avoided the illness if they had not used cannabis according to Professor Robin Murray, of London's Institute of Psychiatry.[90] Twenty percent of (heavy) marijuana users who start early develop schizophrenia. Euphoria turns into schizophrenia by dumping too much dopamine into the brain.

A number of studies show a connection between marijuana and psychosis, and also birth defects. Almost one hundred percent

---

[89] Robert Stutman, a 25-year veteran of the Drug Enforcement Administration (DEA) has served as special agent in charge of several DEA field divisions, including the New York field division, the Nation's largest. He states if he could abolish any drug it would be OxyContin
[90] Kevin Sabet, PhD, *Refer Sanity*, page 33 (2013).

of cocaine users started with marijuana.

The psychoactive substance in marijuana intensifies the state of denial among users, obscuring the drug's potential health harms.[91]

The nationwide total of emergency room admissions for marijuana related incidents went from an estimated 16,251 emergency room visits in the United States related to marijuana use in 1991 to exceeding 374,000 emergency room admissions in 2008 - a nearly twenty-five fold increase in just seventeen years. Interestingly the number of users of marijuana stayed about the same during this period. This suggests that the increase in emergency room visits did not have to do simply with increased numbers of users.[92] One study showed that using marijuana regularly before age eighteen resulted in an average IQ of six to eight fewer points at age thirty-eight (relative to those who did not use marijuana before age eighteen). This astounding finding was still true for those teens who use marijuana regularly but stopped using the drug after the age of eighteen.[93] One study showed that those who had used marijuana on more than fifty occasions had a much higher risk, six times higher, of developing schizophrenia relative to nonusers.[94]

If regular heavy marijuana use reduces a person's I.Q. by six to eight points, and most children have an I.Q. of 100, a loss of six to eight points can be the difference between graduating or not, or going to high school or not. It also interferes with other aspects of their physical, mental and emotional functioning and development. And today's children already have the lowest chances of owning homes, getting jobs, and having healthy children of previous generations in America. In a study in the Journal of Psychiatric Research, research showed that heavy

---

[91] Kevin Sabet, PhD, *Refer Sanity*, page 34 (2013).
[92] Kevin Sabet, PhD, *Refer Sanity* page 36 (2013).
[93] Kevin Sabet, PhD, *Refer Sanity* page 42 (2013).
[94] Kevin Sabet, PhD, *Refer Sanity* page 43 (2013).

marijuana use among young adults and adolescents may affect normal brain development, interrupting an important process called myelinization.

One in eleven marijuana users become addicted. One in six children that use marijuana becomes addicted.[95] In studies of twins, it was discovered that a marijuana smoking twin was five times more likely than the non-using twin to use other drugs.[96]

Smoked marijuana has never been approved by any scientific body as medicine.[97] The most common method of ingestion is smoking. There is no way to measure the amount of the drug that is ingested with this method.

There are approximately two-hundred and forty-five chemicals in marijuana. Only two are great medicine, and they are for only a very few specific medical conditions such as glaucoma. We don't extract the good chemicals. Ninety-two percent of medical marijuana users smoke it.

For those who argue that it is no worse than alcohol, respond:

- Dude - that's your best excuse.
- Alcohol has eight million addicts.
- Even occasional use changes the physical structure of the brain, and we do not know for how long.
- Every neurologist will tell you messing with the brain is bad.
- Children drink more alcohol than they smoke marijuana because alcohol is legal. Legalize marijuana and you say to many teens that it is safe.
- We cannot even prove that marijuana works on non-cancer pain, but we are flooding America with it.

---

[95] Kevin Sabet, PhD, *Refer Sanity* page 150 (2013).
[96] Kevin Sabet, PhD, *Refer Sanity* page 156 (2013).
[97] Kevin Sabet, PhD, *Refer Sanity* page 57 (2013).

CHAPTER FIFTEEN

SYNTHETIC CANNABIS; also known as SYNTHETIC MARIJUANA

"I sometimes wish that people would put a little more emphasis on the observance of the law than they do upon its enforcement."
Calvin Coolidge

Synthetic or designer drugs were created in an attempt to try to get around the existing drug laws. They are very dangerous and illegal. Two thirds of substance abuse emergency room visits for 2013 in the United States were because of synthetic cannabis use. These were originally created by scientists trying to extract the medicinal value items from marijuana. The bad guys find the research and use it to their advantage.

Scientists have to keep on top of these synthetic drugs to test for them, but the drugs are still illegal. Drug dealers perpetuate the common misconception among drug users that the drugs are legal. It may have been true that some of the drugs were not yet illegal when they were first coming on the market but laws were changed in 2010 making such drugs illegal under federal law and many states including Texas. [98]

The leaves and twigs in these synthetic drugs do not come from Cannabis plants–they can be just about any herb which has then been sprayed or soaked with a solution of synthetic chemicals. One study revealed that some of the herbal ingredients listed by the manufacturers could not be found in the products. As far as a buyer

---

[98] Tex. Controlled Substances Act 481.1031.

knows, some of these products may contain nothing but lawn clippings sprayed with these toxic chemicals.

Symptoms

Synthetic cannabis can precipitate psychosis and in some cases it is prolonged. Studies suggest that synthetic cannabinoid intoxication is associated with acute psychosis, mental illness in previously stable individuals, psychotic disorders, and also may have the ability to trigger a chronic (long-term) psychotic disorder among vulnerable individuals such as those with a family history of mental illness.

The list of symptoms is very long and include strokes, vasculitis (which is an inflammation of the blood vessels and a cause of strokes), brain aneurysms, blood vessels in the brain constricting and limiting blood and oxygen flow, abdominal pain, agitation, aggressive behavior, anxiety, arrhythmia, loss of balance, birth defects, blindness, elevated blood pressure, red and bloodshot eyes, permanent brain damage, cardiac problems, becoming catatonic and nonresponsive, claustrophobia, severe cognitive impairment, confusion, chest pains, combativeness, loss of concentration, loss of consciousness, convulsions, coordination, disturbed perceptions, burning eyes, delirium, dizziness, drowsiness, drug craving, gastrointestinal problems, hallucinations, headaches, rapid heart rate, heart attacks, heart palpitations, homicidal ideations, irritability, kidney damage, kidney failure, dangerous behavior, lack of concern for loved ones, mental illness (including long-term mental illness), a change in mood, migraines, nausea, neurological problems, nightmares, numbness, panic attacks, paralysis, paranoia, paranoid delusions, psychotic episodes, psychosis, including chronic psychosis, manic rage, multiple organ failure, muscle spasms, impaired sense of time, respiratory depression, seizures, stumbling, slurring of words, inability to speak, suicidal thoughts, sweating, tremor, tachycardia (rapid heartbeat), disorganized thoughts, inability to control urination, violent outbursts (becoming violent in an instant), extreme violence, vomiting, xerostomia (dry mouth), and even DEATH, and many more problems.

Psychological symptoms are increasing among users who had no history of vulnerability to mental illness. Some users become floridly psychotic. Perfectly normal people have used synthetic cannabis once and then immediately had to be institutionalized for psychiatric care repeatedly.

It is more harsh than marijuana and makes your throat burn and your lungs ache long after you smoke. It sometimes takes more than five minutes for the drug to take affect, so people will use far more of it than they should. Some symptoms last for weeks after use, some are permanent.

There have been so many negative reported events; it keeps any clinical trial from happening because nobody wants to touch it.

Think popcorn. When you have a bag of popcorn and squirt the liquid butter into it, some of the pieces are saturated, while others may just have a hint. The fake weed is the same way. It is believed that those super-soaked batches can be the difference from a "normal" high, and one that induces a scary "Zombie-affect". There have been several stories in the media that have cited people actually eating pets and biting people and having a seemingly Zombie reaction; however, it is called that because it can cause extreme anxiety, paranoia, panic attacks, alienation/disassociation, psychotic episodes and hallucinations, which are the most common reported side effects. The term "couch lock" is associated with synthetic marijuana to describe one effect– an inability to move despite being conscious.

A young man in Farmington Hill, Michigan stole from his father to obtain money for synthetic marijuana and later beat his father to death with a baseball bat for more money to obtain more of this drug. Before the murder he stated that he would have no qualms about murdering his entire family for more.

Some of the brand names of the synthetic marijuana products include: Blaze, Blueberry Haze, Dank, Demon Passion Smoke, fake weed, Genie, Hawaiian Hybrid, K2, legal weed, Magma, Mr. Smiley, Ninja, Nitro, Moon Rocks, Ono Budz, Panama Red Ball, pot-pourri, Puff, Red X Dawn, Sativah Herbal Smoke, Skunk, Spice, Spike, Train, Trainwreck, Ultra Chronic, Voodoo Spice, Yucatan Fire. Some Spice products are sold as "incense," but they more closely resemble potpourri. Like marijuana, Spice is abused mainly by smoking. Sometimes Spice is mixed with marijuana or is prepared as an herbal infusion for drinking. They are marketed as "herbal" products, and people tend to equate "herbal" with "safe".

Educate your children about the hazards of consuming anything that has not been tested, and let them know that these fake marijuana products are anything but natural. Does "2-[(1R,3S)-3-hydroxycyclohexyl]-5-(2-methyloctan-2-yl)phenol)(CP 47,497)" or methylenedioxypyrovalerone sound natural to you? And since these products are not regulated drugs, there is no way to know how big a dose you are getting. No drug is safe if you do not know what it is and how much of it you are taking.

The internet offers easy accessibility and enhanced anonymity. Labels on Spice products often claim that they contain "natural" psycho-active material taken from a variety of plants. Spice products do contain dried plant material, but chemical analyses show that their active ingredients are synthetic (or designer) cannabinoid compounds.

One in every nine high school seniors admitted to having used synthetic marijuana in 2011, according to a University of Michigan survey—even though the substance was linked to more than 11,000 emergency-room visits in 2010. About one-third of those emergency room visits involved teens between ages twelve and seventeen. In fifty-nine percent of the emergency room cases involving synthetic marijuana, that was the only drug found in the person's system. Typically, patients who seek medical care because of using illicit drugs have more than one substance in their system.

Although synthetic cannabis does not produce positive results in drug tests for cannabis, it is possible to detect its metabolites in human urine. The synthetic cannabinoids contained in synthetic cannabis products have been made illegal in many European countries. On November 24, 2010, the United States Drug Enforcement Administration announced it would use emergency powers to ban many synthetic cannabinoids within a month. Prior to the announcement, several states had already made them illegal under state law. In the United States in 2011, many of the cannabinoids were placed on Schedule I of the Controlled Substances Act (and are therefore illegal to possess or use in the United States); the Drug Enforcement Administration claims that said action is to avoid an imminent hazard to the public safety. In

July 2012, the Synthetic Drug Abuse Prevention Act of 2012 was signed into law. It banned synthetic compounds commonly found in synthetic marijuana, placing them under Schedule I of the Controlled Substances Act.

Synthetic cannabinoid manufactured in Asia has profits of five billion per year.

K2 is second most frequently used drug in high school after marijuana, then ecstasy. A person using this can have psychotic episodes months after use.

CHAPTER SIXTEEN

AMPHETAMINES

" Amphetamines cause mania and Parkinson's."[99] Hitler had both mania and Parkinson's and took amphetamines daily and methamphetamines five times per day for four years before his death.[100]

Amphetamine, like cocaine, is a drug that can induce euphoria. It increases one's alertness and initial concentration by lessening the levels of fatigue. This increased wakefulness can however reduce one's appetite. Otherwise known as 'speed', amphetamine stimulates the nervous system. For medical reasons, it is used for the therapeutic management of ADHD, narcolepsy and severe cases of prolonged fatigue.

Adderall, Ritalin, and Vivanse the prescription drugs used to treat attention deficit disorder (see Prescription Drugs above), are amphetamines. Amphetamine-type medications can be habit-forming. Amphetamines when given chronically can produce aggressive, violent, paranoid reactions resembling schizophrenia.[101]

Vivanse or Vyvanse also used to treat ADHD may cause serious (possibly fatal) heart and blood pressure problems if misused or abused. If you use this drug for a long time, you may become dependent on it and may have withdrawal symptoms after stopping the drug. Some side effects are severe skin problems, death/sudden death, insomnia, discomfort, agitation (restlessness),

---

[99] Dr. Daniel Amen, *Healing A.D.D.* (2001) p. 308.
[100] Nassir Ghaemi, *A First-Rate Madness: Uncovering the Links Between Leadership and Mental Illness* (2012).
[101] David D. Burns, M. D. *Feeling Good* (1980) page 675.

anxiety, irritability, severe aggression, sudden mood change, inability to control rage, physical abuse of others, hyper-sexuality, slowed thinking, unstable emotions, psychosis, etc. This does not include the many other negative physical side effects that may occur.

A review on treatment for amphetamine, dextroamphetamine, and methamphetamine on induced psychosis states that about five to fifteen percent of users fail to recover completely.

CHAPTER SEVENTEEN

METHAMPHETAMINE

Interstate 35 and Highway 82 in Texas is a hub between Mexico and major cities in the United States. Gainesville, Texas, which lies at that crossroad is where I was the elected District Attorney. The County also has an unsecured one-thousand three hundred acre municipal airport (a remnant of WWI when German prisoners of war were housed at Camp Howze in Cooke County). Neighboring Love County Oklahoma is the home to Winstar Casino, the largest gambling casino in the world. Gambling casinos are known for significant money laundering. Oklahoma enacted laws regarding the sale of pseudoephedrine (a necessary ingredient for methamphetamine) before Texas so manufacturing of methamphetamine in Cooke County was rampant. A local joke was "What's the biggest pickup line in Cooke County? . . . Nice teeth". Tooth loss is an early byproduct of the use of this drug. Methamphetamine was first called "poor, white trash coke." It was not as popular among African Americans as cocaine.

While I was District Attorney, during one federal raid, more than one-hundred defendants were arrested in a single night in Cooke County, Texas and neighboring Love County, Oklahoma and flown from that airport directly to federal prison in a major investigation of a multi-state operation.

The United States government reported in 2008 that approximately thirteen million people have used methamphetamine—and 529,000 of those are regular users.

Only ten percent of those who drink alcohol become problem drinkers, while seventy-five percent of the users of drugs like crack cocaine or methamphetamine become addicted.

Methamphetamine (more so than most illegal drugs) hijacks the brain. Users do not have the capability to stop using the drug despite harmful consequences. Ten percent of alcohol drinkers become problem drinkers while seventy-five percent of the users of methamphetamine become addicted after their first use. This is because methamphetamines causes portions of the brain to cease to function.

Crack (the freebase form of cocaine that can be smoked) is more dangerous than cocaine. Methamphetamine is more dangerous than crack. Methamphetamine and alcohol are the most physically toxic of drugs. Methamphetamine damages every organ of the body.

The brain scan in Chapter Thirteen shows a loss of brain functioning of a person that has taken methamphetamine. This is especially true in the prefrontal cortex–the part of the brain that controls impulsivity, and judgment, i.e. decision making. The methamphetamine user does not even know that he is not capable of fixing his situation.

Meth labs are usually just run-down, neglected rural homes (the smell is so strong it would be difficult to go undetected in an urban area). This is why methamphetamine tends to be more of a rural problem (at least that is where it is manufactured more frequently). The average cost to clean up the mess that a methamphetamine lab causes is twenty thousand dollars. Twenty to thirty percent of meth labs are discovered due to fires and explosions. One man I prosecuted blew up his boat making methamphetamine on the lake. The boat is now at the bottom of Lake Ray Roberts in Cooke County Texas. Methamphetamine production yields five to seven pounds of toxic waste for every pound of methamphetamine produced. Every meth cook teaches an average of ten other cooks each year.

Almost seventy percent of children found in methamphetamine labs have toxic levels of those chemicals in their bodies. One young girl in Wichita Falls, Texas that was found living in a methamphetamine lab had lost all her teeth. One child died because his mother served him cheese that had been in the same refrigerator as the dangerous chemicals used to cook the meth. In Cooke County, Texas eighty-five percent of the children in foster care were there because of methamphetamine abuse by their parents. Very few of them were ever returned home (unlike most child welfare cases) because the parents were never able to stop using the drug.

Ingredients in methamphetamine are antifreeze, anhydrous

ammonia, drain cleaner, iodine crystals, lye, battery acid (lithium), cold tablets (pseudoephedrine), and paint thinner.

Signs of methamphetamine abuse are rotted teeth, extreme nervousness, brain damage, and more. Methamphetamine users become psychotic and have delusional ideas. The drug can also affect the skin, causing skin abscesses that often become infected because of a weakened immune system. This also leads to periods of sickness. It can lead to blindness, respiratory failure, kidney failure, chest pain, internal bleeding, brittle bones and malnutrition because of lack of eating and increased metabolism. Psychological effects include psychosis and paranoia, aggressive behavior, mood instability, delusions, suicidal thoughts and schizophrenia. Many of these are caused by a mix of sleep deprivation, over stimulation and damage to the brain.

Methamphetamine in large doses over prolonged periods can produce rage and psychosis resembling paranoid schizophrenia.[102]

Cocaine withdrawal symptoms last for three days. Methamphetamine withdrawal symptoms last for six to nine months.

The short-term effects of methamphetamines are loss of appetite, increased heart rate, elevated blood pressure, elevated body temperature, dilation of pupils, disturbed sleep patterns, and nausea. There can also be bizarre, erratic, sometimes violent behavior and hallucinations, hyper-excitability, and irritability, panic and psychosis, convulsions, seizures and death from high doses.

The long-term effects are permanent damage to blood vessels of the heart and brain, high blood pressure (leading to heart attacks), strokes (the leading cause of long term disability), liver, kidney and lung damage; destruction of tissues in nose if sniffed; respiratory (breathing) problems if smoked; infectious diseases and abscesses if injected; malnutrition, weight loss, severe tooth decay,

---

[102] David D. Burns, M. D. *Feeling Good* (1980) page 669.

disorientation, apathy, confused exhaustion, strong psychological dependence, psychosis, depression, damage to the brain similar to Alzheimer's disease, stroke, epilepsy, and death.

Neurotransmitters in the brain are like little ferry boats from one synapse to another. Meth turns your ferry boats into the Spanish Armada-they move slowly.

Treatment for methamphetamine addiction can include cognitive behavioral therapy, motivational interviewing, contingency management, 12-step facilitation therapy, community reinforcement approach, outpatient treatment, and finally medication such as bupropion (which is an antidepressant and should probably only be used as a last resort as it is imperative that the body heal from the pharmaceutical abuse it has endured). Most professionals adhere to the idea that there are no effective pharmacological treatments for methamphetamine dependence at the present time.[103]

The single most important factor for positive treatment outcome will be the degree to which clients are retained in post-residential treatment. Treatment effects do not last very long after treatments stops.

Persons in treatment must be educated about the truth of the effects of the drug. They must get rid of any remaining traces of it, thoroughly cleaning their homes. They must understand that recovery takes time and they should not do this alone. Yet they must separate themselves from the bad influences. They should relive good memories.

They must discover their motive, i.e. parental neglect is a frequent cause. They must look at how their life was taken from them. They must keep a safety net, and keep people nearby. Develop a reward system for going so many days without meth. Read books, and write down thoughts. Do something that will take the mind off the addiction. Expose dealers. Be social. Join a 12-

---

[103] G. Galloway et al A controlled trial of imipramine for the treatment of methamphetamine dependence *Journal of Substance Abuse Treatment* (1996).

step group, like NA, AA or other addiction support group.

There are five stages of recovery from methamphetamine[104]:

1. Withdrawal (days 0–15)-the sleep, eat, and drink stage, with the body and brain in healing overdrive;
2. The Honeymoon (days 16–45)-feeling stronger;
3. The Wall (6 weeks–4 months) seemingly insurmountable wall of depression; boredom, and despair;
4. Adjustment (months 4–6) adjusting, physically, socially, and emotionally, to life without methamphetamine;
5. Ongoing recovery (months 6–12) it's important to remember that methamphetamine addiction is a chronic disease and one is never cured;

Recovery is always ongoing.

Methamphetamine drains the dopamine supply of the brain, resulting in activities that used to provide fun, joy, and pleasure no longer being seen as enjoyable. This is called anhedonia. Treatment for anhedonia is aerobic exercise, Yoga, Tai Chi, and meditation.

Even after a person stops using methamphetamine, this part of the brain takes time to heal. Damaged receptors and transmitters regrow within six to twelve months.

Like other chronic diseases, such as diabetes and hypertension, methamphetamine addiction can be managed. But rewiring and changing-the-brain type healing takes time. And not all methamphetamine addicts heal at the same rate or timetable. Not everyone who goes through treatment for methamphetamine addiction will relapse, but many will. Recovery experts say that the longer a meth addict remains in treatment, the greater the chances to successfully stay off the drug.

Signs that a relapse might be pending (with any substance

---

[104] Stoprxdrugabuse.org (Developmental Model of Recovery)

abuse addiction) are: skipping meetings, hanging out with old friends who use, justifying just one time, using alcohol or other drugs (once begun they gravitate toward more frequent use of the substitute drug, followed by a return to methamphetamine use).

It's not uncommon for chronic methamphetamine users to become homeless, lose their families, go into bankruptcy, and wind up incarcerated. Depressed, filled with self-hatred, yet unable to quit using methamphetamine, many become suicidal. Methamphetamine addicts turn to stealing from family and friends then they often graduate to theft from strangers' homes and places of business-even to armed robbery.

Drug courts combat methamphetamine addiction. Intensive Outpatient Treatment (IOP) is used in drug courts.[105] For methamphetamine-addicted people, drug courts increase treatment program graduation rates by nearly 80%. When compared to eight other programs, drug courts quadrupled the length of abstinence from methamphetamine.[106]

Re-addiction following prison is seventy percent for mixed addicts (those addicted to more than one drug). And even more for those addicted to opiates. With long term treatment the re-addiction percentages are:[107]

- Alcohol 30–50%
- Cocaine 50%
- Meth 50%

Long-term methamphetamine and alcohol use does result in permanent damage to the central nervous system. There is partial recovery of dopamine transporters after prolonged abstinence. The

---

[105] http://www.nadcp.org/sites/default/files/nadcp/best-practice-standards/index.html
[106] NADCP.org
[107] Joseph Lunievicz, director, NDRI, National Development Research Institute, Bureau of Justice *Neuroscience of Addiction* (2012) Webinar.

brain looks almost like normal after thirty-six months if there was no permanent damage, but even then new neural pathways can form and other areas of the brain can compensate for the damaged portions. It can take six months to several years to restore the brain.

This treatment can be done biologically, psychologically, socially, and spiritually.

Addiction is a chronic disease that requires lifelong management.

Relapse is to be expected and usually occurs in the first six months after treatment. According to a study by the Substance Abuse and Mental Health Services Administration (SAMHSA)[108] of 1,652 treatment/interventions for methamphetamine abusers one month after treatment there is a seventy percent relapse rate, six months after treatment there is an eighty-seven percent relapse rate. According to a study by the National Institute of Drug Abuse (NIDA) regarding compliance with any treatment regimen there is a seventy-five percent chance of relapse three months after treatment. [109]

One well-publicized estimate puts relapse rates at 92%. (Rehab centers have countered with their own statistics of methamphetamine users who successfully complete rehabilitation at a 10 to 30% relapse rate.) A crystal meth addict will slip or relapse on average between seven and thirteen times before finally quitting. In one long-term study, three years after treatment fifty percent of methamphetamine abusers had relapsed.[110]

People, places and things that remind the user of the drug increase the chances of relapse. Sanctions should be a minimal amount of punishment necessary to achieve program compliance.

---

[108] http://beta.samhsa.gov
[109] Joseph Lunievicz, director, NDRI, National Development Research Institute, Bureau of Justice *Neuroscience of Addiction, Part III* (2012) Webinar.
[110] Joseph Lunievicz, director, NDRI, National Development Research Institute, Bureau of Justice *Neuroscience of Addiction* (2012) Webinar.

The most likely time of relapse for any drug is in the first month, then the first three months, and then the first six months.

One study found no deficits in motor function, memory, learning, attention, or executive function in methamphetamine users after four years of abstinence.[111]

-----

[111] Cathleen Otero, M.S.W., M.P.A. et al, *Methamphetamine Addiction, Treatment, and Outcomes: Implication of Child Welfare Workers* National Center on Substance Abuse and Child Welfare (2006).

CHAPTER EIGHTEEN

HEROIN

The opium poppy is processed chemically to produce heroin and other synthetic opioids. The byproduct of a simple flower is converted into one of the most addictive drugs known to man. Opiates date as far back as 4000 B.C. Opiates mimic endorphins. Opiates are natural. Heroin is semi-synthetic. Other opiates such as Darvon and Fentanyl are synthetic.

Bayer Pharmaceuticals marketed heroin in 1848 as a non-addictive pain reliever and a cough suppressant. "Heroin, the sedative for coughs" was their ad. Heroin was not made illegal in the United States until 1924. It is still prescribed for pain in the United Kingdom. The incidence of first time heroin users has increased sixty percent in the last decade because it is becoming less expensive. The year 2007 was the year of methamphetamine. The year 2009 was bath salts. In 2014 it was heroin. This is because heroin is an opiate. Prescription opiate-based drugs are so prevalent; persons become addicted and then discover that the illegal drugs are less expensive than the prescriptions. Heroin is half the cost of prescription opiates. Opioids are ninety-three percent of prescription deaths. Getting high on opioids creates a feeling of warmth, safety and well-being. Actor Heath Ledger died from three prescription drugs given to him by three different psychiatrists in 2008 (Xanax, Ambien and OxyContin). Musician Keith Richards obtained heroin from Europe that could be snorted. Kurt Cobain, a lead guitarist for a rock band, died of a heroin overdose. Actor Phillip Seymour Hoffman died of a heroin overdose in 2014. Heroin is also responsible for the deaths of Jim Morrison of The Doors

Almost no one in white, suburban America used heroin forty years ago because it was necessary to stick a needle in your arm. It can now be snorted, smoked or injected. The purity of heroin is up ten tines from what it was fourteen years ago so you don't have to shoot it up now, and it has lost the stigma. It is now a white, suburban drug of choice and is cheaper. In 2002 heroin purity changed because we invaded Afghanistan. Our soldiers were exposed to opium poppy process farms.

A negative test for the drug does not mean that there is no drug, it just means it is above the cutoff for the test to detect it.

Codeine and morphine also come from the poppy flower. Morphine is ten times more potent than codeine. Fentanyl is seventy-five times more potent than morphine.

There are two documented cases where a neonate has died from nursing milk when the mother was on prescription opiates. Codeine is a very fast metabolizer. In the body it quickly turns into morphine.

Many children today obtain an Oxycontin prescription filled by health insurance and sell the pills for $80 each. While selling it they claim to the buyer that it is safe because it came from a doctor. Young people "parachute it" (crush it up in a napkin and swallow or snort). This thwarts the time release feature.

In addition to therapy there are medication-assisted therapies (MAT, e.g., methadone, buprenorphine, naltrexone) to treat dependency in the appropriate cases.[112]

---

[112] Methadone is a long-acting, synthetic opioid agonist. Methadone maintenance therapy (MMT) has been the standard treatment for heroin addiction since the FDA approved its use in 1972, but only in highly regulated outpatient treatment programs (OTPs, i.e., methadone clinics). Naltrexone is an opioid receptor antagonist. The oral form (ReVia) of naltrexone totally blocks the effects of opioids and may also decrease cravings for opioids (as well as for alcohol). A sustained-release, injectable form of naltrexone (Vivitrol) has been shown to be effective.

CHAPTER NINETEEN

COCAINE

C ocaine is derived from the leaves of the coca tree that grows in Latin America. Its distribution and sale, especially for non-medical or non-government authorized purposes, is purely prohibited. However, cocaine is a drug that is widely used among many social classes and races throughout the world.

Brains of cocaine addicts light up when they see cocaine. This activity in the amygdala is blunted when Baclofen is administered. Baclofen is a drug used to treat back injuries. It is now approved for treating cocaine addiction. A cocaine vaccination is on the horizon

Primates will ignore food and water to get to the cocaine to the point of death. They will overdose on cocaine in 5 days.

Speed balling with cocaine is responsible for the deaths of John Belushi, and Chris Farley.

One NIDA study showed that for any drug treatment modality there is a ninety-four percent relapse within five years after treatment for crack and cocaine users, i.e. when cocaine is the drug of choice, they relapse at least once regardless of treatment.

Cocaine can produce psychotic episodes.

CHAPTER TWENTY

DESIGNER DRUGS

Just when we thought nothing could be worse than methamphetamine, along came designer drugs. A common designer drug is known as "bath salts". Bath salts are more addictive than methamphetamines. Bath salts (which really have nothing to do with bath salts) were marketed under the name "bath salts" to avoid apprehension initially. They became publicized with a cannibalistic attack in Miami in 2008. The Centers for Disease Control had to issue a statement that there was not an outbreak i.e. a Zombie apocalypse, because there were so many such incidents in the south. They were originally marketed as a legal alternative to LSD and cost 40-100 dollars per gram. Naphyrone MDPV is the main drug in bath salts. It is ten times stronger than cocaine, and similar to cocaine.

Bath salt symptoms are similar to synthetic cannabis (see above). Designer drugs eat up emergency room services because it takes so many medical health professionals to treat the victims, and it is difficult to know what the victims have taken.

Krocodil is a drug made from codeine. It is cheaper than heroin. Once taken there is an immediate addiction. The life expectancy after use is two years.

Smiles is a hallucinogenic synthetic drug.

Acetyl fentanyl is five times more potent than heroin. Other commonly used designer drugs are Mephedrone AKA Molly (used for energy, sexual stimulation), and Bizarro.

CHAPTER TWENTY-ONE

DRUG OVERDOSE

For the first time in the history of recording causes of death, automobile accidents are the second leading cause of death by accident in the United States. Since 2011 the leading cause of death by accident is drug overdose. According to the Office of National Drug Control Policy (ONDCP), approximately one hundred Americans died from an overdose every day in 2010, totaling 38,000 for the year. Deaths resulting from drugs have doubled over the last decade, now claiming one life every fourteen minutes.[113]

Every day in the United States, 113 people die as a result of drug overdose, and another 6,748 are treated in emergency departments (ED) for the misuse or abuse of drugs. Nearly nine out of ten poisoning deaths are caused by drugs.

Among people age twenty-five to sixty-four years old, drug overdose caused more deaths than motor vehicle traffic crashes. Drug overdose death rates have been rising steadily since 1992 with a 118% increase from 1999 to 2011 alone. In 2011, 33,071 (80%) of the 41,340 drug overdose deaths in the United States were believed to be unintentional, 5,298 (12.8%) were of suicidal intent, 80 (0.2%) were homicides, and 2,891 (7%) were of undetermined intent. In 2011, drug misuse and abuse caused about 2.5 million emergency department visits. Of these, more than 1.4 million emergency department visits were related to pharmaceuticals.

Between 2004 and 2005, an estimated 71,000 children (18

---

[113] Centers for Disease Control.

or younger) were seen in emergency departments each year because of medication overdose (excluding self-harm, abuse and recreational drug use). Among children under age six, pharmaceuticals account for about forty percent of all exposures reported to poison centers.

Pharmaceuticals are the most common drugs involved in overdoses. In 2011, of the 41,340 drug overdose deaths in the United States, 22,810 (55%) were related to pharmaceuticals. Of the 22,810 deaths relating to pharmaceutical overdose in 2011, 16,917 (74%) involved opioid analgesics (also called opioid pain relievers or prescription painkillers), and 6,872 (30%) involved benzodiazepines. (Some deaths include more than one type of drug.)

In 2011, about 1.4 million emergency department visits involved the nonmedical use of pharmaceuticals. Among those emergency department visits, 501,207 visits were related to anti-anxiety and insomnia medications, and 420,040 visits were related to opioid analgesics.

Benzodiazepines are frequently found among people treated in emergency departments for misusing or abusing drugs. People who died of drug overdoses often had a combination of benzodiazepines and opioid analgesics in their bodies.

More than two hundred and fifty million prescriptions for painkillers were written in 2012, enough for every American adult to have a bottle of pills.[114]

In the United States, prescription opioid abuse costs were about $55.7 billion in 2007. Of this amount, 46% was attributable to workplace costs (e.g., lost productivity), 45% to healthcare costs (e.g., abuse treatment), and nine percent to criminal justice costs.

Among those who died from drug overdose in 2011:

- Men were 60% more likely than women to die;
- Whites had the highest death rate, followed by Native

---

[114] www.cdc.gov/VitalSignsCosts

Americans, then Alaska Natives, and then African Americans;

- The highest death rate was among people 45-49 years of age; and the lowest death rates were among children less than fifteen years old because they do not abuse drugs as frequently as older people.

Among people who misused or abused drugs and received treatment in emergency departments in 2011:

- 56% were males;
- 82% were people 21 or older.

Most overdoses occur within the first 48-72 hours of release from jail. It is also the time that most domestic violence occurs. Domestic violence is closely associated with substance abuse.

Prescription errors occur in one in ten adults, and 1 in 4 children.[115]

To break the cycle of recidivism, two stumbling blocks to successful reentry must be removed—drug addiction and unemployment. Jobs and education reduce recidivism, not mass incarceration. Higher education not only leads to increased employment opportunities, but also reduces recidivism by as much as forty-three percent. [116]

---

[115] NPR. 6/9/11 and http://www.cdc.gov/homeandrecreationalsafety/overdose/facts.html
[116] Rand Corporation, Evaluating the Effectiveness of Correctional Education (2013).

CHAPTER TWENTY-TWO

YOUTH

"Just as your fortune depends upon how your money is invested, so the success of your life depends upon how your time is invested."
Leone Kester

The frontal lobe of the brain is still forming in teenagers. This forms until age twenty-five. This is the part of the brain that controls impulsivity - reasoning, judgment, and thinking.[117] It is as if teens are driving a Ferrari with Fred Flintstone brakes. Mark Twain said "When a boy turns thirteen, seal him in a barrel and feed him through a knot hole. When he turns sixteen, plug up the hole." This is a colloquial reference to the undeveloped prefrontal cortex in teens.

America is in the worst drug epidemic this country has seen. Today the majority of people that die from drug overdose and usage never see a drug dealer. Before 1985 seventy percent of drug users were men. Now drug users are fifty percent men and fifty percent women.

Since 2010 the number one cause of death in America is drug overdose (more than car accidents, cancer, heart problems, etc.). There were 40,000 drug overdoses in 2013, and 23,000 of those (more than half) were pharmaceutical i.e. prescription drugs. This is more than crack, cocaine and heroin combined.

It is no surprise that in recent surveys sixty-eight percent of high school graduates said drugs were a major stressor, and

---

[117] Barbara Strauch, *The Primal Teen: What the New Discoveries about the Teenage Brain Tell Us about Our Kids* (2004).

seventy-one percent said their high schools were drug infested. Asbestos is far less prevalent and less toxic.

Fifty percent of all college students binge drink (approximately six drinks in two hours) and/or abuse drugs monthly. Twenty-three percent of college students today meet the definition of alcohol or drug addiction. On average, 2,600 students are injured daily on college campuses because of drugs or alcohol.

It is estimated that more than one thousand female college students are raped on college campuses daily due to drugs or alcohol (it is the facilitator of the crime). These assaults are rarely reported. Five to six students die daily on college campuses due to the effects of drugs or alcohol.

With children age twelve and over drug dependence has quadrupled in recent years. The younger a person is when they start, the more difficult it is to ever put them in remission.

Ten percent of addicts become addicted after age twenty-one. Ninety percent of addicts become addicted before age twenty-five. The younger a person is when they start, the more difficult it is to ever put them in remission. Erowid.org is a website where children go to learn about drugs. The developers of this website appear to be a cross between pharmacologists and hippie drug users. It gives them tips like "caution, do not drive" on the label on a prescription drug means it will get you high.

In 1968 age sixteen was the average age that persons started abusing controlled substances, today that age is twelve. Today the fourth grade is the first year students are most at risk for alcohol abuse. Forty percent of people who start drinking before age 15 become alcoholics. Today at age eleven most children get high via inhalants. Pam (for those of you who make dinner via reservations, this is cooking oil spray) is the most huffed product.

Forty years ago the cost of marijuana was ten to twenty dollars for an ounce. Now an eighth of an ounce of marijuana costs fifty dollars, so users turn to other more dangerous alternatives.[118]

---

[118] The hydroponic plants are more in the neighborhood of $400 per ounce. This

Today's children know that if they seal broken Sharpies (thick permanent marker ink pens) in plastic sandwich bags for five minutes, it will get them higher than marijuana (and it is much cheaper).

Forty years ago no one died from marijuana. Now synthetic cannabis is responsible for two thirds of emergency room visits for drug abuse. While it is true that synthetic cannabis is not marijuana,-many in a youthful market do not know the difference.

Children in the past killed themselves but did not die from using LSD. PCP use might have increased testosterone levels and resulted in some ass kickings, but you didn't die from it. Now there is no room for error.

If you, as an adult, go out with another couple and you sit down to dinner and the first thing they say is "let's get shit faced"; you would know there was something wrong. Yet this is the way many parties with children start. Unlike adults who generally drink to relax, children drink alcohol to get blitzed. That is why it is a problem for them.

Remember, the frontal lobe of the brain is not developed until age twenty-five or later. There is nothing to tell them "you are getting drunk - stop it." Their brains have not fully developed: reasoning, judgment, and thinking.

Children who do well in school are somewhat less likely to abuse drugs and alcohol than those who do poorly. Those engaged in team sports have the highest rate of substance abuse, followed by those who engage in no sports. Those who engage in individual sports have the lowest rates of drug abuse. This is due to the fact that their sense of self-esteem is higher.

Many creative achievers were either orphaned or had little contact with their father, but they frequently had a very involved, loving mother who expected a lot from them.[119]

---

is a method of plant production by means of suspending the plant roots in a solution of nutrient-rich, oxygenated water.

[119] Mihaly Csikszentmihalyi, *Creativity* (1996).

More white high school students are using drugs than any other race because they are getting it from their parent's medicine cabinet. Montana and Alaska now have the highest per capita drug use among children. Private schools generally have an eighteen percent higher rate unless they are faith based – then the percent is significantly lower.

Children use terms such as "farming" (pharmaceuticals), "fruit salad party", and "skittle club" for the practice of bringing drugs from their parent's medicine cabinet to a party where they are mixed indiscriminately in a large bowl, and children ingest them by the handfuls.

When pop stars such as Miley Cyrus smoke salvia in a bong and get high on You Tube for all to see, we are not sending a message of abstinence to our youth.

CHAPTER TWENTY-THREE

WHAT PARENTS SHOULD BE TEACHING THEIR CHILDREN.

TALKING TO YOUR CHILDREN ABOUT DRUGS

"The future depends on what we do in the present."
Mahatma Gandhi

Education about the health dangers of drugs is the most important lessons parents can impart to avoid substance abuse problems with children. And they must start early – grade school is not too soon. Young people ages ten to eighteen say their parents are the most important influence on their decision to drink or not drink. They will listen to what you have to say. While much of what we can do for or teach our children was covered in the earlier chapter *What Citizens Can Do-Top Ten Things*, here are many more:

Here's what parents need to know now...

Peer pressure is the main reason children give for using drugs. Tell them - drug dealers will do anything to get you hooked. They just want to make money. Some just want to control you.

Be honest with your children. If you only tell children "if you use drugs you will die" they will know it is a lie and won't believe you about the important things.

Addiction is the number one most diagnosed mental illness in children in the United States today since 2013.

Start talking with your children about the dangers of drugs before they set foot in junior high school. By high school, it may be too late.

The biggest problem this country faces is prescription drugs. It's not coming from dope peddlers; it's coming from doctors and your medicine cabinets. Today young people are much more likely to abuse prescription medications than marijuana or LSD. In fact, one in five high school students have taken a prescription drug that they didn't get from a doctor. Even over-the-counter medications such as cough suppressants are abused.

Abuse of prescription drugs often is riskier than abusing illegal drugs. Many teens—and even parents—incorrectly assume that anything prescribed by a doctor can't be all that dangerous. In truth, many prescription medications are extremely dangerous when not used as intended. For example, OxyContin is a time-release pill designed to suppress pain over six to eight hours. Drug abusers crush these pills into powder so that the full dose is absorbed at once. Either this year or next, fatalities from misuse of prescription medications (alone – not including illegal drugs) are likely to surpass auto accidents as the single leading cause of accidental death in the United States.

One in five teens meet the criteria for addiction. One out of seventy go to rehab. The relapse rate in teens is ninety percent.

Two-thirds of substance abuse emergency room visits are for synthetic cannabis i.e. K2. Children are falsely told that synthetic cannabis and designer drugs are legal but they are very illegal and very dangerous. This is sold on internet providing anonymity to drug dealers. Some synthetic drugs cannot be detected like other drugs that are being shipped through the mail.

Those who start drinking as teens or preteens are approximately twice as likely to become alcoholics as those who wait until their twenties. Alcohol kills more teenagers than all other drugs combined. It is a factor in the three leading causes of death among fifteen to twenty-four-year-olds: accidents, homicides and suicides. Children who drink are seven times more likely to use other illegal drugs and fifty times more likely to use cocaine than young people who never drink.

The average prescription for opioids has sixty pills. The average patient takes only five or six of these (because they no longer need them, or they develop some unpleasant side effect). So we end up with unused, superfluous medicine in our homes. And thanks to the lobbyists for the big corporations that sell these drugs, a person must pay the same for five pills as is paid for sixty.

In 1995 direct advertising was allowed by pharmaceutical

companies to the public. Remember when we started being bombarded by Viagra commercials? That same year OxyContin was first put on the market and marketed as non-addictive.

The average physician has thirty minutes training on opioids (of four years of medical training). Veterinarians get more training on opioids. Prescription opioids kill more people than heroin and cocaine combined.

Prescription drugs for attention deficit hyperactivity disorder (ADHD – commonly diagnosed in children and therefore prevalent) are Adderall and Vivanse. These drugs are amphetamines (AKA speed) and cause mania and Parkinson's. This early introduction to children in our country that drugs are O.K. and necessary to function is sending the wrong message. Adderall is the most abused prescription drug in America. It has numerous side affects including aggression.

How you act - you become. Fake it until you make it. Your thoughts become moods, moods become actions, your actions become habits, and your habits become who you are. So always have thoughts that are full of positive energy and love. Cary Grant who is arguably one of the most sophisticated, classiest, elegant movie stars that ever graced the silver screen would say that he acted like the man he wanted to be for so long that he finally became that man. Dr. Wayne Dyer reminds us that "you are the sum total of your choices."[120] Dyer's book *Your Erroneous Zones* (1976) is about escaping the trap of negative thinking and taking control of your life. It is a quick read and the best self-help book available for young adults.

_____

[120] Wayne Dyer, *Your Erroneous Zones* (1976)

CHAPTER TWENTY-FOUR

THE SOLUTIONS-WHAT EVERY PARENT MUST DO

"You must do the thing you think you cannot do."
Eleanor Roosevelt

For information on how to fight drugs in your community:

- Drugfreeworld.org A non-profit public benefit corporation. There is a free video, documentary, booklets, and more.
- Talk to your child about alcohol:
- National Institute on Alcohol Abuse and Alcoholism: Niaaa.nih.gov

In the past I have pledged significant amounts of money to children in my family if they could make it to age eighteen without taking a drink of alcohol or ingesting any illegal substance. They have lived up to the challenge. And I have been happy to pay up on eighteenth birthdays. They have told me along the way that several times when others tried to get them to drink they advised their acquaintances about the pledge to me and they were actually grateful that they could use that excuse. They also thought that others secretly envied them for the pact we had made. Some lived in communities where alcohol and drug use were prevalent and thankfully they never had any desire to abuse them.

Research shows that the best way to influence your child to avoid drinking is to develop a strong, trusting relationship. Why? First, when they have that bond, it follows that they feel good about themselves and are therefore less likely to fall to peer pressure and drink alcohol. Second, your good relationship fosters the desire for them to try to live up to your expectations because they want to please you and maintain their close tie.

To build this strong bond, establish open lines of communication to make it easy for them to speak honestly with you. Spend one-on-one time with your children giving them your undivided attention. Ask open-ended questions about how they feel about things. Establish rules for their behavior with consequences and let them know it is okay to blame your rules when others pressure them to engage in unsafe behavior.

Avoid criticism and offer acceptance and appreciation for their accomplishments and efforts. Respect your child's viewpoints and privacy (then they will more likely do the same for you). And when children say that alcohol is worse than marijuana, in an attempt to justify marijuana use, you can respond: "Is that the best you've got?" One third of all traffic fatalities are alcohol related; more than10,000 lives lost each year along with hundreds of thousands of injuries and life-altering injuries.

Educate your children about the consequences of a criminal conviction:

- It is difficult to get a job;
- Student grants and loans will be denied;
- Disciplinary action at school;
- Public assistance; health care, housing ineligibility;
- Federal law imposes a lifetime ban on food stamps and federally funded public assistance for drug felons;
- State licenses, contracts, and some other federal benefits are restricted as to drug offenders;
- Passports;
- Possession of a firearm is prohibited;
- Right to vote affected;
- Jury service will be denied in front of a large group of other citizens;
- Ability to hold public office affected;
- Driver's license could be suspended;
- Citizenship, if applicable, could be affected;
- Military Service (includes deferred adjudications);
- Employers, landlords, mortgage lenders, insurance companies, schools, and volunteer agencies often require you to report criminal convictions, and will conduct

background checks for criminal convictions when evaluating applicants.
- Each subsequent offense will bring extra conditions to a bond or to enhance penalties.
- If the conviction is for driving while intoxicated, there is a zero tolerance for minors drinking and driving (in Texas and many other states), i.e. any amount of alcohol or illegal drugs.
- Loss of driver's license;
- Community service hours (24-100);
- Fines and court costs, monthly probation fees, surcharge fees;
- Cancellation of insurance and/or increased insurance rates;
- Monthly probation reporting;
- Mothers Against Drunk Driving (M.A.D.D.) Victim Impact Panel (lasts three hours);
- Multiple court appearances;
- The ignition interlock device required for many probations ($75 per month);
- Mandatory jail time in some instances;
- "Home visits" by the probation officer;
- Interference with employment-time missed from work;
- Future employability problems;
- Possible loss of a professional license;
- Ignition Interlock Devices (and the accompanying expenses); and
- Property forfeiture.

Tell your teens about the repercussions of social media. The new social media environment is fertile ground for many forms of self-destructive behavior, much of which adversely affects relationships and families. What you put on social media could affect the rest of your life. It could be used against you in court, e.g. people on probation can get revoked for talking about being out drinking or other violations of probation.

I had a case where promiscuous language by a sexual assault victim seriously compromised the case. Social media should come with a Miranda-style warning, advising that "everything you say can and will be used against you in a court of law for the rest of your life." If you put a photo of yourself naked out there on the internet, ten years from now someone is forwarding it to your employer. Four out of ten employers will not hire an applicant after they check out their social media sites. The main reason for this rejection is inappropriate photographs.[121] Sexting is costing people their college scholarships and job offers. In a world where law school graduates/lawyers have to intern for free for six months or more just to get a job interview this is a crazy risk to take with the rest of your life. Also, predatory adults on the internet are manipulating and blackmailing children with the information they mine from the internet.

Tell children that the problems with drug abuse come with long term use. Get education programs in your schools. Schools must use scientifically validated programs. The DARE program taught us that the police are not the best ones to treat our children about drug abuse. Train clergy. Clergy are the most frequent line of defense.

The most important place for children to receive their education is in the home. Parents and families must talk to their children. Let them know the families are on the children's side. Families must be informed and a good source of information about drugs and alcohol. Practice or role play different scenarios with children to build their skills in avoiding peer pressure.[122]

---

[121] National Public Radio 6/23/13.

[122] Resources to assist parents in speaking with children:
National Council on Alcohol and Drug Dependence (NCADD) -- https://ncadd.org/for-youth/233-overview - and establish yourself as the trustworthy source of information. Enterhealth: Recommendations for Parents on How to Talk with Their Children about Alcohol and Drugs http://www.enterhealth.com/sites/default/files/linked/Tips-For-Talking-About-Drugs-and-Alcohol.pdf. National Institute on Drug Abuse (NIH)-Family Checkup: Positive Parenting Prevents Drug Abuse

Stay involved in your children's lives, look in their purses and backpacks, check their electronic devices, know who their friends are, be nosy.

---

http://www.drugabuse.gov/family-checkup Be sure to download the PDF Substance Abuse and Mental Health Services Administration (SAMHSA) Underage Drinking Prevention - http://beta.samhsa.gov/underage-drinking

CHAPTER TWENTY-FIVE

MASS MURDERERS

"We are not enemies, but friends. We must not be enemies. Though passion may have strained, it must not break our bonds of affection. The mystic chords of memory will swell when again touched, as surely they will be, by the better angels of our nature."
Abraham Lincoln

Remember from Chapter One, the Secret Service study on school shootings indicated that all the shooters suffered from depression.[123] With mass murderers the front of the brain (frontal cortex) is thin. They are unable to empathize. This is the number one factor in common with these individuals. It can manifest itself in the torturing of animals.

In 1966, prior to the Texas Tower incident where thirteen were killed and thirty three wounded on the University of Texas at Austin campus, the shooter went to a psychiatrist stating "I'm having thoughts of going up in the Texas tower with a long rifle and shooting people at random." This was ignored because he did not look like a sociopath. The shooter was a bank teller with a high I.Q. who suddenly decided to shoot forty-six people. His I.Q. of 138 put him in the top 0.1 percentile of the human population (I.Q. above 130 - 2.2 % of population; below 70 – 2.2% of population). Prior to this shooting, the shooter left a message that it was his wish for his brain to be examined to determine what went wrong. A nickel size tumor pressing on his hypothalamus and amygdala was found upon autopsy.

---

[123] Dr. Daniel Amen, *Change your Brain, Change your Body* p. 112 (2010).

The disease of frontotemporal dementia has fifty-seven percent of its sufferers engaging in socially violating behavior compared to only 7 percent of Alzheimer's patients.[124]

The shooters names should not be used in the media (to avoid glorifying their horrific acts). The news media should be reminded of this each time there is such a tragedy. A lengthy study was conducted and released in 2014 after the Newtown, Connecticut murders at Sandy Hook Elementary (twenty children, six teachers slaughtered in their classrooms). It was determined that while the Asperger's disorder that the shooter suffered from was not the cause of the shooting, the continued failure to treat the disease was in fact the cause. While only the shooter is responsible, parents, school officials and medical personnel did not obtain proper treatment for the murderer before the murders occurred.

With more attention given to the mentally ill, perhaps tragedies that have occurred in an Aurora, Colorado theater, at Columbine High School, in Arizona with Gabby Gifford, in a Texas Luby's cafeteria (twenty-four dead), and a mall in Oregon, might never have occurred.

---

[124] David Eagleman, *Incognito, The Secret Lives of the Brain* (2011).

CHAPTER TWENTY-SIX

THE SOLUTIONS – A CONTINUUM OF CARE

"Truth never damages a cause that is just."
Mahatma Gandhi

When someone says "I need help" how long is that window of opportunity open? Fifteen minutes? If the service provider (counselor, psychologist, doctor, etc.) says "come back in thirty days" we could not think that was very effective. Do you know how many drills you can steal at Walmart in thirty days? Yet that is what we do in the criminal justice system. People are released on bond, or held without services in a concrete cell until their desire to change dissipates and the opportunity is forever lost.

Drug addiction cases should be on a different track than other criminal offenses.

Left to their own devices without intensive supervision by a judge, approximately twenty-five percent of offenders never arrive for a single treatment session. And among those who do show for treatment, most drop out prematurely before receiving any benefits. The power and authority of the court is necessary to keep them engaged in treatment long enough to experience any lasting gains.

The facts of each criminal case must first be evaluated to determine the proper treatment. Treatment is a highly cost-effective alternative; it is about one-tenth of the cost to treat a person rather than putting him or her in jail. If it is a non-violent offense and the complaining witness is agreeable it might be appropriate to place a defendant on a conditional dismissal. With a defendant that exhibits the lowest risk and lowest needs, it may only be necessary to insure that the person stay on their medication. If the person has more needs Supportive Outpatient Treatment (SOP) or Intensive Outpatient Treatment (IOP) may be warranted (depending on their level of dependence). The goal is to get them out of the jail as soon as possible before they decompensate and start costing the county an average of $300 per day (as opposed to $58-70 per day that the general population costs).[125]

In Dallas protocols were developed for dealing with the mentally ill. Here is the one that addresses substance abusers charged with low-level drug cases i.e. possession of small amounts of a controlled substance.

PROTOCOL/MODEL FOR DEALING WITH LOW LEVEL DRUG CASES IN THE MENTAL HEALTH DIVISION (WITH DEFENDANTS HAVING A MENTAL HEALTH DIAGNOSIS)

1. Identify defendants charged with low-level drug offenses who are suspected of having a mental illness at book-in in the jail. Begin the program with all State Jail level offenses that meet this criteria. Check with Drug Court to determine there is no interference with their program.
2. Have the cases assigned to the Mental Health Division. A prosecutor reviews the case and criminal history to determine suitability for the program.
3. Have a defense attorney assigned expeditiously.
4. Case management: Have the defendant evaluated by ADAPT[126] to:
   a. Determine the diagnosis;
   b. Investigate family history, service history, records;
   c. Assess the necessity of services.

---

[125] Texas Tribune Anaylsis: Pay for Health Care or Pay the Jailer (June 20, 2014).
[126] Adapt of Texas provides community support and clinic services within a seven-county area in and around Dallas, Texas. It is associated with Metrocare, the local mental health authority.

Consider the following conditions:

Medication;

- SOP-Supportive Outpatient (substance abuse);
- IOP–Intensive OutPatient (substance abuse);
- IPS–Integrated Psychotherapeutic Services, a step up for those continuing to use; meet two to three times per week , very intense, twice as much as IOP;
- Other conditions, i.e. 12-step;
- Transicare - case management, peer support, behavioral-health transportation services, which has Qualified Mental Health Professionals, 24/7 access;
- Housing;
- Employment, if capable;
- Assign a Metrocare casemanager;
- Attend Metrocare classes as appropriate, e.g. Understanding Schizophrenia;
- Insure medication compliance and supply before release from jail.

5. Have the defendant assigned to a mental health provider.
6. First Court Setting. Place the Defendant on a written conditional dismissal setting out the terms. Enter into Personal Recognizance (PR) bond with appropriate conditions: meet with health care provider, attend specific classes, stay away from specifically named persons, no weapons, etc.
7. Consider placement in the misdemeanor Jail Diversion program.
8. Monitor treatment and services. The defendant checks in regularly with the court with the assigned caseworker. The sufficiency of the bond is evaluated.
9. Resolution of case:
   1. If successful, dismissal;
   2. If not successful, re-evaluation

Determine whether circumstances exist to continue on the

program.

CATS[127] / PSI[128]

Probation Services including Treatment:

1. NEXUS-(lowest level) 45 days (Contract residential treatment in the community, women only);
2. ATLAS[129] (second level);
3. Wilmer[130] (third level, if eligible):
    a. DDC Wilmer–Dual Diagnosis[131] Court–90 day program,
    b. JTC Wilmer–Judicial Treatment Center–6 month program.
4. SAFPF [132]– six months plus three months of aftercare. Special Needs SAFPF (9 months)

If the defendant is unable to complete the program, he or she must serve time.

In exceptional circumstances, dismiss due to inability to comply with terms and conditions.

(end of Protocol)

It is crucial that the defendants are identified early. This increases the incentive to complete the program and avoid a return to jail. It is also crucial that they receive aftercare. Think of what

---

[127] Comprehensive Assessment Treatment Services.

[128] Pre-sentence Investigation Report, required by Texas law before a defendant can be placed on probation.

[129] Achieving True Liberty and Success, a highly structured mental health court in Dallas.

[130] Wilmer is a local Intensive In-Patient Facility for substance abuse.

[131] Dual diagnosis means one of each: mental illness and alcohol or substance abuse.

[132] Substance Abuse Felony Punishment Facility.

we do in regard to cancer aftercare: annual check-ups for years. We don't generally do those things with recovery from addiction.

The mentally ill and/or drug addicts cannot get help on their own. At www.brainplace.com there are brain scans of people using other controlled substances. See for yourself how drugs affect the brain.

Families will thank you for sending their loved ones to in-patient treatment – before and after such treatment. They will not thank you for sending them to SAFPF.

Recovery is like climbing Mount Everest. If you slip, you cannot give up. And you don't go to the bottom and start over. You just rest, regroup and start over. Jail (or SAFPF if the there is no addiction or a strong incentive to recover via other therapies such as intensive outpatient treatment) will make a defendant worse, rather than trying to start over. It could be harsher than a relapse in some cases.

Also, consequences should be swift and immediate and not overly harsh. Supposed you went to a doctor with an infected toenail and he said "we have to amputate." Wouldn't you want a less invasive treatment first, perhaps antibiotics?

Given the state of many defendants' health at the time of arrest, it would be unnecessarily exposing the taxpayers to liability for defendants to be incarcerated with low-level offenses that are no threat to public safety.

CHAPTER TWENTY-SEVEN

ACCOUNTABILITY AND SPECIALITY COURTS

"The most beautiful thing we can experience is the mysterious. It is the true source of all art and science."
Albert Einstein, *What I Believe in Forum* (October 1930).

Accountability courts (courts that hold the participants accountable and engage the participants in specific treatment to change behavior) are the solution for addiction and nonviolent offenders. Drug courts are the primary example of accountability courts and they work. Drug Courts have more supervision than regular probation given in regular courts. However, you do not have to be a "drug court" to implement their evidence based, scientifically proven, best practices. Start with treatment as listed above in the protocol for dealing with low-level drug offenders, considering the least restrictive first, i.e. SOP (Supportive Outpatient treatment). If SOP is not successful then-IOP[133] (Intensive Outpatient). If IOP is not successful then-IPS (Integrated Psychotherapeutic Services), a step up for those continuing to use (participants meet two to three times per week, very intense, twice as much as IOP). If IPS is not successful then-Inpatient treatment. If Inpatient treatment is not successful then: SAFPF.[134]

It is very important in these courts to not mix persons who are not compliant with the program with those who will be

---

[133] http://www.nadcp.org/sites/default/files/nadcp/best-practice-standards/index.html
[134] Substance Abuse Felony Punishment Facility

successful in treatment. A punishment facility such as SAFPF should only be used when all else fails, and punishment is the only option. SAFPF is a punishment facility. It is cruel to punish a sick person for being sick.

Most substance abusers have a diagnosed mental illness. This is known as dual diagnosis. Depression is a sickness. Substance abuse is a sickness. Both are listed in the DSM-V[135] as mental illnesses. Many with depression attempt self-medication with alcohol. Alcohol is itself a depressant, so the victims find themselves in a vicious downward spiral.

For jurisdictions wanting to implement scientific based programs, IOP is far better, more successful, and less disruptive than SAFPF. The research is unequivocal: Drug Courts (or the methods used there which include IOP) significantly reduce drug abuse and crime and do so at less expense than any other justice strategy; and according to rigorous and replicated studies.

The prosecutor works closely with the defense attorney in negotiating appropriate plea agreements which focus on accountability, treatment and rehabilitation. Having been trained in treatment court philosophies and practices, the prosecutor and defense counsel appropriately communicate with one another and the team regarding offender case status, and participate in team discussions regarding any matter which may result in participants receiving sanctions or incentives.

It is the position of the National Association of Drug Court Professionals, NADCP [136](based on scientific research) and the Texas Association of Drug Court Professionals TADCP that there is a damaging and negative effect for individuals charged with addiction related offenses to be incarcerated more than six days. Also, consequences should be swift and immediate and not overly

---

[135] The American Psychiatric Association Diagnostic and Statistical Manual of Mental Disorders, Fifth Edition (2013).

[136] NADCP was started in 1989.

harsh. Treatments should start with the least invasive to the individual and become gradually more intense if not successful. Relapses are to be expected. There are numerous studies and scientific papers on the websites supporting this. [137] [138]

Providing too much treatment or too much supervision is not merely a potential waste of scarce resources, it can increase crime or substance abuse by exposing individuals to more seriously impaired or antisocial peers, or by interfering with their engagement in productive activities such as work, school, or parenting. [139]

More than six days of incarceration contributes to recidivism. Courts should employ short, staccato sentences in drug cases.

Specialty courts are those that specialize in a specific area, such as mental health.

The disproportionate number of mentally ill defendants (schizophrenia spectrum, bipolar disorder and major depressive disorders) in the criminal justice system, especially jails and prisons, is well documented and undisputed. Numerous multisite studies have shown that mental health courts reduce recidivism.[140]

Texas is home to 155 drug courts and 19 innovative Veterans Treatment Courts. The evidence based reforms implemented have saved an estimated $2 billion in new prison spending since 2007, led to the closure of three prisons and six juvenile lock-ups, brought about a thirty-nine percent reduction in

---

[137] www.NADCP.org
[138] www.TADCP.org
[139] Lowenkamp, C.T. & Latessa, E.J., *Understanding the Risk Principle: How and why correctional interventions can harm low-risk offenders. Topics in Community Corrections* (Washington, DC: U.S. Department of Justice, National Institute of Corrections) (2004).
[140]Allison D. Redlich et.al., *Is Diversion Swift? Comparing Mental Health Court and Traditional Criminal Justice Processing* (2012). http://gainscenter.samhsa.gov/cms-assets/documents/62079-970135.isdiversionswift.pdf

the parole failure rate, and reduced the statewide crime rate to levels not seen since the 1960s.

Some of the specialty/accountability courts in Dallas are[141]:

- 4C SAFPF Re-entry.
- ATLAS-(Achieving True Liberty and Success).
- Community Prosecution Diversion.
- Jail Diversion (mental-misdemeanor) –DDC – Judge Stolz and Magnis (Dual Diagnosis Court aftercare).
- Mental Health (competency restoration).
- DIVERT (addiction)–(Diversion and Expedited Rehabilitation and Treatment).
- Domestic Violence Court–(Misdemeanor).
- DWI court (felony).[142][143]
- DWI court (misdemeanor).
- ESTEEM–Experiencing Success Through Empowerment, Encouragement and Mentoring.
- Juvenile.
- PRIDE-(positive recovery intensive divert experience) (misdemeanor prostitution initiative).
- STAR–(Strengthening transition and recovery) (felony

---

[141] The Texas Governor's web site shows the specific specialty courts by county http://governor.state.tx.us

[142] As a result of the effectiveness of DWI courts, the following have issued official resolutions in support of such courts: American Judges Association, Governors Highway Safety Association, International Association of Chiefs of Police, Mother's Against Drunk Drivers, National Alcohol Beverage Control Association, National District Attorneys Association, and the National Sheriff's Association. Even the Wine and Spirits Wholesalers is a leading voice on responsible access and distribution of alcohol.

[143] The National Highway Traffic Safety administration (NHTSA) reported 10,076 deaths in 2013 involving an alcohol impaired driver, and 17,000 deaths in 2003. The death toll has dropped due to strong laws, tough enforcement, the work of specialty courts, and vigorous public education.

prostitution initiative)

- STATC-(Successful treatment of addiction through collaboration.)
- Veterans.
- IPP–Intensive Probation Violation Program.

Georgia has a drug court and mental health court in each judicial district of that state (111).

The two primary goals of mental health courts are to reduce recidivism and increase engagement in community treatment. Mental health courts average an eight percent reduction in recidivism. Participants charged with more serious crimes such as those involving a victim are less likely to be rearrested than those charged with less serious crimes such as drug offenses.[144] Prior to enrollment in mental health courts, participants have twice as many crisis treatment episodes as those who receive treatment as usual. Participants in mental health courts had lower re-arrest rates and fewer post-eighteen month incarceration days after mental health court, lowered substance abuse, and a more frequent diagnosis of bipolar disorder rather than schizophrenia or depression.[145]

A defining feature of mental health courts is the requirement that enrollees appear periodically for status reviews before the judge.[146] Participants who complete the programs have fewer arrests and longer delays until the next arrest. Participation must be voluntary to avoid a subgroup of offenders being treated specially and guilty pleas are required for enrollment.[147]

---

[144] http://gainscenter.samhsa.gov/grant_programs/adultmhc.asp
[145] Henry J. Steadman PhD., et. al., *Affects of Mental Health Courts on Arrests and Jail Dates, a Multisite Study* (2010) http://gainscenter.samhsa.gov/cms-assets/documents/62075-221384.effectsofmhconarrestsandjaildays.pdf
[146] Allison D. Redlich et al., *The Use of Mental Health Court Appearances in Supervision* University of Albany, State University of New York (2010).
[147] Alison D. Redlich et al., *Enrollment in Mental Health Courts: Voluntariness, Knowingness, and Adjudicative Competence American Psychology Law*

Brainstormer

Society/Division 41 of the American Psychological Association (2008).

CHAPTER TWENTY-EIGHT

DRUG COURTS WORK

"Stay with tradition and you ensure that you'll always be the same, but toss it aside, and the world is yours to use as creatively as you choose."
Dr. Wayne W. Dyer, *Your Erroneous Zones* (1976)

Celebrities Matthew Perry and Martin Sheen are strong advocates for drug courts. They regularly speak at the National Association of Drug Court Professionals (hereinafter NADCP) to encourage the successful, science-based work done by these courts.

These courts treat those defendants with DSM-V[148] substance use disorders. The research is unequivocal: drug courts (or the methods used there which include IOP) significantly reduce drug abuse and crime and do so at less expense than any other justice strategy; according to rigorous and replicated studies.

Training at the NADCP results in a 500% increase in cost benefits to those jurisdictions where the trained participants return and implement what they have learned at such conferences. This is because the changes in science are taught at the conferences. Drug courts are the paradigm, the distinct concept, the systematic arrangement of evidence based, best practices. Drug courts incorporate weekly counseling sessions, fifteen months of treatment (eighteen to twenty-four months with high risk offenders), positive judicial and counselor attributes, frequent drug

---

[148] The American Psychiatric Association Diagnostic and Statistical Manual of Mental Disorders, Fifth Edition (2013).

and alcohol testing. And since these are drug courts and not treatment programs, the goal is to protect the community.

Drug courts combat methamphetamine addiction. For methamphetamine-addicted people, drug courts increase treatment program graduation rates by nearly 80%.[149] When compared to eight other programs, drug courts quadrupled the length of abstinence from methamphetamine.[150]

Drug courts use a Risk and Needs Assessment (RANT) web-based program to evaluate participants.[151]

Low risk/low need–emphasis should be on prevention;
Low risk/high need–emphasis on treatment;
High risk/low need–emphasis on accountability;
High risk/high needs–accountability and treatment.

The most resources will need to be spent on the high risk/high needs individuals. Judges can create a color-coded matrix to readily determine which quadrant a defendant is in and the corresponding services and level of care necessary.

Participants in these categories should be kept separate. If the defendants are capable of working they should not be in drug court. They may need some other kind of help, but drug court participants should be in such need that the program is all they can do.

A low risk track should include weekly urine samples, no court check-ins and approximately eight treatment sessions. Suggested eligibility requirements are no prior charges, a high

---

[149] http://www.nadcp.org/sites/default/files/nadcp/best-practice-standards/index.html
[150] http://www.nadcp.org/sites/default/files/nadcp/best-practice-standards/index.html
[151] Risks-and-Needs Quadrants and Associated Practice Recommendations for Drug Offenders can be seen at Douglas B. Marlowe J.D., Ph.D. *An Analysis of Prognostic Risks and Criminogenic Needs* Chapman Journal of Criminal Justice (2009)

school diploma, and no history of prior police contacts. Any failures (i.e. a positive drug test) results in a transfer to a different program.

Sanctions that are too low make people worse. It is like "boiling the frog." A frog in water will not realize that the water is becoming gradually hotter and will not jump out of the water. People get used to the sanctions.

Sanctions that are too high, on the other hand, can prove too burdensome and you may create learned helplessness. If too much structure is required, the situation can worsen. You must consider the ratio of benefit to burden.

Goals can be proximal (short-term goals) or distal (long-term goals). For distal goals you must have low sanctions and high rewards, i.e. when they are new to the program. Distal becomes proximal. Those goals in the future eventually become the present. Abstinence is a proximal goal.

If due to addiction there is a triggered binge pattern, cravings or compulsions or withdrawal symptoms, you are dealing with a neurologically damaged brain. For those individuals it takes three to nine months to become proximal.

If you use jail for early sanctions, you are not a drug court.

If there is no drug problem, do not send them to rehab.

CHAPTER TWENTY-NINE

THERAPIES/ TREATMENTS

Treatment

"What does the Lord require of thee but to do justly, to love mercy, and to walk humbly with our God."
Micah 6:8.

If a person can stop with a threat alone, they were not an addict. Treatments may include psychosocial rehabilitation programs, psychotherapy, behavioral treatment services, medical treatment, psychotropic medications, etc., but there is also much that can be done to improve the environment to assist those suffering from mental illness. Individuals must consult their own doctors to determine the best course of treatment, but some remedies, such as taking herbs, cannot hurt you and have the potential for great relief so why not try them? Recovery can be a long-term process that frequently requires multiple episodes and methods of treatment.

Healing the Addicted Brain by Harold C. Urschell, III, M.D.[152] is a *New York Times* Bestseller detailing a science-based alcoholism and addiction recovery program. This is the best, most comprehensive book to give someone ready to combat the disease of alcoholism or substance abuse. This book has holistic (focusing

---

[152] Dr. Urschell is the Chief of Medical Strategy for EnterHealth. www/EnterHealth.com

on the whole person and system) approaches to curing addiction. The EnterHealth Program used at Urschell's clinic and set out in *Healing the Addicted Brain* claims to have a 90% recovery rate compared to 20-30% of other programs. The book has photos of Single-photon Emission Computerized Tomography, SPECTS, scans of normal versus addicted brains. *Healing the Addicted Brain* is very comprehensive covering counseling (changing thoughts, combating triggers and cravings; dealing with emotions, maintaining goals), substance abuse programs, the 12-Step Recovery Program, medications, dual diagnoses, the family, lapse and relapse, health and nutrition (reducing processed foods, sugars, etc.), and regaining enjoyment in life.

Vivitrol and suboxone both reduce cravings and make it almost impossible to get high from alcohol, heroin, and prescription opiates. Campral repairs the damaged brain. Then there are the other medicines for mental illnesses.

Other therapies could include exercise (boosts neurotransmitters, norepinephrine, and serotonin), anger management, sunshine and/or vitamin D (to avoid SAD Seasonal Affective Disorder), yoga, meditation, etc.

Detoxification should be the first step in in-patient treatment. Generally, insurance companies will not pay for in-patient treatment if the person has been clean for more than thirty days (and sometimes as low as 10 days). These corporations (insurance companies) consider it a waste of resources to require in-patient treatment when the person is not in crisis. Insurance companies will pay for Intensive Outpatient treatment (IOP) in those situations. They know that the clients have already gone through detox and the worst stages of withdrawal. Criminal justice professionals must understand this and stop warehousing sick addicts in jails.

The more down-and-out a person is, the more they need positive reinforcement.

Research shows that positive reinforcement, i.e. incentives, is more powerful for changing behavior.[153] If they do not care about positive rewards, you are probably dealing with a serious drug abuser.

Positive reinforcement in courts, as in parenting, is more affective in changing behavior than sanctions. "Punishment often engenders behavioral suppression: fear, anger, as well as escape and avoidance responses. The effects of punishment is transitory with the punished behavior returning when the punishment is removed."[154] Punishment teaches what not to do. Positive incentives teach what to do. Participants should be punished for a negative test, but praised for the fact that they are attending treatment. They may know that they are not doing right. They don't know how to do right. This is why positive reinforcement is so important.

The best treatment centers use a holistic approach with a variety of rehabilitative techniques such as:

- Detoxification
- Counseling
- 12-step programs
- Substance abuse programs
- Medication
- Nutrition (reducing processed foods, sugars, etc.)
- Health awareness
- Anger management
- Exercise
- Sunshine
- Yoga
- Meditation
- Stress reduction training

---

[153] Joseph Lunievicz, Director, NDRI, National Development Research Institute, Bureau of Justice; Webinar: *Neuroscience of Addiction, Part III* (2012).
[154] Judge William Meyer NADCP.

- Music Therapy[155]
- Also: supplements, equine therapy, acupuncture, tai chi, saunas, etc.

Electronic health records (EHRs) are crucial to real-time access of pertinent clinical information (e.g., diagnoses, co-morbidities, medications, treatment goals and crisis plans). EHRs should be available to all members of the treatment team to foster collaboration, coordination and consistent care.

---

[155] Music can in some cases transcend Parkinson's, Alzheimer's, amnesia depression, insanity, and even schizophrenia. Oliver Sacks, *Musicophilia* (2008) p. 332.

CHAPTER THIRTY

COUNSELING

"Make failure your teacher, not your undertaker."
Zig Ziglar

"The state of your life is nothing more than a reflection of your state of mind."
Dr. Wayne W. Dyer

We must all become aware that we are responsible for everything happening in our lives. Those who were subjected to neglectful parenting as children will have to learn this through counseling.

Counseling increases socially adaptive behavior, modifies maladaptive or problem behaviors, and replaces them with behaviors and skills that are adaptive and socially productive. This is also referred to as "behavior management, behavior training, or behavior therapy," and similarly related terms.

Understanding addiction and its impact on the brain allows us to view relapse in a realistic context to determine appropriate treatment response, sanctions and incentives to help clients stay engaged in treatment and succeed through graduation in accountability courts.

Chronically expressing worries often irritates others and makes a person seem less powerful, perhaps even less mature. A person's day-to-day thoughts and behaviors have a powerful effect on brain chemistry.

Good counseling teaches optimism and how to learn from

and then forget mistakes. If you do not experience love, acceptance, and forgiveness for yourself, you are not able to give or feel those qualities for other people.

Those who can, should read self-help books or the Bible.[156] If there is insufficient time to read the entire Bible, read the Book of Proverbs. Other religions also have books that are beneficial to self-growth. A limitless approach will pull in those with no faith to possibly find faith. One of the reasons Alcoholics Anonymous is so successful is because religion is not allowed to regulate the goals.

Counseling teaches how to break negative thought patterns. Drug addicts, mentally ill, and criminals in general tend to ruminate. This is a source of unhappiness.

Those in counseling can learn to change aspects of their lives that they can and accept aspects that they cannot change without letting them continue to rule their lives.

Automatic negative thoughts (ANTS) should be stamped out, like ants at a picnic. Counseling should teach one to examine the thought. Have a vivid imagery of the thought turning around and working out well for the person.

Clients are mentally vulnerable and should be identified as "a person in long term recovery". The answer for many mental illness problems is more love, respect, and understanding (as it is with many problems in the world). A good counselor or therapist will allow someone to receive love, respect, and understanding. And remember - you can have the best therapist in the world, but at the end of the day you have to be your own therapist. When the client is not with the therapist, they must be both client and therapist.

---

[156] All books by Dr. Wayne Dyer, Dr. Phil, Minister Joel Osteen, Zig Ziglar's films and tapes, Dale Carnegie's books, and numerous other authors are excellent.

er.

CHAPTER THIRTY-ONE

HAPPINESS

"Remember, happiness doesn't depend upon who you are or what you have; it depends solely upon what you think."
Dale Carnegie

"The secret of happiness is freedom. The secret of freedom is courage."
Thucydides

C alm is the new happy. One of the most important, ultimate goals of counseling is to restore or instill happiness. Authentic happiness comes from developing one's strengths.[157] When people are thanked in front of other people they can be on a high for days or weeks.[158] This is why drug courts can be effective. Participants are publicly congratulated for their positive behavior. For many of them this is the first time they have ever received any positive recognition publicly.

Counseling will assist those with limited skills to inject self-esteem and happiness into their lives. Stress is the underlying reason for many crimes. Happy people produce less of the stress hormone cortisol. Smiling, hugging, giving and receiving love all reduce stress. Hugs create oxytocin, a hormone that creates happiness. Staring into the eyes of a loved one creates oxytocin. This is also true if you stare into the eyes of a beloved dog (but not a cat). A pet can reduce stress and be a companion for a person

[157] Martin Seligman, *Authentic Happiness* (2002).
[158] Martin Seligman, *Authentic Happiness* (2002).

suffering from mental illness.

Hope brings happiness. Participants in accountability courts need to be guided to wish for goals that are just beyond reach, and when they achieve goals, make new ones.

They should receive guidance on how to unclutter their lives. A good start is to make a list of things for which they are grateful and focus on those. This can be difficult for many people that are in the criminal justice system, but they will accomplish this. An attitude of gratitude is critical for good mental health. There is always something for which to be grateful.

Counseling can get individuals to a place mentally where they can begin to care for themselves via physical exercise, health maintenance, diet, etc. Pain is inevitable, but a lot of suffering is optional.

Truly happy people are distinguishable from others because they have a rich repertoire of friends.

Happiness is found in the present. Too much dwelling on the worries of the future or the mistakes of the past interferes with happiness. Meditation can help a person train their brain to be in the present. Tibetan Buddhist monks find inner peace and off-the-charts happiness levels as measured in brain scans by meditating quietly on compassion and loving kindness.[159] Great masters and teachers have always known that positive acts and thoughts attract positive things.[160] People with a sense of purpose live longer and have less stress.

The number one most important thing you can do to increase happiness is SMILE. Even when you don't feel like smiling-smile anyway. Smiling will bring out the best in those around you. Force yourself to do this in the beginning. The habit will become second nature. Put a pencil in your mouth to force a smile. Even a forced smile will make you feel happier. Engage in

---

[159] Susan Cain, *Quiet, the Power of Introverts in a World that can't stop Talking* (2013) page 190.
[160] Rhonda Byrne, *The Secret* (2006).

unrealistic optimism. Just the physical act of smiling can make one feel happier. Those who smile appear more competent to others. It takes more muscles to smile that to frown. It is an inexpensive face lift.

Yawning cools off the brain. Yawning is contagious and is a sign of empathy and it improves memory.

Counseling teaches the consumers to not get too hungry, angry, lonely, or tired (HALT).

Turn your mistakes into lessons. Disconnect from technology when you can. Take chances. Try to experience new culture, food, or places when you can. Take breaks. Get plenty of rest. Exercise and keep moving so you can have a restful night of sleep. Respect honesty and truthfulness, to do less leads to stress and anxiety. Don't compare yourself to others, celebrate your uniqueness.

Never argue with a fool. People watching will not know which is which. There is amazing power for the speaker in the statement "that's true you're absolutely right."

Remember that most of the world's problems can be solved with love. Many mental illnesses come from a lack of love or happiness (albeit in an indirect way): drug abuse in utero, neglect as a child, etc. When we can, we must try to reverse the damage and prevent harm from happening in the future. Always remember that Utopia, Paradise, Shangri-La, are within us. The Kingdom of Heaven is within us. We can help others find peace, happiness and fulfillment, and we are better at helping others if we find these gifts for ourselves first. Use your words to share your love. Create happiness. Choose happiness.

Stormer's Abbreviated List For Happiness

- Smile.
- Be and live in the present.
- Breathe–deeply.
- Have good relationships, be in love.
- Laugh.
- Make others happy. Help others.
- Give to another, that which you wish for yourself.

- Be positive.
- Surround yourself with positive, loving, supportive friends.
- Have good nutrition.
- Free yourself from negative thoughts. Stamp them out.
- Be at peace/happy.
- Exercise, be physical, it increases endorphins.
  - Do yoga.
  - Be healthy/fit.
- Meditate – especially on compassion and loving kindness, meditation can help improve focus.
- Clear clutter, unclutter your life, let go of things (attachments, identification with work, etc.).
- Give. Pass your unused possessions to the less fortunate.
- Listen to music (good music).
- Stick to a routine; repetitive behaviors are calming.
- Begin everyday with an expression of gratitude.
- Practice gratitude. Cultivate an attitude of gratitude.
- Cultivate the inner condition for happiness for yourself.
- Cultivate loving kindness for others.
- Spend time in the sunshine.
- Give and receive hugs.
- Yawn, it cools off the brain.
- Hope, dream big.
- Wish for things that are just beyond your reach.
- When you achieve your goals make new ones.
- Surround yourself with beautiful things.
  - Go to art museums.
  - Watch fun, happy, beautiful movies.
- Change what you can for the better.
- Be spiritual.
- Live in the moment.
- Be socially connected.
- Be intellectually connected.
- Have good posture.
- Stay intellectually fresh:
  - Learn new things.
- Intend to feel good.

- Pretend to feel good. Fake it until you make it.
- Let go of the ego.
- Strive for simplicity.
- Stay detached of outcomes.
- Love yourself.
- Live fearless.
- Accept others. When you judge others you are not able to love them.
- Avoid stress.
- Adopt a pet.
- Get a (relaxing, fun, stress free) hobby.
- Forgive-yourself and others.
- Shut off media (televisions, social media, phones, etc.).
- Smile and watch the healing in others begin.

DON'T
- Don't ruminate.
- Don't lose balance in your life.
- Don't drink too much alcohol.
- Don't gossip.
- Do not dwell on those things you cannot change.
- Avoid materialism.
- Avoid entitlements.
- Avoid violent movies and video games and do the same for your children.

CHAPTER THIRTY-TWO

TWELVE-STEP PROGRAMS

"I didn't come to AA to save my soul, I came to save my ass. It was years before I realized they were connected."
(Alcoholics) Anonymous

When in recovery, studies have shown that people who help others find sobriety are more likely to stay sober than those who do not help others. By staying active and engaged and improving the community, participants avoid isolation, find purpose in life, improve their physical health, make new friendships, enhance their self-esteem, feel valued, and make a difference for others. Such programs help them stay focused on a recovery-oriented lifestyle and increase their resilience against mental illnesses like depression.

Twelve-step programs' success rates vary but it is believed that they may have:

12-25% success when used alone,
75-95% success with a holistic approach,[161]
36-82% success with marijuana,
58% percent is the highest success rate with other drugs.[162]

Non-religious community based alternative to AA /NA:

Smartrecovery.org

----

[161] For example: individual and group therapy, family therapy, psychiatric, wellness and nutrition, etc.
[162] Kevin Sabet PhD, *Reefer Sanity* (2013) page 161.

Unhooked.com
Cfiwest.org

If a defendant needs to be restricted from a geographic area as a condition of probation or bond, area restrictions must be reasonable. Ask if the defendant has a compelling need to go to the area. A condition (of probation or a dismissal of the criminal charges) could be "cannot go anywhere where alcohol is the primary thing that is sold."

CHAPTER THIRTY-THREE

INTENSIVE OUTPATIENT TREATMENT

*"Treat people as if they were what they ought to be and you help
them to become what they are capable of being."*
Johann W. von Goethe (1749-1832)

Intensive Outpatient Treatment is an outpatient treatment program that delivers no less than six hours per week of chemical dependency counseling.[163] A Qualified Credentialed Counselor (QCC) is a licensed chemical dependency counselor or one of the practitioners listed below who is licensed and in good standing in the state of Texas as defined by the DSHS[164]:

(A) Licensed professional counselor;
(B) Licensed master social worker;
(C) Licensed marriage and family therapist;
(D) Licensed psychologist;
(E) Licensed physician (MD or DO);
(F) Licensed physician's assistant;
(G) Certified addictions registered nurse; or
(H) Licensed psychological associate; and
(I) Nurse practitioner recognized by the Board of Nursing as a clinical nurse specialist or
nurse practitioner with specialty in psyche-mental health[165].

A degree can now be obtained in Behavioral Science

---

[163] Tex. Administrative Code Title 37, Part 6, Chapter 163, RULE §163.40 (23).
[164] Texas Department of State Health Services.
[165] Tex. Administrative Code Title 37, Part 6, Chapter 163, RULE §163.40 (26).

(formerly it was only psychology).

Best Practices are evidence based substance abuse treatment programs that address concepts such as criminogenic risks and needs, responsivity, and cognitive behavioral treatment, and programs that possess the following hallmarks:

(A) Validated treatment assessments that include criminogenic risks and need factors;

(B) A treatment regimen that focuses on changing criminogenic risks and needs, behaviors,

and thinking patterns;

(C) A treatment regimen that includes a specific, cognitive behavioral program that has been

recognized in professional criminal justice journals;

(D) Responsivity in addressing offenders' needs and employment of qualified staff; and

(E) Measurable outcomes to reduce substance abuse, dependency, or addiction as well as

other criminogenic risks and needs.[166]

Structured Activity is a planned, interactive, scheduled event that is overseen by staff in which participants actively take part in an activity related to recovery, health, life skills, or interpersonal skills.[167] Supportive Outpatient Treatment is a program that delivers no less than two hours per week of chemical dependency counseling.[168]

---

[166] Tex. Administrative Code Title 37, Part 6, Chapter 163, RULE §163.40 (5).
[167] Tex. Administrative Code Title 37, Part 6, Chapter 163, RULE §163.40 (31).
[168] Tex. Administrative Code Title 37, Part 6, Chapter 163, RULE §163.40 (32).

CHAPTER THIRTY-FOUR

TOPICS COVERED IN TREATMENT

"There is a law in psychology that if you form a picture in your mind of what you would like to be, and you keep and hold that picture there long enough, you will soon become exactly as you have been thinking."
William James (1842 - 1910)

Below is a list of the variety of topics that may be covered in an intensive-inpatient or outpatient treatment therapy. These might be used in individual counseling or in group therapy.

- Why did you start using (boredom, fun, depression, to escape, childhood, stressors, peer pressure, medicate for mental illness, family, energy, relaxation, etc)?
- Why do you continue (addicted, kill the pain, like the feeling, social, peer pressure, etc.)?
- Different drugs;
  - o The effect of different drugs on the brain.
  - o The effect of different drugs on people's lives.
- Family group therapy, intervention with the family.
- Self care: nutrition, sleep.
- Neuroscience–disease of the brain.
- Addiction: ways to stay clean.
- Loving you, building self-esteem.
- Kindness to yourself and others.
- Relationships.
- Negative thoughts and how to handle them.
- Consequences and boundaries.
- Sexually transmitted diseases (HIV and aids are more common in drug addicts).

- Child Protective Services, their point of view, becoming friends with them.
- Parenting.
- Stages of addiction.
- People the counselor has helped in the past and those that could not be helped.
- List and discuss five things each participant is passionate about.
- Values–asking each person what values are important, feelings, character defects.
- Qualities–what you look for in others.
- Cigarettes and the deadly chemicals in them.
- Who you should forgive and who should forgive us.
- Problem solving, ask each about problems they have and how to solve them.
- PAWS–Post Acute withdrawal symptoms.

Motivational Interviewing:
- What problems has your addiction caused?
  - What are the benefits of being clean?
  - Being clean outweighing being addicted.
- Community roles, what role you play in the community.
- Deep relaxation.
- Positive imagery (how you would like to look, like your life to be, build the craving then build up a positive coping skill).

The participants may have homework that could include keeping a journal of thoughts and feelings related to substance abuse or writing an essay on a drug-related topic. They also discuss current events or past events such as actor Robin Williams' addiction and suicide in August, 2014 or bestselling author and pastor Rick Warren's son who committed suicide even though by all accounts he had everything a person would need to avoid such an end, i.e. loving parents, a supportive church, surrounded by individuals that were knowledgeable about helping others, travel to other countries to help others, etc.

The participants may also role play how to say no, e.g. one

participant is the drug dealer, and another is the one to say "no".

Participants in therapy might review movies such as *Saving Private Ryan*, and then discuss how we as Americans might not unite like that now due to drugs; or a movie such as *The Secret,* a documentary by Rhonda Byrne, about the laws of attraction and how we attract certain things (good and bad) into our lives by our behavior. Another example of a movie useful in therapy is *Twenty-eight Days* with Sandra Bullock which examines the recovery journey through therapy.

Therapy can include conditions similar to probation where participants could do community service projects that are visible to the community and, have the media invited to cover the events, e.g. a community garden where produce is provided to the elderly, planting of public areas with daffodils bulbs and other plants in conjunction with the city recreation/parks department if there is one, maintenance of the public cemetery, Habitat for Humanity, etc.

Consumers of therapy can role-play situations such as the following: A man on probation picked up an acquaintance and gave him a ride. As they were driving the acquaintance made a phone call and was obviously making a deal to sell drugs. He asked the probationer to pull over at a gas station where he sold the drugs to an undercover officer. The delivery of drugs charge was upheld against the probationer. How could the situation have best been handled?

Therapy might include contrition, apologizing to people they harmed, contacting people they used drugs with and: tell them goodbye or ask them to get help.

According to the National Institute on Drug Abuse, it takes a minimum of thirty-six months and often much longer for an adequate dosage of treatment to be effective. If we do not allow enough time for treatment to take effect, then we are terminating drug court participants early that need the treatment and the drug court environment the most. It is critical that those running drug courts understand the difference between proximal goals (what can be achieved immediately) and distil behavioral goals (behavior that will take some time to achieve) and operate their drug court sanctions accordingly.[169]

Thirty-day programs are not the most effective because most relapses occur within the first ninety days. It takes many years for the brain to recover from some illnesses.[170]

Some of the classes offered in the Dallas County, Texas jail are:

1. Anger Management: Learn to express and manage anger in healthier ways. Some believe that sweat lodges are effective in assisting those who need anger management.
2. Mental Health Awareness: Learn how to stay healthy by making specific plans to deal with problems and crisis.
3. Social Skills: Learn proper ways to interact with others in various social settings.
4. Healthy Relationships: Learn techniques necessary to build and maintain healthy relationships.
5. Think Again: Learn how to modify unhealthy thoughts, emotional patterns and learn problem-solving skills to prevent future legal issues.
6. Life Skills: Learn how to cope with different life skill situations.
7. Co-occurring Psychiatric and Substance Use Disorders (COPSD): Learn how to manage mental illness and reduce the use of alcohol and/or drugs.
8. Coping with Trauma: Learn to let go of dangerous relationships and gain control over the effect trauma has on your emotions.

---

[169] Joseph Lunievicz, Director, NDRI, National Development Research Institute, Bureau of Justice.
[170] Joseph Lunievicz, director, NDRI, National Development Research Institute, Bureau of Justice.

9. Coping with Mood Disorders: Learn what mood disorders are and how to deal with them.
10. Relapse Prevention: Learn what happens to the body, mind and emotions after putting down drugs and alcohol.
11. WRAP: Wellness Recovery Action Plan.
12. Discharge Planning: Preparing inmates with necessary community resources (housing, medication, food, etc.) upon their release from jail.

Here are some of the other organized classes/groups done in coordination with the Inmate programs:

1. AA recovery.
2. Rosalana-Yoga, Interplay, and Art.
3. El Centro College Art program.
4. New Circle tools: Volunteer men mentors.

There are a number of other activities the inmates do with the Mental Health Officers (professionals trained in mental health working in the jail).

Twelve Steps for Providers:

1. Engage the client.
2. Contact collaterals, gather information.
3. Screen for and detect COD co-occurring disorders.
4. Determine severity of MD (mental disorders) and SUD (substance abuse disorder).
5. Determine appropriate care setting.
6. Determine diagnosis.
7. Disability and functional impairment.
8. Identify strengths and supports.
9. Identify cultural and linguistic needs and supports.
10. Identify additional problem areas to be addressed.
11. Determine readiness for change.
12. Plan treatment.

CHAPTER THIRTY-FIVE

ANGER MANAGEMENT

"If there is any great secret of success in life, it lies in the ability to put yourself in the other person's place and to see things from his point of view, as well as your own."
Henry Ford

*P*eace is Every Step by Thich Nhat Hanh (1992) is the book used at Vernon State Hospital in Texas (where the violent, mentally ill criminals are sent) to teach anger management. It emphasizes that one should not act out their anger, as that fuels the fire. Instead, one should examine, analyze and let go of the anger. Contrary to what most of us have been told, it is not healthy to express anger. When we dwell on something that has been done to us and on how to express it, the feeling gets worse. Blood pressure goes down when people decide to express friendliness and not anger.[171]

Empathy is the best antidote for anger. Empathy is the ability to understand the thoughts and motivations of another. The angry person must be taught to put themselves in the shoes of the person with whom they are angry.

Anger management consists of: awareness, postponement, role-playing, journaling, verbal acknowledgment, talking it out, labeling the feeling, etc.[172]

Participants must be taught awareness and that eliminating the anger before it occurs is the healthiest choice.

---

[171] Martin Seligman, *Authentic Happiness* (2002).
[172] Wayne Dyer, *Erroneous Zones* (1976) page 223.

Blood sugar spikes and hunger contribute to anger outbursts and mood swings.

CHAPTER THIRTY-SIX

GENDER - SPECIAL CONSIDERATIONS WITH FEMALE VICTIMS OR DEFENDANTS

"People become really quite remarkable when they start thinking that they can do things. When they believe in themselves, they have the first secret of success."
Norman Vincent Peale

A woman's brain experiences more stress over the same event as a man's brain.[173] Men have more processors in the amygdala, a part of the brain regulating fear and aggression.[174] This explains why men are more likely to anger quickly and take action in response to immediate physical danger.

It is estimated that seventy to ninety-five percent of women with drug abuse problems were sexually abused as children.

Post Traumatic Stress Disorder (PTSD) prevents them from changing their circumstances. Women raised by mothers who were in concentration camps during the holocaust suffer from inter-generational trauma.

Stephanie Covington *A Woman's Way through the Twelve Steps* (1994),[175] is recommended for women in recovery.

Women need to be in groups that form relationships with other women. Recovery groups of eight are recommended and the

---

[173] Luanne Brizendine, *The Female Brain* (2006).
[174] Luanne Brizendine, *The Female Brain* (2006).
[175] Other recommended books are: Stephanie Covington Beyond Trauma: A Healing Journey for Women (2003) and Lisa Najavits Seeking Safety: A Treatment Manual for PTSD and Substance Abuse (2001).

classes are called "Chasing Butterflies" because no one wants to go to a group called "trauma." Participants are welcomed to the group with introductions and grounding and relaxation type exercises are taught and used at the end of each session thereafter (exploring the five senses via a body scan: thinking of five things you can see, four things you can touch, three things you can hear, two things you can smell, and one thing you can taste).

The second session starts with a quiet time, a review, and then the course begins to evaluate traumatic events. Next, there is education about power versus abuse. Finally, guided imagery is used to take the person to a safe place psychologically.

The third session deals with healing trauma by learning self-care and resilience: persons who have not been well-loved must learn better coping skills. Hyper-vigilance and hyper-arousal are like having your foot on the brake and the gas at the same time. Changes in the brain are explained. Boundary exercises are taught (e.g. approaching each other from the back and side). Those subjected to long-term sexual abuse have more difficulty establishing boundaries.

In the fourth session, there is an emphasis on healing the trauma, healthy relationships, and an introduction to the relationship wheel (respect, mutuality, and compassion). The group is given definitions of these qualities.

Session five addresses relationships, what brings joy, endings, and appreciation for others in the group and what the group has accomplished. The participants should now have a sense of sanctuary in their lives (a good environment). Participants receive a certification of completion.

Regarding assaults on women, it is estimated that ten to sixteen percent of women will be raped in their lifetime. Of those, only eighteen percent report the assaults. Only five percent of college women report assaults.

Alcohol does not cause sexual assault. Alcohol is the weapon.

Men who are more at risk to be victims of sexual assault are: adolescents, youth, inmates, and men in the military. Seventeen percent of college campus sexual assault victims are male. This is twice the number usually cited. Male victims of sexual assault are more likely to be injured and less likely to report than women.

It is estimated that two to eight percent of sexual assaults reported are false reports.

There is much disbelief of victims because it requires great empathy to put oneself in the shoes of the complaining witness.

Of the participants in drug courts the following statistics are found:

- 91 % have suffered trauma.
- 65% were raped by a non-relative.
- 38% were raped by relative.

Sexual assault victims who end up in drug court indicate that the sexual assault was the worst trauma of all traumas that they experienced. In addition, sexual assault victims are at a nineteen times greater risk of developing post-traumatic stress disorder (PTSD).

Twelve-step programs that require the participants to admit their powerlessness must be cognizant of interpretation by sexual assault victims. The distinction should be emphasized that there may be a surrendering to a higher power that is unlike any surrendering in the context of an assault or long-term abuse.

"Co-dependent" is the term used that means having one's life revolve around another person's addiction or desire.

A male child who had adverse childhood experiences is many times more likely to be a drug user.

CHAPTER THIRTY-SEVEN

HEALTH AND MENTAL ILLNESS.

"If we all did the things we are capable of doing, we would literally astound ourselves."
Thomas A. Edison

Accrding to bestselling author Dr. Daniel Amen, seventy-five percent of our health care dollars are spent on illnesses that are a result of bad decisions.[176]

To enhance recovery and encourage individual wellness, try these techniques which focus on interactions between the mind, body and behavior to affect physical functioning and promote health:

Meditation increases calmness and relaxation.

Yoga improves physical fitness and relieves stress.

Acupuncture relieves pain and helps manage stress.

Saunas can drive toxins out of the body. It is best if they are used two to three times per day for thirty days (note, the toxins are stored in the fat cells of the body and therefore, working in the hot sun and sweating can have the opposite affect and actually cause an addict to crave the drug of addiction).

A clean and properly functioning colon will remove toxins from the body. Consider doing a colon flush periodically (with natural fruit juices, psyllium, and herbs). Supplements also help to remove toxins from the body.[177]

While it is true that your thoughts create feelings and those

---

[176] www.amenclinic.com
[177] Complementary and alternative medicines (i.e. supplements) www.mentalhealthamerica.net/list-cam-treatments

feelings create actions or lack thereof, to heal, one must at times take the opposite approach, i.e., actions first, feelings second.

Your brain has its own receptors that produce the chemicals you need e.g. opioids. It is an internal pharmacy. Placebos work for serous neurological affects such as Parkinson's. The production of opioids starts in the temples and then goes to the mid-brain.

Education

"The world is a dangerous place to live, not because of people who are evil, but because of people who don't do anything about it."
Albert Einstein

The best things to do for your children scholastically are:

- Read to them.
- Talk to them about college plans.
- Set and live the example. Take a class yourself. Read.

Diet

"Nothing will benefit human health and increase chances of survival of life on Earth as much as the evolution to a vegetarian diet."
Albert Einstein

If it came from a plant, eat it. If it was made in a plant, don't eat it.

Every time you eat or drink you are either feeding a disease or fighting it.

The Osage Indians are the tallest of the Native American tribes in America. The oral history of the Osage Indians indicates that before they were forced onto reservations and forced to eat the white man's diet they had healthy lives where they frequently and regularly lived to be one-hundred years old, and could cover by foot one-hundred miles in a day even at a very advanced age.

In the 1960s Americans spent 17.5% of their income on food and 5.2% on healthcare. Now those numbers have virtually flipped. Perhaps if we spent more of our money on healthy food we would not have to spend so much on healthcare.[178]

The Salem witch trials, hysteria and hallucinations may have been a manifestation of a postencephalitic disorder. Ergot poisoning may have played a part. "Ergot, a fungus containing toxic alkaloid compounds similar to LSD, can infest rye and other grains, and if contaminated bread or flour is eaten, ergotism may result. This happened frequently in the Middle Ages, and it could cause agonized gangrene (which led to one of it popular names, St. Anthony's fire). Ergotism could also cause convulsions and hallucinations very similar to those of LSD. In 1951 an entire French village succumbed to ergot poisoning. Those affected endured several weeks of terrifying hallucinations and often compulsions to jump from windows as well as extreme insomnia."[179]

Iodine deficiency is believed to be the number one cause of mental retardation. Processed food does not have iodine.

Consider becoming a vegetarian. Those who switch to vegetarianism find that they are healthier, stronger, have more energy, and are more mentally alert than ever. A vegetarian diet reduces the chances of cancers, heart disease, diabetes, osteoporosis (resulting from too much protein in the diet), etc. It reduces exposure to toxins (mercury in seafood, growth hormones, antibiotics, tranquilizers, and thousands of other drugs routinely used in corporate owned animals; deadly salmonella, and mad cow disease). A vegetarian diet reduces pre-mature aging (rotting meat in the body releases free radicals). A meatless diet makes you slower to exhaust and quicker to recover from fatigue.

This is not to mention all the other beneficial side effects

---

[178] Michael Pollan, *In Defense of Food* (2009) p. 259.
[179] Oliver Sacks, *Hallucinations* (2012) p. 245.

such as reducing global warming, using natural resources more efficiently, reducing pollution, and restoring biodiversity (overfishing of seafood). Eighty percent of other countries will not accept American meat because of the drugs in the meat.[180] This is why American women have issues with facial hair. Such unnatural hair growth is a result of the hormones in our meat. Estrogen in chicken and beef can cause breast growth in men. Seven people can be fed for a whole year from the grains and soy needed to produce the meat, poultry and dairy products eaten by the average American.

A study released in May of 2013 revealed that turkey meat sold in the United States had fecal matter in fifty percent of the products and ninety percent of the products had antibiotics. In China twenty-two tons of rat meat labeled as lamb was sold to the public.[181] Commercially grown cantaloupes had e-coli from cattle fecal matter from a neighboring ranch over which the water source was derived. This resulted in deaths and a nationwide recall in 2012.

Humans are herbivores. Digestive juices are one-twentieth the strength of carnivores. It takes a carnivore three hours to digest meat (digestive tracts are short). It takes a human twelve to eighteen hours (digestive tracts are very long). Flesh is putrefying in the gut in that time. Human teeth are designed for grinding, not tearing flesh.

Cooked meat destroys enzymes that aid digestion. This leads to pancreatic cancer. Nitrosamines (carcinogens) are formed when alcohol or tobacco reacts with preservatives in meat. Sodium nitrate gives meat its red color. It is poisonous. Even milk can have carcinogenic hormones and contain pus and blood. I do not; however, recommend cutting out dairy products as milk helps the body create serotonin–which helps us feel good.

---

[180] Industrially raised cattle consume eighty percent of the antibiotics in the United States.
[181] National Public Radio 5/3/13.

Diseased animals, euthanized pets, animal control kills, road kill, rotting animals on ranches are all taken to rendering plants. They are steam cooked there to separate the fats (used in cosmetics, lubricants, soaps and candles) from the proteins (used for dog food and feed lots i.e. forcing herbivores to eat their own kind resulting in mad cow disease, etc).

And the moral side of the issue (reducing the suffering of animals), some animals in slaughterhouses are still alive when they are skinned and dismembered after being tased with an electrical weapon.

If all this just seems like too much (reducing gluten and sugar and processed foods, vegetarianism, and other diet changes) the corporations will supply the demand. If we all expected healthy choices, corporations would stop forcing their carcinogenic, highly processed, sludge on the American people. It is simple supply and demand.

While these are just a few reasons to reconsider your diet, on the lighter side-remember an apple a day will keep anyone away if you throw it hard enough.

Nutrition and Mental Health

DON'T EAT
- Highly processed, genetically modified food.
- Fructose, sucrose, corn syrup-filled.
- Antibiotiked, cornstarched, color dyed.
- Herbicided, pesticided, hormone laden, glutenized.
- Hydrogenated, trans-fat, salty, sugary, supersized.
- Radiated, toxic food.
- Excessive food.
- Anything incapable of rotting.
- Food with unrecognizable ingredients.

DO EAT
- Fresh, organic vegetables, nuts, eggs, avocados, and spices.
- Dairy, as it allows your body to produce serotonin.
- Seafood is generally good (avoid mercury), oysters raise

your progesterone level which improves mood.

- Eat only real food, the kind your great grandmother would recognize.
- Eat mostly plants.

The more one studies mental illness, the more one realizes the inevitable connection between mental illnesses and nutrition. The old axioms "you are what you eat" and "food is medicine" are never more relevant. The brain is more sensitive to nutrition than the heart.

The two best things you can do for your mental health nutritionally are:

1. Cut out sugar.
2. Cut out grains with gluten.

The two most important things you can do nutritionally to avoid Alzheimer's and avoid contributing to the symptoms of schizophrenia are:

1. Cut out carbohydrates.
2. Eliminate gluten.[182]

There is no cure for Alzheimer's, but preventative measures can be taken.

If someone would have told me even ten years ago what I now know to be true about what the government allows in our food today, I would have smiled and backed away slowly from that person. I would have thought they had the same mental illnesses that the people I now prosecute have (it is a common symptom of mental illness for the mentally ill to believe that the government is putting toxins/poisons in their food). While the government may

---

[182] Dr David Perlmutter, *Grain Brain* (2013).

not be putting toxins in our food, they certainly allow big corporations to do so.

To improve the brain via nutrition: increase water intake, restrict calories, eat fish and good fats (eggs, avocados, etc), and consume dietary antioxidants. Inflammation in the brain is an important player in brain degeneration. Antioxidants fight this.

Omega-3 deficiencies are associated with depression, suicide, and homicide.[183] Omega-3 deficiencies are also linked to schizophrenia and attention deficit hyperactivity disorder. Omega-3 can be obtained through flaxseed (vegetarian) or fish.

The brain is about 80% water, hydrate it. Dehydration reduces cognitive performance and the ability to function. Dehydration can raise stress hormones which can damage a brain over time. Liquids should be unpolluted with artificial sweeteners, sugar, caffeine, or alcohol. Caffeine is a diuretic (dehydrates). Green tea is also good for brain function. Many herbal teas are great for physical and mental health and should be consumed regularly. Drinking water reduces anxiety, toxins and a host of ailments. Alcohol interferes with the brain and kidney function and causes excess excretion of fluids, which can then lead to dehydration.

While there are numerous benefits to eating less, it is important for the brain in that it triggers certain mechanisms in the body to increase the production of nerve growth factors, which are helpful to the brain. Researchers use the acronym CRON (calorie restriction with optimal nutrition).

DHA, one form of omega-3 fatty acids found in fish, makes up a large portion of the gray matter of the brain. The fat in the brain plays a vital role in how our brain cells function. Neurons are also rich in omega-3 fatty acids. Recent research has revealed that diets rich in omega-3 fatty acids may help promote a healthy emotional balance and positive mood, possibly because DHA is a main component of the brain's synapses

---

[183] Michael Pollan, *In Defense of Food* (2009) p. 181.

Consume lots of dietary antioxidants. To understand antioxidants one must first understand free radicals. Tiny molecules called free radicals are made when a cell converts oxygen into energy. Free radicals rid the body of harmful toxins when produced in normal amounts. Free radicals damage cells, causing cell death and tissue damage when produced in toxic amounts. This results in an inflammation in the brain causing brain degeneration. This is known as oxidative stress. Free radical formation plays a major role in the deterioration of the brain with age. Antioxidants fight the damaging affect (think rust) of free radicals.

The top antioxidant foods (which reduce chances of disease and aging in the body and brain) are blueberries, blackberries, kale, strawberries, spinach, raspberries, brussel sprouts, plums, broccoli, and beets. Vitamin E, Vitamin C, and beta carotene inhibit the production of free radicals. A number of studies have shown that dietary intake of antioxidants from fruits and vegetables significantly reduce the risk of developing cognitive impairment.

Calorie Restriction/Weight Restriction

"Great things are done by a series of small things brought together."
Vincent van Gogh

In poor countries people die of starvation. In rich countries people die of overeating. Reduced calories improve memory and other cognitive function.[184] Fasting improves health. Fasting also increases longevity. One Mr. Singh (the world's oldest marathon runner), a one-hundred-and-one-year-old Indian man who runs marathons of over seven hours in length claims that his happiness and the secret to his longevity lies in what and how much he eats.

---

[184] Dr David Perlmutter, *Grain Brain* (2013) p. 133.

He has never had surgery, shows no signs of heart disease, and never takes medicine. He eats a simple diet of fresh food and in a child's type portion.[185]

Calorie restriction was the first effective treatment in medical history for epileptic seizures. Fasting confers profound neuroprotection, increases the growth of new brain cells, and allows existing neuronetworks to expand their sphere of influence, i.e. neuroplasticity.[186] Reduced calories, improves memory, and other cognitive function.[187]

During the Great Depression (1929-1933) there was a drought and food was scarce, yet life expectancy in the United States increased by six years. Eighty years ago nutritionists at Cornel University working with animals discovered that reducing calorie intake increased longevity in those animals.[188] Some lab animals with calorie restriction have as much as a forty percent longer life span than those that are fed to obesity.[189]

The risk of Alzheimer's and cognitive decline is tripled for those with low physical activity.[190] Weight gain contributes to diabetes. Diabetes doubles one's chances for Alzheimer's.

The bigger the belly, the smaller the brain's memory center - the hippocampus. As your hippocampus shrinks, your memory declines. As the hippocampus shrinks, the risk is higher for small strokes in the brain. Clinically obese people have significantly less brain tissue, while the overweight had four percent less brain tissue compared to normal weight individuals. Much of the tissue was lost in the frontal and temporal globe regions of the brain, the place

---

[185]   http://www.documentarytube.com/eat-fast-and-live-longer-bbc-horizon-2012.

[186] Dr David Perlmutter, *Grain Brain* (2013) p. 135.

[187] Dr David Perlmutter, *Grain Brain* (2013) p. 133-135.

[188]   http://www.documentarytube.com/eat-fast-and-live-longer-bbc-horizon-2012.

[189]   http://www.documentarytube.com/eat-fast-and-live-longer-bbc-horizon-2012.

[190] Dr David Perlmutter, *Grain Brain* (2013) p. 203.

from which we make decisions and store memories, among other things.[191]

More body fat results in a dramatically increased risk for dementia. The Mediterranean diet (good for the brain) is rich in olive oil, nuts, beans, fish, fruits and vegetables, and wine with meals.[192] Lean protein, complex carbohydrates, and foods rich in omega-3 fatty acids (large, cold water fish, such as tuna and salmon, walnuts, Brazil nuts, and olive oil) are essential to brain function.

Individuals with the lowest calorie intake have the lowest risk of Alzheimer's disease and Parkinson's disease.[193] Physical exercise, caloric restriction, and the addition of certain nutrients like curcumin and omega-3 fat reduce the effects of epilepsy, anorexia nervosa, depression, schizophrenia, and obsessive-compulsive disorder.[194] The more fat on your body, the more toxins it stores.

Exercise

"You have only to endure to conquer . . . you have only to persevere."
Sir Winston Churchill

Exercise increases longevity, reverses memory decline in elderly people and increases growth of new brain cells in the brain center.[195] Exercise is more effective for depression than antidepressants.[196] Exercise reduces the chances of dementia.[197]

---

[191] Dr David Perlmutter, *Grain Brain* (2013) p. 121.
[192] Dr David Perlmutter, *Grain Brain* (2013) p. 124.
[193] Dr David Perlmutter, *Grain Brain* (2013) p. 134.
[194] Dr David Perlmutter, *Grain Brain* (2013) p. 132.
[195] Dr David Perlmutter, *Grain Brain* (2013) p. 132.
[196] Dr. Daniel Amen, *Change your Brain Change your Body* by (2010) p. 112.
[197] Dr. Daniel Amen, *Change your Brain Change your Body* by (2010) p. 113.

"When people start habitually exercising, even as infrequently as once per week, they start changing other unrelated patterns in their lives, often unknowingly. Typically people who exercise start eating better and become more productive at work. They smoke less and show more patience with colleagues and family. They use their credit cards less frequently and say they feel less stressed. It's not completely clear why, but for many people, exercise is a keystone habit that triggers widespread change, and there is something about it that makes other habits easier."[198]

Those who exercise forty minutes, three times per week grow their hippocampus (houses memory) by two percent over the year they have been exercising.[199] *There is no medicine that can do this.* Exercise promotes angiogenesis, increasing the blood vessels in the brain.[200] It brings more oxygen to every part of the brain which improves brain function.[201] Exercise promotes the creation of new mitochondria which encourages the growth of new cells, new synapses, new blood vessel branchings, and builds muscles.[202] Low levels of DHA, found in fish oil, are found in adolescents who are incarcerated and have behavior problems, in children with ADHD, and in people with dementia and Alzheimer's disease. DHA is responsible for enhanced learning. In one study children that ate fish more than once per week had an overall school grade fifteen percent higher than those who consume less than one serving per week. [203]

Exercise increases oxygen to the prefrontal cortex, increasing learning, decreasing anger impulses. Exercise causes the brain to grow more brain cells/neurons, increases intelligence, and increases problem solving abilities. Exercise boosts neurotransmitters, norepinephrine, and serotonin making one have

---

[198] Charles Duhig, *The Power of Habit* (2012) p. 108.
[199] Dr. Majid Fotuhi M.D., PH. D. *Boost Your Brain* (2013) p. 65.
[200] Dr. Majid Fotuhi M.D., PH. D. *Boost Your Brain* (2013) p. 27.
[201] Dr. Majid Fotuhi M.D., PH. D. *Boost your Brain* (2013) p. 69.
[202] Dr. Majid Fotuhi M.D., PH. D. *Boost your Brain* (2013) p. 69.
[203] Dr. Majid Fotuhi M.D., PH. D. *Boost your Brain* (2013) p. 80.

an overall feeling of wellness, and feel better about themselves. Exercise allows the natural amino acid tryptophan to enter the brain, enhancing mood.

People who exercise have healthier diets, take more responsibility for their own health, and seek more social support. They manage stress better. They have higher self-esteem. They sleep better and are less likely to be roaming the streets getting into trouble. To prepare for the role of a woman addicted to prescription drugs due to chronic pain in the movie *Cake* (2014), actress Jennifer Aniston stopped exercising. She became irritable, tired, hungry all the time, and suffered other noticeable ill effects.

Breathing exercises are useful in stress and anger management. Aerobic exercise improves the brain.

Epigenetics, nurture altering nature, what we do today via exercise, nutrition, etc., can alter our DNA not only for ourselves but for those generations to come.

To avoid that rundown feeling, cross streets carefully.

Herbs and Spices – And other Mental Nutrition

"In the fields of observation, chance favors only the prepared mind."
Louis Pasteur – 1854

New research in nutrition and weight loss has revealed that ingesting certain nutrients in foods, teas, herbs, and spices can change the chemical balance of the brain. Addictive eating causes imbalances in brain chemistry. Neurosurgeon Dr. Braverman has identified the effects of certain nutrients on four brain chemicals- acetylcholine, dopamine, GABA, and serotonin that allow the brain to fire at just the right moment for your body to function at the optimal level. When one of these four chemicals is out of balance, your brain will compensate by sending signals that can damage and eventually destroy your health (mental and physical). Dr. Braverman's solutions emphasize the consumption of herbs, spices, and teas to alter brain and body metabolism. Dr. Braverman's book *Younger (Thinner) You Diet: How*

Understanding Your Brain Chemistry Can Help You Lose Weight, Reverse Aging, and Fight Disease has charts that indicate which spices and herbs to use for different mental challenges that a person might face.[204]

Acetylcholine affects memory. If you don't have acetylcholine you won't remember that you're out of RAM. Dopamine is the brain's reward system (produces a feeling of euphoria). GABA calms you and lowers anxiety. Serotonin affects mood, and sleep regulation.

Norepinephrine affects one's metabolic rate (controlling how fast and effectively calories are burned). Endorphins affect pain relief, and cravings.

Examples of the effects of some nutrients from a mental standpoint are:

- Ashwagandha extract is effective in boosting measures of cognition in people with bipolar disorder and reduces stress.
- Chamomile reduces depression and anxiety.
- Curcumin has antidepressant qualities.
- Rosemary keeps the brain chemical acetylcholine from breaking down. This deficiency has been noted in patients with Alzheimer's disease.
- Sage protects acetylcholine in the brain.
- St. Johns Wort - a natural herbal treatment is helpful in raising serotonin levels and calming the cingulate part of the brain. It is just as effective as anti-depressants without the side effects. In Germany it is prescribed seven times more often than Prozac.
- Turmeric has antidepressant qualities.

---

[204] Dr. Eric R. Braverman, *M.D. Younger (Thinner) You Diet: How Understanding Your Brain Chemistry Can Help You Lose Weight, Reverse Aging, and Fight Disease* (2009).

A ketogenic diet (coconut oil) has been used as a treatment for epilepsy and now Parkinsons, Alzheimer's, ALS, and autism. Ketogenic diet has been shown to reduce amyloid in the brain. It increases glutathione, the body's natural brain protective antioxidant in the hippocampus.[205] Beta-hydroxybutyrate (beta HBA) is a superior fuel for the brain it can be found in coconut oil. It stimulates the growth of new brain cells.[206]

Vitamins

Lack of Vitamin D is associated with schizophrenia and Alzheimer's.[207] A lack of this vitamin is the cause of many diseases and ailments.[208]

Those deficient in Vitamin D are sixty percent more likely to develop cognitive decline. Those with the highest intake of vitamin D have a seventy-seven percent reduction in Alzheimer's. Low Vitamin D is linked to depression, chronic fatigue, Parkinson's, and declined mental function.[209] It reduces the symptoms of bipolar disease, depression, and memory problems.

Vitamin D is found in sunshine or can be provided via supplements. This is so important for health that jail standards require that inmates receive a minimum amount of sunshine each day.

Cholesterol

People with high cholesterol are less likely to suffer from

---

[205] Dr David Perlmutter, *Grain Brain* (2013) p. 137.

[206] Dr David Perlmutter, *Grain Brain* (2013) p. 183.

[207] Dr David Perlmutter, *Grain Brain* (2013) p. 89.

[208] Soram Khalsa, M.D., *The Vitamin D Revolution: How the Power of This Amazing Vitamin Can Change Your Life* (2009).

[209] Dr David Perlmutter, *Grain Brain* (2013) p. 192.

dementia.[210]

HDL and LDL cholesterol are both good for the brain. It is only when LDL is combined with sugar that it is bad. A good source of cholesterol is eggs. Eggs and avocados contain the type of fat that is good for the brain and body.

While herbs, spices, teas and proper nutrition may not be a substitute for medicine in a particular case, they cannot hurt you (in moderation) why not try them.

Gluten and Other Poisons

As easy as (eliminating) apple pie.
Author Unknown

Today's wheat is not the wheat of the Bible and it is not even your grandmother's wheat. Today's wheat (gluten) is biochemically different. The wheat today is a product of aggressive hydrogenation and genetic modification. Today's Franken-wheat has herbicides and pesticides inside the seed.

Wheat, rye, barley and even oats are the most common food products with gluten. Single ingredient products are gluten free. Gluten is found in bread, pasta, pizza, cookies, crackers, muffins, cupcakes, pretzels, waffles, donuts, cakes, cereal, etc.

Gluten is the sticky stuff that helps us bake. Our bodies were not designed to digest it. We are all allergic to wheat on some level.

Gluten leads to dementia, gluten encephalopathy, seizures, hallucinations, neurological impairment and magnifies the symptoms of bipolar disease and schizophrenia.[211] Wheat gluten destroys the intestinal lining in people with Celiac disease. Celiac

---

[210] Dr David Perlmutter, *Grain Brain* (2013) p. 76.
[211] Dr. William Davis, *Wheat Belly* (2011).

Disease has increased fourfold in the past fifty years.[212]

One out of 133 people in the United States have Celiac Disease but less than ten percent of them know about it.[213] Symptoms of Celiac Disease are cramping, diarrhea, weight loss, anemia, migraine headaches, arthritis, neurological symptoms, infertility, short stature (in children), depression, chronic fatigue, incontinence, dementia, gastrointestinal cancer, and a variety of other ailments.

One in ten adults suffers from gluten sensitivity. There is no test for it. Gluten sensitivity causes a variety of neurological disorders. According to the New England Journal of Medicine over fifty diseases are linked to gluten. The symptoms of gluten sensitivity include digestive symptoms (bloating, irritable bowel syndrome, diarrhea, etc.), depression, joint pain, brain fog, migraines, skin rashes, leaky gut, etc. Gluten sensitivity increases inflammation in the body.

Movement disorders are related to gluten sensitivity. Anything in a package could have gluten even if it is labeled "gluten free."

Order eggs (scrambled, omelets, etc.) in a restaurant today and you will probably be eating pancake batter which is used frequently to extend the amount and make it less expensive. Real unadulterated eggs served in restaurants, seem to be more the exception than the rule (of course this is not the case with boiled or fried eggs). This can be a real problem for someone who is gluten sensitive or worse for someone who has Celiac Disease.

Low glycemic foods are good for your brain. Gluten (high glycemic) is bad for the brain.

As if gluten were not bad enough by itself, wheat exorphins (not gluten) cause the wheat to be addictive and are likely to cause the behavioral distortions in people with schizophrenia, autism and

---

[212] Dr. William Davis, *Wheat Belly* (2011) p. 82.
[213] Dr. William Davis, *Wheat Belly* (2011) page 77.

ADHD.[214] Eating two slices of whole wheat bread is really little different, and often worse, than drinking a can of sugar sweetened soda or eating a sugary candy bar.[215] As we eat more our health declines and the cycle continues. Look at pictures of your ancestors, obesity was rare in earlier days.

"In lab animals, administration of Naloxone blocks the binding of wheat exorphins to the morphine receptor of the brain cells. Yes, opiate blocking Naloxone prevents the binding of wheat derived exorphins to the brain. The very same drug that turns off the heroin in a drug abusing addict, also blocks the effects of wheat exorphins." [216]

During food shortages toward the end of World War II bread became scarce and Celiac symptoms in children decreased. Celiac symptoms in children began to increase in the Netherlands when Swedish relief planes dropped off bread. Gluten of wheat, barley, and rye was the source of the life-threatening struggles.[217] Sugar and grains contribute to Alzheimer's and depression. Nine out of ten headaches are nothing more than gluten sensitivity.[218]

There are many gluten-free varieties of your favorite products. Psyllium husks can be used in non-gluten baking to hold bread together. Psyllium is used as a thickener for ice creams and other desserts. It is a dietary fiber that is not absorbed by the small intestine. It reduces constipation, irritable bowel syndrome, and diarrhea while it reduces cholesterol, blood sugar, chances of heart disease, and many other ailments.

Genetically modified organisms (GMO) seeds do not reproduce. They have insecticides and other unnatural poisons spliced into their genes. When consumed over time, they can produce cancer and other maladies. They are modified to resist

---

[214] Dr. William Davis, *Wheat Belly* (2011) page 174.
[215] Dr. William Davis, *Wheat Belly* (2011) page 33.
[216] Dr. William Davis, *Wheat Belly* (2011) p. 49.
[217] Dr. William Davis, *Wheat Belly* (2011) page 76.
[218] Dr David Perlmutter, *Grain Brain* (2013) p. 139.

pests. The most genetically modified food is corn with soy taking a close second. Others are wheat, fruits, vegetables, or animals raised for food and fed GMO feeds.

Aspartame is made from genetically modified bacteria. It tricks the brain into thinking something is sweet. Aspartame may be associated with Parkinson's (Michael J Fox, Robin Williams, Linda Ronstadt).

At my fortieth year high school class reunion the best looking couple stood out as not aging. Both were fit, no wrinkles, big smiles, no grey, full head of hair, bright eyes and teeth, great skin, etc. In talking to John I learned that they had a granddaughter diagnosed with Celiac disease so the entire family had eliminated gluten from their diets. I thought, "that little girl may have saved her family's lives."

The health benefits that can be derived from eliminating gluten and being vegetarian (toxins, hormone, tranquilizers, other drugs, disease, GMO grain fed, antibiotic laden, fecal matter, pus, blood, destroyed enzymes in cooking, carcinogenic compounds, poisonous sodium nitrate for coloring, etc.) is so extensive it would require another book on each subject.

Meditation

Master your mind by quieting your mind
Author Unknown

To the mind that is still, the whole universe surrenders.

Be aware of your breathing until you are no longer aware of your breathing.

Mindful meditation, yoga, tai chi, and prayer all change the structure of the brain.[219] It works by relieving stress. Chronic stress can release toxic levels of the hormone cortisol into the

---

[219] Dr. Majid Fotuhi M.D., PH. D. *Boost your Brain (2013)* p. 96.

bloodstream. Those who engage in meditation have less chance of developing brain disease. [220]

Meditation can be used to manage chronic pain and illness. It can help the body heal itself. It is useful in anxiety, depression, and stress reduction. Meditation improves memory, creativity and compassion. It helps cure addiction. It can alter the functioning of the brain. Meditation lowers blood pressure, and relaxes muscles. One study showed that meditation results in a growth of the hippocampus, which plays an important role in memory and learning. It is useful in treating post-traumatic stress disorder.

Athletes train. A workout of the body on a physical level builds muscle. Like muscle memory (e.g. as musicians experience), meditation becomes wisdom. Meditation is training the mind to focus and improving the function of the brain.

The posterior cingulate is the part of the brain associated with memory. The cells there start to fire when you think of something stressful. When you let go of those stressful thoughts and become aware of your breath, it quiets down the brain.

There is societal exhaustion with use of cell phones, the internet, and electronic gadgets. Meditation can transform classrooms, and heal veterans. Google offers their 52,000 employees free lessons in mindfulness meditation.

"Long term meditation produces significant alterations in cerebral blood flow in parts of the brain related to attention, emotion, and some autonomic functions."[221] Meditation increases blood flow to the prefrontal cortex. Maintaining a calm and focused mindset makes new blood vessels grow and network connections between brain regions become stronger.[222]

Meditation increases the size of the hippocampus (memory), the temporoparital junction, and the cerebellum (areas involved in learning, emotional regulation, and perspective taking),

---

[220] Dr David Perlmutter, *Grain Brain* (2013) p. 139.
[221] Oliver Sacks, *Hallucinations* (2012) p. 248.
[222] Dr. Majid Fotuhi M.D., PhD, *Boost your Brain (2013)* p. 33.

and boosts BDNF. [223] [224] It strengthens the pathways leading to more synapses and greater oxygen flow in those areas. It improves sleep and reduces inflammation, blood pressure, and heart rate. It increases one's ability to pay attention, process information, and regulate their moods and emotions. It thickens the cortex of the brain and reduces aging.[225]

Aromatherapy can be incorporated into meditation and yoga exercises. It is instrumental in elevating mood and eliminating stress.

Yoga

If your body is tense, your mind will follow.
Author Unknown

"All that we are is a result of what we have thought."
Buddha

"A man is what he thinks about all day long."
Ralph Waldo Emerson

"Our life is what our thoughts make it."
Marcus Aurelius 18 centuries ago

"There is no way to peace, peace is the way."
A.J. Muste

---

[223] Dr. Majid Fotuhi M.D., PhD, *Boost Your Brain* (2013) p. 98-100.
[224] Create a thicker, denser, healthier cortex and hippocampus by boosting the Brain-derived Neurotrophic Factor (BDNF), AKA fertilizer for the brain, increasing oxygen flow and maximizing healthy brain activity. Dr. Majid Fotuhi M.D., PhD, *Boost Your Brain* (2013) p. 40.
[225] Dr. Majid Fotuhi M.D., PhD, *Boost your Brain (2013)* p. 98-100.

Yoga, like meditation, has many health benefits. It improves posture, calms the brain, and helps relieve stress and mild depression. It relieves menstrual discomfort, improves digestion, and relieves headache, back pain, and fatigue. Bone production is stimulated when tension and resistance are applied on tendons. It promotes happiness and a general sense of well-being. Daily yoga cures insomnia per numerous studies including one from Harvard.

Yoga centers attention on making the spine elastic, massaging the various organs of the body and improving the functions of the glands, lungs and heart. It returns the body to a youthful condition for enjoyment of pleasure and relaxation.

CHAPTER THIRTY-EIGHT

SPECIFIC MENTAL ILLNESSES -MENTAL ILLNESS AND WHY IT SUCKS

MENTAL ILLNESS AND CRIME

"Speak up for those who cannot speak for themselves. For the rights of all who are destitute. Speak up and judge fairly. Defend the rights of the poor and needy."
Proverbs 31:8-9

"The test of our progress is not whether we add more to the abundance of those who have much, it is whether we provide enough for those who have too little."
Franklin D. Roosevelt

"Serious mental illness is relatively rare, both in the general population and in the justice system, but the over-representation of people with serious mental illness in the justice system is significant."[226]

Disease is an abnormal bodily condition that impairs normal functioning and can usually be recognized by signs and symptoms. Chronic illness requires ongoing, changing, treatment at different levels of intensity with specific components.

---

[226] Alison MacPhail and Simon Verdun-Jones, *Mental Illness and the Criminal Justice System* International Centre for Criminal law Reform and Criminal Justice Policy (2013).

Seventy percent of the incarcerated mentally ill suffer from addiction, and more than that have experimented with illegal substances in an attempt to self-medicate. In my own experience, I have found it to be very rare for a severely mentally ill person that is charged with a criminal offense to not have a substance abuse problem also. It is usually unknown if the substance abuse caused the mental illness.

Six percent of Americans suffer from a serious mental illness.[227] There is an overlap because it is estimated that the prevalence in the human population is:

4% sociopaths. (1% have Antisocial Personality Disorder)
0.8 % bipolar.[228]
0.3% have schizophrenia.
0.3 % have Schizoaffective disorder.[229]
5.3 % have depression.[230]
.26% substance/medication-induced depressive disorder.[231]
10-15% have personality disorders (more with sex offenders).

One million people in the United States have schizophrenia and half receive no treatment.

Forty-nine percent of the people in the United States will suffer from a psychiatric illness at some point in their lives per the National Institute of Health. Sigmund Freud said we all suffer from some level of mental illness. We all have some level of these characteristics, e.g. depression, anxiety, bipolar. It is only when

---

[227] American Psychiatric Institute 2011.

[228] The American Psychiatric Association Diagnostic and Statistical Manual of Mental Disorders, Fifth Edition (2013) p.136.

[229] The American Psychiatric Association Diagnostic and Statistical Manual of Mental Disorders, Fifth Edition (2013) p 107.

[230] David D Burns, M. D., *Feeling Good* (1980).

[231] The American Psychiatric Association Diagnostic and Statistical Manual of Mental Disorders, Fifth Edition (2013) p. 178.

our behavior starts affecting others around us that it is labeled as a mental illness. You do not want a person with no obsessive compulsive disorder (OCD) tendencies at all[232] as your attorney, doctor, accountant, bridge maker, etc. You want someone who will pay intense and strict attention to detail.[233]

In the Dallas jail, the most frequently diagnosed mental illnesses are: bipolar disorder, followed (in order) by schizophrenia, schizoaffective disorder, intellectual disability (formerly mentally developmentally disabled) (mentally retarded)[234], and then other, less frequently diagnosed mental illnesses such as: Major Depressive Disorder, Post Traumatic Stress Disorder PTSD, Traumatic Brain Injury TBI, Borderline Intellectual Functioning BIF, followed by others.

In 2006 the Canadian Medical Association Journal published a study that diagnosed the characters in *Winnie the Pooh* with crippling mental problems (but psychology students were doing this before that time). Keeping these characters in mind helps one to remember the symptoms of different illnesses. Their diagnoses were as follows:

- Winnie the Pooh: intellectually disabled, addict (always in search of honey), eating disorder;
- Tigger: Attention Deficit Hyperactivity Disorder. He is prepared to try any substance or matter that comes along his path which could indicate a substance abuse problem;
- Kanga Roo: Social Anxiety Disorder, overprotective mothering, and co-dependent;
- Owl: Dyslexia, narcissistic, (note: he is extremely bright

---

[232] The best book for curing excessive compulsive disorder is by Edna B. Foa, Ph.D. and Reid Wilson, Ph.D *Stop obsessing how to Overcome Your Obsessions and Compulsions* (2001).

[233] I personally am CDO, that is the same as OCD but with the letters in the right order-a little mental health humor.

[234] Defined by the Texas Health and Safety Code 591.003.

despite his disorder);

- Rabbit: Obsessive-compulsive disorder, and narcissistic;
- Eeyore (donkey): Depressive Disorder;
- Piglet: Generalized anxiety disorder, panophobia (not in the DSM or dictionary)(fears everything), OCD; and
- Christopher Robin: Schizophrenia, auditory hallucinations where all of the above mentioned characters are formed in his mind.

If a person's intelligence quotient (IQ) is less than 70 they are considered to be intellectually disabled[235] (the new politically correct term for the outdated term "mentally retarded" and later term "mentally developmentally disabled"). To have this diagnosis of intellectual disability the symptoms must occur before age 18.

50-70 I.Q. is mild intellectual disability (85%),
35-40 moderate (10%),
20-25 Severe (3 – 4 %),
Below 20 profound (1- 2%),
100 IQ is the mean.

Most lawyers and doctors generally have an I.Q. of an average of 125. Below 65 or above 145 other personality issues tend to manifest. Any I.Q. over 140 is considered to be genius. Borderline Intellectual Functioning (BIF) is not intellectual disability and is represented by an I. Q. in the 71 – 84 range. Seven percent of the population has BIF and it is a frequent diagnosis of criminal defendants.

There are many degrees of mental illness.

It is estimated that intellectually disabled (mentally

---

[235] Intellectual disability (formerly mentally developmentally disabled or mentally retarded) is defined in section 591.003 of the Health and Safety Code. The term "mentally retarded" is still used throughout the Code of Criminal Procedure and the Health and Safety Code.

retarded) individuals generally, spend an average of four times as long incarcerated as other individuals charged with similar offenses, due to their inability to advocate for themselves. In September of 2010 Dallas Sheriff Lupe Valdez stated that of the 7,100 inmates in the jail, 2,200 had a mental illness. That is thirty-one percent. As stated earlier, twenty-four percent of book-ins in the Dallas jail was individuals with a diagnosed mental illness. If they are twenty-four percent of book-ins and thirty-three percent of the jail population, this is proof that the mentally ill are not getting out on bonds and are serving more time in jail. It is worse in other areas as Dallas has many programs and individuals in place to alleviate this issue, but even with all our efforts in Dallas we still keep those sick individuals in jail longer.

There are also unmet needs in the community. In Texas 2.6 million have a diagnosed mental illness. The mental illnesses of schizophrenia, bipolar, and depression are the only three that are eligible to receive services from the State and they make up about one-fourth of those with mental illnesses. In addition, less than one-half of those actually received community based services. People with mental illness are significantly more likely to be victims of both violent and non-violent crimes, for a variety of reasons. Their symptoms make them vulnerable to homelessness and substance abuse.

My friend, Dr. Dave Bunger, attorney, psychologist, professional musician, composer, sound technician, and more (and an I.Q. that puts him in the top .03 percent of the population) was a psychologist at Terrell State Hospital and has interviewed countless mentally ill individuals. He states that people subjected to long-term sexual abuse will also suffer from the mental illness of borderline personality disorder (cannot sustain relationships). This is why those charged with prostitution all seem to suffer from borderline personality disorder among other mental illnesses. They also all seem to suffer from drug addiction, almost all have PTSD, almost all have another original diagnosis like bipolar or schizophrenia, and some have traumatic brain injury (TBI) from being beaten and abused. In almost forty years in the criminal justice field, I have never seen a woman charged with prostitution that did not suffer from a mental illness.

Personality disorders common with sex offenders are:

borderline personality disorder, avoidant personality disorder and narcissistic personality disorders.

Borderline personality disorder was demonstrated by illustration via characters Glen Close played in the movie *Fatal Attraction* or the one Kathy Bates played in the movie *Misery*.

Avoidant personality disorder is illustrated by the character Adam Sandler plays in *Punch Drunk Love* or the character William Hurt plays in *Accidental Tourist.*

Narcissism is portrayed by the character Frazier Crane on the sitcom *Frazier*, Vivian Leigh in the movie *Gone with the Wind,* and Tom Cruise in . . . well any Tom Cruise movie. Some may say Donald Trump is a narcissist. Some may say Steve Jobs was a narcissist. This is because they are such perfectionists.[236] They believe they can do the job better than anyone else. Narcissists can be confident, articulate, and intelligent.

Patients can generally be divided into two categories. The first category is schizophrenia, bipolar, and severe depression. These are brain diseases that need to be treated by a neurologist rather than a psychiatrist. The others are patients that just have difficulty living in our society. They can be treated by a therapist.

---

[236] Jeffrey Kluger, *The Narcissist Next Door: Understanding the Monster in Your Family, in Your Office, in Your Bed—in Your World* (2014).

CHAPTER THIRTY-NINE

BRAIN SCANS, NEUROPHYCHIATRY AND FREE WILL

"Imagination is more important than knowledge. For knowledge is limited to all we now know and understand, while imagination embraces the entire world, and all there ever will be to know and understand."
Albert Einstein

D r. Daniel Amen,[237] a clinical neuroscientist and psychiatrist, has a clinic that is the world leader in applying brain imaging science to clinical practice. His book *Change your Brain, Change Your Life* (1998) has brain scans showing other disorders that are discernable on brain scans, including but not limited to: aggression, Alzheimer's, stroke, depression, obsessive compulsive disorder (OCD), pre-menstrual stress syndrome (PMS), anxiety, attention Deficit Disorder (ADD), and even heavy caffeine and nicotine use. A brain can be monitored to determine when a person is being truthful with eighty-five percent accuracy. It is more effective than a lie detector test. Not only can mental illnesses show up on a brain scan, they can cause physical side effects, e.g. Conversion Disorder can cause a person to become blind or deaf.

Single-photon Emission Computerized Tomography Scans (SPECT) allows the doctor to analyze the function of internal organs. They can also show which areas of a brain are more or less

---

[237] Dr. Amen is skilled in brain nuclear imaging (one of only a handful of brain imaging researchers).

active. The empty spaces on the scan indicate no activity.[238]

After a year of abstaining from drugs and alcohol, brains show a marked improvement.

With frontotemporal dementia, a disease that results in loss of brain tissue, fifty-seven percent display socially violating behavior that results in trouble with the law compared to only seven percent of Alzheimer's patients.[239] In fact, David Eagleman puts a great deal of free will as it relates to criminal activity in question in his book *Incognito, The Secret Lives of the Brain*. Eagleman sets out the average number of violent crimes committed annually in the United States by the population carrying a specific set of genes. If you carry the genes you are eight times more likely to commit aggravated assault, ten times more likely to commit murder, thirteen times more likely to commit armed robbery and forty-four times more likely to commit sexual assault.[240]

"It turns out that social stress of being an immigrant to a new country is one of the critical factors in developing schizophrenia. In studies across countries, immigrant groups who differ the most in culture and appearance from the host population carry the highest risk. In other words, a lower-level of social acceptance into the majority correlates with a higher chance of a schizophrenic break. In ways not currently understood, it appears that repeated social rejection perturbs the normal functioning of the dopamine systems. But even these generalizations don't tell the whole story, because within a single immigrant group (say, Koreans in America), those who feel worse about their ethnic differences from the majority are more likely to become psychotic. Those who are proud and comfortable with their heritage are mentally safer."[241]

---

[238] Brainplace.com – to view SPECTS.
[239] David Eagleman, *Incognito, The Secret Lives of the Brain* (2011) p. 156.
[240] David Eagleman, *Incognito, The Secret Lives of the Brain* (2011) p. 158.
[241] David Eagleman, Incognito, *The Secret Lives of the Brain* (2011) p. 211.

CHAPTER FORTY

ANTISOCIAL PERSONALITY DISORDER AKA SOCIOPATHS

*"We can choose how we want to feel, by choosing how we behave.
We feel the way we behave. So if you don't like the way you feel,
then change your behavior."*
Thomas D. Willhite

When I speak publicly about this disorder, I give this analogy to help teach the differences between these disorders. A normal person will swerve to avoid a dog; a sociopath will run over the dog; a psychopath will jump the curb to hit the dog on the sidewalk. Or if you are a dog hoarder, like my good friend Wendy, you stop, pick up the dog and take it home. While this explanation is perhaps not scientifically correct, it still has a pedagogic value.

It is estimated that four percent of the population are conscienceless sociopaths who have no empathy or affection for humans or animals. The development of sociopathy is due half to genetics and half to non-genetic influences.[242] Dr. Martha Stout's (Harvard Medical School) book *The Sociopath Next Door* (2006) is highly recommended to anyone who believes they are dealing with a sociopath.

Avoid sociopaths if at all possible. Persons with antisocial personality disorder are sociopaths. They have no conscience. These people would drain you of everything they can. A psychiatric expert in Dallas while attempting to explain to a jury in

---

[242] Martha Stout PhD, *The Sociopath Next Door* (2006).

layman's terms exactly what sociopaths are testified "they lack of moral fiber".

While sociopaths can be a difficult population to deal with in the criminal justice system (I always tell defense attorneys representing such clients to be careful, watch their backs and expect grievances to be filed against them with the State bar), those with antisocial personality disorder can do well. When the sociopath is shown that it is in *their* best interest to engage in the desired behavior - they get with the program and deliver.

For a character study on a sociopath, think of Hannibal Lector played by Anthony Hopkins in the movie *Silence of the Lambs*. Obvious sociopaths are Charles Manson, and Timothy McVeigh. However, sociopaths are not all serial killers: Leona Helmsley (the Queen of Mean) and Bernie Madoff may very well have been sociopaths. Sociopaths are drawn to positions of power so you may expect to see them in politics and on court benches (I have practiced in front of a few).

Psychopaths have a smaller amygdala. Altruists (persons with great empathy, a person that would donate a kidney to a stranger) have a larger amygdala.

A psychopathic predatory criminal can be identified by their recklessness, single-mindedness, not being shocked at things that would appall other people, being calm in conflict, and a need to be in control. A troubled abusive childhood is an important factor in predicting violent criminality.[243] Risk assessments should be conducted on all criminal defendants. This is being done by many probation departments in Texas.

---

[243] Gavin De Becker, *The Gift of Fear: Survival Signals that Protect us from Violence* (1997). Oprah Winfrey stated that every woman in America should read this book.

CHAPTER FORTY-ONE

ATTENTION DEFICIT DISORDER - ADD

"People are disturbed not by things, but by the views we take of them."
Epictetus

"Children with ADHD (Attention Deficit Hyperactivity Disorder) are significantly more likely than peers without ADHD to develop conduct disorders in adolescence and antisocial personality disorders in adulthood, consequently increasing the likelihood for substance use disorders and incarceration."[244] ADHD is common among children and adolescents who display excessive anger and irritability.[245] Those with ADHD are more susceptible to angry outbursts.

Attention deficit disorder can have its origins in the genetic, physiological or environmental realms. ADHD is correlated with smoking during pregnancy.[246] It is also related to diet, history of child abuse, neglect, multiple foster placements, neurotoxin exposure (e.g. lead), infections (e.g. encephalitis), or alcohol exposure in utero.[247] Influences in ADHD symptoms are visual and hearing impairments, metabolic abnormalities, sleep disorders,

------

[244] The American Psychiatric Association Diagnostic and Statistical Manual of Mental Disorders, Fifth Edition (2013) p. 63.
[245] The American Psychiatric Association Diagnostic and Statistical Manual of Mental Disorders, Fifth Edition (2013) p 64.
[246] The American Psychiatric Association Diagnostic and Statistical Manual of Mental Disorders, Fifth Edition (2013) p 62.
[247] The American Psychiatric Association Diagnostic and Statistical Manual of Mental Disorders, Fifth Edition (2013) p 62.

nutritional deficiencies, and epilepsy.

ADHD results in slow activity in both frontal lobes.[248]

I have a close personal friend with a genius I.Q. who is the most talented person I know and yet suffers from ADHD. If you have a friend or loved one with ADHD one of the best resources today is the book *Healing ADD Revised Edition: The Breakthrough Program that Allows You to See and Heal the 7 Types of ADD* by Dr. Daniel Amen (2013).

Children on medications for ADD, i.e. Ritalin, have twice the future rate of drug abuse. One-third of children on these medications develop symptoms of OCD behavior in the first year. Ritalin is called "kiddie cocaine" by some in the business. Drugs used to treat ADHD have resulted in permanent Tourette's syndrome.[249]

Organic food, no sugar and clean water and air are essential for those with ADHD. The best way to deal with ADHD is to focus on getting proper nutrition, which includes supplementing with powerful super-foods. Cleansing the body of built-up toxins and feeding it with rich nutrients is the number one priority when trying to maintain mental clarity and boost energy and focus. Remember to avoid excessive caffeine, refined sugars and processed foods, because these things only help to intensify the undesirable symptoms.

To treat ADHD the most important aspect of nutrition is (1) taking a good probiotic and (2) a gluten free diet. When looking for a probiotic (1) choose a high culture (at least 15 billion); (2) with multiple strains (L for the little intestine and B for the big intestine); (3) delayed release; and (4) potency.

Your brain is seven percent fat. We are told all kinds of diets are the best: only meat, only this or that, only that which is made by fairies in an ancient forest, but the best diet is simply *low in carbohydrates and gluten free*. A high fat, low carbohydrate diet

---

[248] Dr. Majid Fotuhi M.D., PhD, *Boost Your Brain* (2013) p. 32.
[249] Dr. Majid Fotuhi M.D., PhD, *Boost Your Brain* (2013) p. 156.

is the best thing for brain and body: olive oil, coconut oil, wild fish, avocados, nuts and seeds, and yes-eggs. Twenty-five percent of cholesterol in the body ends up in the brain. Cholesterol is good for the brain.

Every food we eat affects our DNA. We are in control of our genetic destiny. A body is continually growing brain cells. You can grow new cells in the brains memory center-the hippocampus.

To ease ADD symptoms try exercise, an elimination diet, and supplementation with fish oil, zinc, acetyl-l-carnitine, and SAMe.[250] A study in Holland showed that children who were put on an elimination diet and had only lean protein, fruits, vegetables, rice, and pear juice had the same positive response rate they had when given Ritalin, a common medication for ADD.[251]

Neurofeedback, a type of biofeedback that uses electroencephalography or EEG, is helpful in the treatment of concussion, ADHD, epilepsy, migraines, insomnia, anxiety and other disorders.[252] It is better than medication because the results are lasting.

ADHD is a medical diagnosis as opposed to a moral failing. Such a diagnosis is helpful to people. The diagnosis lifts a weight off the shoulders of the afflicted and their families. Then intervention and healing can begin to help avoid future problems.

---

[250] Dr. Daniel Amen, *Change your Brain Change your Body* (2010) p. 182.
[251] Dr. Daniel Amen, *Change your Brain Change your Body* by (2010) p. 183.
[252] Dr. Majid Fotuhi M.D., PhD, *Boost Your Brain* (2013) p. 105.

CHAPTER FORTY-TWO

BIPOLAR DISORDER

Bipolar disorder average age of onset is the mid-twenties.[253] It almost always begins with a depressive episode.

Hitler was bipolar and it was aggravated by daily injections of amphetamines and methamphetamine, five times per day for the last four years of his life.[254]

Vitamin D reduces the symptoms of bipolar disease.

Bipolar disorder may require long-term medication.[255]

This disorder has extremes of highs and lows, manic states with delusions of grandiosity followed by depression. This is why it was formerly referred to as manic/depressive. It is more common among first degree biological relatives. Persons with this disorder can suffer from unemployment, panic disorders, anxiety disorders, sleep disorders, alcohol use disorder, and substance abuse issues.

Bipolar mood disorder is linked with artistry. A very dear friend of mine suffers from bipolar disorder. He is brilliant and one of the best classical guitarists you will ever hear even though he has had very little formal training on the instrument. When he plays his guitar you are certain you are in heaven-it is so filled with power and emotion. Remember the owl from *Winnie the Pooh*. It is a mistake to associate mental illness with a lack of intelligence or ability.

Suicide risk is greater for those who suffer from bipolar

---

[253] The American Psychiatric Association Diagnostic and Statistical Manual of Mental Disorders, Fifth Edition (2013) p. 136.
[254] Nassir Ghaemi, *A First-Rate Madness: Uncovering the Links Between Leadership and Mental Illness* (2012).
[255] David D Burns, M. D., *Feeling Good* (1980) p.490.

disorder and there may be an association between genetic markers and increased risk for suicidal behavior.[256]

---

[256] The American Psychiatric Association Diagnostic and Statistical Manual of Mental Disorders, Fifth Edition (2013) p. 138.

CHAPTER FORTY-THREE

DEPRESSION

"Grief that is continually repressed becomes chronic depression, a very unnatural emotion."
Neale Donald Walsch[257]

"For as he thinks within himself, so he is."
Proverbs 23:7,

"For there is nothing either good or bad but thinking makes it so."
Shakespeare[258]

A study in 2014 holds that having depression makes you live longer – turns out even disease doesn't want to hang out with you. With this subject, I had to start with a joke because in reality there is nothing funny about depression.

Ten percent of Americans suffer from depression. Anyone who has suffered the loss of someone close to them and the depression of great grief knows the deep, dark, dank prison that depression can be and how the brain does not function properly for a while and recovery takes time. Research indicates that only sixteen percent of depression is due to genetic influence. For most individuals, life influences appear to be the most important causes.[259] Depression is stress on the neurotransmitters causing a depletion of the brain chemicals norepinephrine and serotonin and

---

[257] Neale Donald Walsch, *Conversations with God, Book III* (1998) p. 438
[258] *Hamlet,* Act two, scene 2
[259] David D Burns, M. D., *Feeling Good* (1980).

increase of the hormone cortisol.[260]

Depression is the fourth most frequently diagnosed mental illness in the Dallas County Jail. Women suffer from depression at a ratio of 2:1 compared to men.[261] Forty years ago the mean age for onset of depression was 29.5: today it is 14.5 years.[262] In the United States 5.3% of the population at any given time will have depression.[263] The lifetime risk is 7 to 8% in adults, higher for women.[264] A Johns Hopkins study found that lawyers suffer from depression at a rate 3.6 times higher than the general employed population.

Adverse childhood experiences, stressful life events, first-degree family members of individuals with major depressive disorder, substance use, anxiety, borderline personality disorders and more, all contribute to depression.[265] Depression is now looked at as an inflammatory disorder. Look at the chapter on "Nutrition and Mental Health" to learn more about the causes and solutions to inflammation.

A depressed person has excessively slow theta activity on the right side of the brain. Anxiety results in too much beta activity on the right side of the brain.[266] Depression is associated with the shrinkage of the hippocampus (memory) of 8 to 10% and brain atrophy.[267] Depressed people over age sixty-five have a twenty-four percent increase in cognitive decline per one study.[268]

There are three types of effective treatment for depression:

---

[260] William Styron, *Darkness Visible* (1990).

[261] Luanne Brizendine, *The Female Brain* (2006).

[262] David D Burns, M. D., *Feeling Good* (1980).

[263] David D Burns, M. D., *Feeling Good* (1980).

[264] David D Burns, M. D., Feeling Good (1980).

[265] The American Psychiatric Association Diagnostic and Statistical Manual of Mental Disorders, Fifth Edition (2013), p. 166.

[266] Dr. Majid Fotuhi M.D., PhD, *Boost Your Brain* (2013) p. 32.

[267] Dr. Majid Fotuhi M.D., PhD, *Boost Your Brain* (2013) p. 189, 192.

[268] Dr. Majid Fotuhi M.D., PhD, *Boost Your Brain* (2013) p. 193.

antidepressant medications[269], individual and group psychotherapy, and bibliotherapy.[270] Cognitive behavioral therapy may actually change brain chemistry.[271] Bibliotherapy is reading therapy and may be as effective is a full course of psychotherapy or treatment with the best antidepressant drugs.[272]

Exercise, meditation, yoga, deep breathing exercises and prayer help with depression.[273] Spiritual people are happier and more satisfied with life than those that are non-spiritual. They have lower rates of depression.[274]

Blockage of blood and oxygen to the brain causes dementia, Alzheimer's, depression, anxiety, memory loss, eyesight and hearing problems. While exercise is better than antidepressants for treating most depression, the most effective treatment for severe depression is still cognitive therapy and antidepressants.

Three effective principles of cognitive therapy are: all our emotions are generated by our thoughts, depression is the constant thinking of negative thoughts, and the majority of negative thoughts that cause us emotional turmoil are wrong or at least distortions of the truth, but we except them without question.[275] One can defeat depression by changing the negative thinking patterns that cause it. Self-help books can actually have significant antidepressant effects in a person suffering from major depression.[276] Thoughts create feelings. Feelings create moods.

Epictetus, the ancient philosopher, professed that it is not the events that determine your state of mind, but how you decide to

---

[269] Very few people remain on antidepressants for more than a year. David D Burns, M. D., *Feeling Good* (1980) p. 467.

[270] David D Burns, M. D., *Feeling Good* (1980).

[271] David D Burns, M. D., *Feeling Good* (1980).

[272] David D Burns, M. D., *Feeling Good* (1980).

[273] The effect of prayer can be seen in brain scans. Prayer in the context of God as a friend elevates mood and helps with depression.

[274] Martin Seligman, *Authentic Happiness* (2002).

[275] David D Burns, M. D., *Feeling Good* (1980).

[276] David D Burns, M. D., *Feeling Good* (1980).

feel about the events. Dr. Daniel Amen refers to the need to stamp out the "ANTS" (automatic negative thoughts) repeatedly in his books and gives many ideas for how to divert and redirect negative thinking and best accomplish this.

Researchers followed two groups of similar patients one of which was to read the Burns book - David D Burns, M. D. *Feeling Good* (1980)-within a month. The group that read the book experienced a significant reduction of depressive symptoms compared to the other group. Furthermore their symptoms did not seem to return. Although a book is not a cure-all for everybody, research studies indicate that two-thirds of patients suffering from moderate to severe depression improved substantially or recovered completely within four weeks of reading the book, *Feeling Good,* even without any professional treatment.[277]

As science has now proven that bibliotherapy is effective for depression all defendants suffering from depression in jail should be required to read (if they are capable). Specifically to read *Feeling Good* by David D Burns M.D., and other similar self-help and motivational books, such as: *Your Erroneous Zones* by Dr. Wayne Dyer (or any Wayne Dyer book), *The Secret* by Rhonda Byrne, *How to Win Friends and Influence People* by Dale Carnegie, *The Power of Positive Thinking* by Dr. Norman Vincent Peale (2003), *The Four Agreements: A Practical Guide to Personal Freedom (A Toltec Wisdom Book)* by Don Miguel Ruiz and Janet Mills (1997)[278], *The Power of Now: A Guide to Spiritual Enlightenment* by Eckhart Tolle (1999), *The 7 Habits of Highly Effective People: Powerful Lessons in Personal Change* by Stephen R. Covey (2013), *The Last Lecture* by Randy Pausch and Jeffrey Zaslow (2008), books by Pastor Joel Osteen, or listen to the

---

[277] www.feelinggood.com
[278] The four agreements: First -be impeccable with your word, Second - don't take anything personally, Third - don't make assumptions, Fourth - always do your best. If you honor these four agreements you will have a beautiful life. You will become the embodiment of God according to the author.

timeless Zig Ziglar motivational tapes, and more. All jails should have reading lists with books such as these available to all defendants.

The reverse side of this is that those incarcerated should not be exposed to anything negative (as much as such can be prevented). This includes violent movies and yes, violent sports.[279] Why allow defendants to watch boxing for days on end when they could be learning how to change their lives for the better? We have the ability to control what is viewed in prison cells via television screens. Laughter increases blood flow which improves heart health and boosts the immune system. Watching funny movies as opposed to violent ones improves health.[280] We must use that power. Only positive self-help information should be allowed to reach those inmates. Happy, hopeful thoughts have an overall calming effect on the brain, while negative thoughts inflame brain areas often involved with depression and anxiety.

While few may take advantage of this opportunity, start with the low-hanging fruit, those that do want to help themselves. They can be a role model and morale booster to those around them. Positive re-enforcements (and if necessary – sanctions) can be developed to encourage others to improve themselves.

The brain is more sensitive to nutrition than the heart according to Dr. David Perlmutter, author of *Grain Brain.* Ten percent of Americans suffer from depression.

To begin to cure depression from a nutritional standpoint:

- Cut out sugar
- Cut out grains (gluten is a major cause of depression).

----

[279] The attempted assassin of President Reagan and assassin of James Brady in 1981 became obsessed with the 1976 film *Taxi Driver*, in which a disturbed protagonist plots to assassinate a presidential candidate. The character was partly based on the diaries of the attempted assassin of George Wallace. Life imitates art.
[280] Dr. Majid Fotuhi, M.D., PhD, *Boost Your Brain* (2013) p. 194.

- Low vitamin D is linked to depression, chronic fatigue, Parkinson's, and declined mental function.[281] Vitamin D deficiency is associated with schizophrenia, dementia, and depression.[282]
- Herbs for depression: St John's Wort, vervain, and curcumin. Turmeric is better than the antidepressant Prozac. Also, inositol decreases depression. Curcumin is an herb that works as an antidepressant. It has no side effects. It is all natural. It is the main ingredient in the herb turmeric. The recommended dosage is 500 milligrams twice a day for two to six weeks. Chamomile reduces depression and anxiety.
- Onions and capers reduce depression caused by chronic stress. Black grapes reduce depressive symptoms and increase serotonin and dopamine levels.
- Reduced cholesterol results in depression. Eat avocados and eggs.
- Fast food contributes to depression.
- Sunshine is important. Weather affects mood. Seasonal affective disorder or SAD can be alleviated by bright light. Alcohol is a depressant. Avoid alcohol.

People with depression have an increased risk of heart attack, stroke, and dementia-conditions that arise from inflammation. Depression is the leading cause of lack of productivity in employment.

Memory lapses that are so pronounced they are mistaken for early signs of dementia are common with a major depressive episode. In some individuals, especially the elderly, it can be the initial presentation of irreversible dementia.[283]

---

[281] Dr David Perlmutter, *Grain Brain* (2013) p.192.
[282] Dr. Majid Fotuhi M.D., PhD, *Boost your Brain (2013)* p. 88.
[283] The American Psychiatric Association Diagnostic and Statistical Manual of Mental Disorders, Fifth Edition (2013) p 164.

Misery and depression are always states of mind and are self-perpetuated. Drugs are problematic in treating depression because once a person stops taking the medication, they tend to become depressed again.[284] Most of our barriers and limitations are self-imposed and barriers are put up mainly by our conscious mind.[285]

Medications that increase serotonin in the brain normalize activity in the cingulate: Prozac, Zoloft, Paxil, among others. Prozac controls the ability to shift attention between topics. It serves as a "lubricant" for the brain's shifting mechanism. When taking these medications, one becomes less stuck on thoughts.

Depressed patients should not be treated with psychotropic medicines alone. The medication must be used in conjunction with psychotherapy.[286] Borderline personality disorder is a chronic and severe depression.[287] This can be treated with specific antidepressants. Antidepressants do not become effective for several weeks. This results in many patients discontinuing the medication.

Benzodiazepines, Ativan, and Klonipin prescribed for anxiety and insomnia are responsible for overdoses, addiction, Alzheimer's, and memory loss. Prescriptions are growing at twelve percent per year. These drugs are not for long-term use.

An effective therapist will help the patient diagnose their mood, identifying the emotions associated with the mood (pointing out that they feel the way they think). This is done by identifying the cognitive distortions, labeling the distortion (e.g. all or nothing thinking, overgeneralizations, mental filtering [picking a single negative detail and dwelling on it exclusively], disqualifying the positive, jumping to conclusions, magnification or minimization,

---

[284] Albert Ellis and Robert A. Harper, *A Guide to Rational Living* (1961).

[285] Sydney Rosen, *My Voice will go with You: the Teaching Tales of Milton Erickson* (1982).

[286] David D Burns, M. D., *Feeling Good* (1980) p.457.

[287] David D Burns, M. D., *Feeling Good* (1980) p.485,566.

emotional reasoning [e.g. "I feel it therefore it must be true"], labeling and mislabeling, personalization [seeing oneself as the cause of a negative external event for which they are not responsible], etc.), analyzing the distortions (developing rational responses for their automatic thoughts), building self-esteem by defending themselves and defeating guilt, and eventually eliminating automatic negative thoughts.

Focusing on what you like about your life and on what you like about others is a powerful way to keep your prefrontal cortex healthy. Fight depression first with exercise then social interaction, listening to music, improved health, meditation, and sufficient sleep. Consider learning a musical instrument. The concentration and focus required for such an undertaking is very good for the brain.

Persons in the advanced stages of depression do not receive much benefit from psychotherapy.[288] This is why it is so crucial to treat depression early. There is no quick acting remedy for serious depression.

Mental health, on some levels, is the acceptance of responsibility for life. However, it is hard to tie your own shoelaces when you do not have any shoes. We must extend a helping hand to those in need to get them back on the bandwagon of life.

Depression should not be taken lightly. In one murder case that I prosecuted, C.M. a loving husband rose from his living room chair, walked to the kitchen, and choked his wife of forty plus years to death. The act was totally unprovoked. By all accounts the two never argued, he was an excellent father, and had never been abusive in any manner. His major diagnosis: depression. He later said that voices/God told him if he did not do this he would be forced to murder their only child (a grown daughter). At the trial the daughter (and only child) held the courtroom spellbound as she took us through the range of emotions she felt. She was in one

---

[288] Williams Styron, *Darkness Visible* (1990).

person the victim and defender; devastated by the loss of her mother and still wanting her father to receive treatment instead of incarceration. He was found not guilty by reason of insanity and has been in a mental hospital now for years - too sick to be released. He was receiving treatment for depression, if only he had been monitored more carefully, perhaps a life could have been saved.

In another case I prosecuted, T.R. decided that Satan was going to walk to her office door at eight o'clock the next morning. She took a gun to work and waited. The first employee that walked through her office door just happened to be her best friend. She shot and killed him. Her major diagnosis was depression. She had been up all night blogging incoherently for days before the murder but had done nothing to alert her co-workers that she was on the verge of a breakdown. If only someone would have reported her mental state to the police, she could have been taken to a mental hospital and a tragedy could have been averted.

I have had a friend for fifty years, Lee. He suffers from chronic, severe depression. He is a very smart and talented writer, songwriter, poet, and musician. Lee says that sometimes he likes to just give in to his disease because it makes him more creative. Sufferers such as these need understand that they are a person in long-term recovery, a mentally vulnerable individual that must fight for good mental health and not take it for granted. Because mental illnesses like addiction can cross that line of no return. Making it very difficult, if not impossible, to get back to where you were. A digression could have a long-term effect on you, your family, and your community. Once again fear, like peer pressure, can motivate substance abuse and even mental illness. Fear of losing family, friends, loved ones, possessions, home, faith, or in Lee's case, a fear of failing to overcome obstacles and be all that you could be.

In summary, treatment for depression is via three methods: antidepressant medications, individual and group psychotherapy, and bibliotherapy. Exercise is better than antidepressants if one is not in the late stages of the disease. We must protect our thoughts from negativity and violence. Nutrition and sunshine are crucial. Exercise, meditation, yoga, deep breathing exercises and prayer help with depression.

Go to www.feeling good.com for free psychotherapy in your geographic area.

CHAPTER FORTY-FOUR

POST TRAUMATIC STRESS DISORDER –PTSD

*"Society wins not only when the guilty are convicted, but when
criminal trials are fair; our system of the administration of justice
suffers when any accused is treated unfairly."*
Brady v. Maryland, 83 S.Ct. at 1197.

Individuals in the criminal justice system with PTSD are one
and one half times more likely to reoffend than those without
this disorder.[289]

Anyone that is subjected to extensive trauma for an
extended period of time can develop PTSD. Cortical steroids bathe
the brain when one is traumatized. Dendrites, the part of the
neurons that will catch the cortical steroids, shrink. People
suffering from to PTSD have a smaller hippocampus.[290]

Post-traumatic responses occur on a continuum: mild
distress, irritable; then: more serious distress or impairment that
can change personality, sleep disruptions, panic attacks, rage,
addictive behaviors and finally: sever stress that impacts jobs or
relationships, and a need for professional help. Persons with PTSD
cut off relationships, isolate, take risks, and engage in self-harming
behaviors e.g. using drugs and alcohol. The largest growing
population of the homeless is veterans with PTSD. When Johnny
comes marching home, he is often ignored. Veteran's courts are
designed to address many issues unique to our returning military
members, i.e. PTSD, substance abuse, and traumatic brain injury.

---

[289] *Adult Drug Court Best Practice Standards Vol. II* (National Association of
Drug Court Professionals 2015) p 13.
[290] Dr. Majid Fotuhi M.D., PhD, *Boost Your Brain* (2013) p. 192.

There are twenty million veterans in America. The Veteran's Administration (V.A.) is the largest health care provider in the United States. The Department of Defense is the largest government agency followed by the V.A. Many Vietnam veteran's developed PTSD because they were vilified when they returned home. Most people are eighteen to twenty-one years of age when they enter the military. They are exposed to trauma before their brain's prefrontal cortex is fully developed. We have a moral responsibility to our veterans who we sent into danger that risked their lives for us. The Texas Veterans Administration estimates that approximately 4,000 veterans are homeless in Texas. More than half of veterans suffer from physical or mental problems. One in five have PTSD or other significant mental illness. Twenty-two veterans commit suicide each day in Texas.

The primary reason Veterans are arrested is substance abuse. The other major reason is PTSD (irritability, anger, etc.).

PTSD deregulates the nervous system. Persons who feel angry, depressed, or guilty are more likely to turn to substance abuse. They then become more vulnerable to becoming traumatized, e.g. car accidents, rape, etc.

Twenty to forty percent of persons with PTSD have a Substance Abuse Disorder (SUD) also. An even larger percent of those with a SUD suffer from PTSD.

Women experience PTSD at twice the rate of men (10% v. 5%). [291] Not all trauma leads to PTSD. Impersonal events e.g. a hurricane or earthquake do not result in as much trauma as personal trauma, e.g. violent assaults, war, etc. Sexual trauma is more likely than most trauma to cause one to end up with PTSD because it is so personal.

---

[291] Kessler et al., Post Traumatic Stress Disorder in the National Comorbidity Survey *Archives of General Psychiatry* 52, 1048- 1060 (1995); D.F. Tolin and E.B. Foa, Sex difference in trauma and posttraumatic stress disorder; A quantitative review of 25 years of research *Psychological Bulletin* 132, 959-992 (2006).

A study of PTSD victims after 911 showed that those who had had PTSD in the past and recovered from it recovered better than others who had not had that experience.

PTSD is triggered by loud noises, being in a crowded room, and isolation. Intensive therapy is needed to change the way one reacts to the triggers.

McKamey Manor is San Diego's year-round haunted house where the attendees are subjected to extreme trauma for four to seven hours. They sign a waiver and can be forced to strip of their clothing, eat unknown rancid foods while blindfolded, may be locked in a coffin, assaulted, etc. In Jackson, New Jersey there is a roller coaster that has a forty-one story drop of doom, Zumanjaro. Violence in movies has tripled since the 1980s. Grisly movie franchises such as "Saw" are an example of invited/welcome stress. The types of things that could cause one person to have traumatic stress may be an exciting experience for another.

Three parts of the brain are affected by PTSD. The amygdala (emotional reactions, fight or flight alarm system), hippocampus (relay station for sorting memories), and the prefrontal cortex (logic, reasoning, planning, impulse, control, organizing). With PTSD the amygdala can start firing and not stop. One is in a constant state of alarm.

There are genes that give you vulnerability to PTSD. PTSD can depend on genetics, severity, duration, proximity. PTSD is mitigated or worsened by: childhood experience, personality characteristics, family history, social support, etc..

There are three evidence based treatments for PTSD: (1) Cognitive Processing Therapy, (2) prolonged exposure/stress inoculation training (fear based model, go to the places that make them anxious and stay there, also go to the memory, tape record it and play it back several times), and (3) Movement Desensitization Reprocessing (MDR - eye-movement desensitization) (have the person give you a mental image of the process, then with alternating bilateral stimulation, e.g. moving waving fingers in front of their eyes, they reprocess the memory). When given this, the amygdala quiets down. In cognitive therapy the counselor starts by finding something in common with the person and talks about that. The objective of PTSD therapy is to help the participant absolve themselves of guilt and expose them to tolerable doses of memories to gradually desensitize them to the associated panic and anxiety.

Epigenetics demonstrates that you transfer your fears and memories to your descendants. In a study where mice were shocked when they came near cherry blossoms, their children and grandchildren experienced fear when they came near cherry blossoms. As we now know that some mental illness derive from trauma, i.e. PTSD, traumatic brain injury, foreigners being more susceptible to schizophrenia due to the trauma they experience in the new culture, etc. It is possible that by protecting people from traumas, we are protecting future generations from mental illness.

CHAPTER FORTY-FIVE

SCHIZOPHRENIA

*"The true measure of a person is not what they have accomplished
but what they have overcome."*
Cindy Stormer

Surviving Schizophrenia, by Dr. E. Fuller Torrey, is the bible for helping families with a loved one with that disease. Schizophrenia is a no-fault, neurobiological illness involving chemical imbalances in the brain. It is highly treatable.

People with schizophrenia suffer from hallucinations, including verbal hallucinations. A Dallas defendant once stated "Judge, there is a Mexican in my penis that won't stop talking". When the Judge asked "what is he saying", the man answered "I don't know? I don't speak Spanish."

Schizophrenia is more common than Alzheimer's disease, HIV, multiple-sclerosis or Type I diabetes. Lifetime prevalence for schizophrenia is .3 or .7 percent.[292] Onset of first psychotic episode is early twenties for males and late twenties for females.[293] Mental disorders such as schizophrenia and bipolar do not usually manifest until the subject is in their late teens.

Euphoria turns into schizophrenia by dumping too much dopamine into the brain.

Those suffering from schizophrenia find it difficult to ignore some stimuli the rest of us ignore. This can become the raw

---

[292] The American Psychiatric Association Diagnostic and Statistical Manual of Mental Disorders, Fifth Edition (2013) p.102.
[293] The American Psychiatric Association Diagnostic and Statistical Manual of Mental Disorders, Fifth Edition (2013)102.

material for hallucinations. There are psychological exercises that can teach them to shut out the stimuli by training them to focus on simple instructions.

Since a common symptom of schizophrenia is hallucinations, believing that a relative is an imposter is common. This occurs when there is a disconnection between the temporal cortex (face recognition area) and the amygdala, the gateway to the limbic system, which generates emotional responses to particular faces.[294] There is a link between increased religious feeling and temporal lobe epilepsy. Seizures in this part of the brain can result in intense spiritual experiences.[295]

The first symptom of schizophrenia is frequently a mere feeling there is another presence near. Though it is hotly contested by some mental health professionals, there is a small group of psychiatrists that adhere to the theory that if schizophrenia is treated aggressively at a very early stage, it can be cured in a small percentage of cases. The treatments involve intense nurturing in every aspect of their lives: tutoring, art therapy, nutrition, avoiding social isolation, etc. Those psychiatrists contesting the theory that schizophrenia can be cured hold that roughly two-thirds of schizophrenia-like symptoms are misdiagnosed as schizophrenia. Whether or not this nurturing and love is a cure for mental illness, we cannot fault those families that struggle with this very difficult mental disease.

The best treatments for schizophrenia involve dopamine inhibitors.

Marijuana, carbohydrates, and gluten contribute to schizophrenia. Gluten magnifies the symptoms of schizophrenia.[296] During World War II, the men and women of Finland, Norway, Sweden, Canada, and the United States required fewer hospitalizations for schizophrenia when food shortages made bread

---

[294] V.S. Ramachandran, *Phantoms in the Brain* (1998).
[295] V.S. Ramachandran, *Phantoms in the Brain* (1998).
[296] Dr. William Davis, *Wheat Belly* (2011) p. xi, 46.

unavailable. There was an increased number of hospitalizations when wheat consumption resumed after the war was over.[297]

Medication is still the best solution for those who are destructive or violent (or those that hear voices encouraging destructive or violent acts). Relapse rates are lower when medication is combined with family therapy and social skills training.

Music therapy is beneficial to schizophrenic patients. There are parts of the brain that schizophrenia does not seem to affect. Nathaniel Ayers, Julliard trained violinist, was a homeless man with schizophrenia. He could still play the violin with great skill. Tom Harrel, acclaimed jazz trumpeter and composer, had schizophrenia and virtually constant hallucinations, but was not psychotic when playing.[298] Famous people with schizophrenia are Peter Green, guitarist and founder of the band Fleetwood Mac, and Brian Wilson, bass player and singer in the band The Beach Boys.

There are so many tragic stories of people who did not receive needed help and the devastating results. One third of the homeless have a mental illness and that mental illness is mostly likely to be schizophrenia. The risk of suicide is fifty times higher for those suffering from schizophrenia. Just a few cases I handled: M.A. who shot her grandmother to death in the parking lot of a mental health facility, W. H. who shot his grandfather to death as he slept, B.S. who stabbed her roommate to death, S.R. who murdered his parents thinking they were holograms, R.S. who shot a man to death in the living room of his home. . . Too many lives are being lost because we fail to timely recognize the signs and meet the needs of sick people in our society.

---

[297] Dr. William Davis, *Wheat Belly* (2011) p. 46.
[298] Oliver Sacks, *Musicophilia* (2008).

CHAPTER FORTY-SIX

SCHIZOAFFECTIVE DISORDER

"What lies behind us and what lies before us is a small matter
when
compared to what lies within us. "
Ralph Waldo Emerson

S chizoaffective disorder is a condition in which a person experiences a combination of schizophrenia symptoms (hallucinations or delusions) and mood disorder symptoms (mania or depression). Schizoaffective disorder is not as well understood as other mental health conditions. This is largely because schizoaffective disorder is a mix of mental health conditions and somewhat unique in each affected person. The word schizoaffective has two parts: "schizo" refers to psychotic symptoms and "affective" refers to mood symptoms.

A person may be given a diagnosis of schizoaffective disorder if they have episodes of mental ill-health and experience: psychotic symptoms, similar to schizophrenia and mood symptoms of bipolar disorder and have both psychotic and mood symptoms at the same time or within two weeks of each other. The mood symptoms of schizoaffective disorder are much like bipolar disorder (manic depression), and may be divided into "manic type", "depressive type" or "mixed type" – just as bipolar disorder is.

Schizoid personality disorder (SPD) is a personality disorder characterized by a lack of interest in social relationships, a tendency towards a solitary lifestyle, secretiveness, emotional coldness, and apathy. SPD is not the same as schizophrenia, although they share similar characteristics such as detachment and blunted affect. There is, moreover, increased prevalence of the disorder in families with schizophrenia.

Schizoid personality can develop as a result of intense

negative relations with the child's mother in the first year of life.[299]

---

[299] Melanie Klein, *Envy and Gratitude* (1957).

CHAPTER FORTY-SEVEN

TRAUMATIC BRAIN INJURY

"If I can stop one heart from breaking, I shall not live in vain. If I can ease one life from aching, or cool one pain, or help one fainting robin unto his nest again, I shall not live in vain."
Emily Dickinson

The brain is our most fragile, delicate organ. Cut or bruise your finger, it may hurt but it will heal. Cut or bruise your brain, and it is long lasting, permanent damage. Defendants in the criminal justice system have received their injuries from a variety of sources, e.g. a woman who was gang raped and severely beaten, football players, victims of car accidents, etc. One man I prosecuted for almost murdering his entire family had previously been hit by a drunk driver and suffered traumatic brain injury. He woke up one day and went through his home with a barbell and knife, beating and stabbing his family members, inflicting severe injuries. By all accounts he was a normal, loving father before this incident. Out of body experiences can occur when the brain is not receiving enough blood, and may happen if there is a cardiac arrest or arrhythmia, massive blood loss, or shock.[300] This may be the cause of hallucinations that lead to criminal activity.

Chronic traumatic encephalopathy, CTE, is a result of brain injuries. These are common in sports. "Tony Dorsett (Dallas Cowboy) is losing his mind" was the lead story on the cover of *D Magazine* in February of 2014 with an article that set out his degenerative brain condition caused by repeated head trauma from

---

[300] Oliver Sacks, *Hallucinations* (2012) p. 257.

football injuries. It manifests itself in bouts of anger, dementia, depression, etc. Julius Whittier, is a former Assistant District Attorney in Dallas and was the University of Texas' first African-American football player. Once a brilliant trial attorney he is now totally disabled and suing the National Collegiate Athletic Association (NCAA) for fifty million dollars for brain injury and early onset of Alzheimer's. Dr. Bennet Omalu (the movie *Concussion* is based on his work) indicates that ninety percent of NFL players suffer from CTE.

Even minor trauma in the brain (boxers, military, blast victims, football, sports, etc.) can add up over time and result in cognitive decline and dementia.[301] In the majority of concussions there is no obvious sign of injury. Traumatic brain injury can be treated with progesterone and DHA to improve recovery.[302]

Many people that suffer from traumatic brain injury also turn to substance abuse later.

---

[301] Dr. Majid Fotuhi M.D., PhD, *Boost Your Brain* (2013) p. 225.
[302] Dr. Majid Fotuhi M.D., PhD, *Boost Your Brain* (2013) p. 231.

CHAPTER FORTY-EIGHT

SUICIDE

The suicide leaves their skeleton in the survivor's closet.
Author Unknown

E very suicide threat must be taken seriously. Those who speak of suicide are the most likely to actually commit the act. Suicide occurs almost twice as often as homicide. Texas loses one child per day to suicide. Suicide is the leading cause of death in jails. The suicide rate in jail is nine times higher than in the community. Veterans have a higher risk of suicide due in part to physical health problems associated with their service, unemployment, and higher rates of mental illness.

In many jails, when jail administrators believe a person is likely to commit suicide, the inmate's clothing is taken, leaving them naked and barefoot in a cold, cement cell, further contributing to the debilitation of their mental state. Suicidal inmates in the Miami Dade jail in Florida are usually kept naked. The beds in the cells are designed so they can be strapped spread-eagled onto it. Cells are kept cold near 50° to keep inmates under their blankets and not causing trouble.[303]

Every person coming into the Dallas County jail receives a health care screening.

Although not everyone that commits suicide show signs, some signs that a person might be contemplating such an act are sleeping most of the time, withdrawing, moments of rage, and of

---

[303] Pete Earley, *Crazy A Father's Search through America's Mental Health Madness* (2006).

course every threat to harm oneself must be taken seriously.

Many of the shooters in the mass shootings were really trying to commit suicide. Mentally ill children should go on a media (and violent video games) diet. They should not be exposed to violence.

One in six children in schools today contemplate suicide, one in thirteen attempts it. Ninety percent of those who commit suicide suffer from mental illness. Suicide risk is higher in individuals that suffer from bipolar disorder.[304] Approximately one-third of individuals with bipolar disorder report a history of suicide attempts.[305] "Suicidal behavior is seen in the context of a variety of mental disorders, most commonly bipolar disorder, major depressive disorder, schizophrenia, schizoaffective disorder, anxiety disorder (. . .PTSD. . .), substance use disorders (especially alcohol use disorders), borderline personality disorder, antisocial personality disorder, eating disorders, and adjustment disorders."[306]

Non-suicidal self-injury occurs when an individual inflicts painful injuries to the surface of his or her body. This is done to reduce negative emotions, such as tensions, anxiety, and self-reproach or to resolve interpersonal difficulty.[307] It could be a predictor of suicidal tendencies, and it is a predictor of substance abuse.[308]

Richard Free got hooked on Adderall (prescribed to treat Attention Deficit Disorder). Like many college students, Free

---

[304] The American Psychiatric Association Diagnostic and Statistical Manual of Mental Disorders, Fifth Edition (2013) p. 138.
[305] The American Psychiatric Association Diagnostic and Statistical Manual of Mental Disorders, Fifth Edition (2013) p. 138.
[306] The American Psychiatric Association Diagnostic and Statistical Manual of Mental Disorders, Fifth Edition (2013) p. 803.
[307] The American Psychiatric Association Diagnostic and Statistical Manual of Mental Disorders, Fifth Edition (2013) p. 804.
[308] The American Psychiatric Association Diagnostic and Statistical Manual of Mental Disorders, Fifth Edition (2013) p. 805.

began taking the drug to help him focus even though he did not have a mental illness. Free was borrowing drugs from friends. The affects of the addiction became so strong Free eventually killed himself.

Many famous people have committed suicide, depriving the world of great talent and value: Vincent van Gogh, Virginia Woolf, Ernest Hemingway, Sylvia Plath, actor Robin Williams . . . Even Rick Warren, pastor, author of *The Purpose Driven Life* (2002), a New York Times bestseller and self-help book for discovering meaning and purpose in your life, lost his son to suicide. Pastor Warren stated that his son had everything to fight depression, including a huge church family to support him, yet he was lost to the vortex of depression. Another famous person that committed suicide was Adolph Hitler.

If a parent cannot convince the teen to obtain help, the parent should get help themselves to learn how to deal with the problem of drug addiction.

When a facilitator at a mental health awareness event or panel starts the talk with –"Who here has been affected by or knows someone personally with a mental health issue?" and the entire room stands (as they almost always do), this is very effective in reducing the stigma that people think is associated with mental health. MetroCare partners with Mental Health America for training lay persons in the community on how to identify mental health issues, guide people into services, and reduce stigma in the community. NAMI also does this training. It is a two day course. The nominal fee ($50) is waived for teachers.

My daughter and paternal grandfather committed suicide. Other close relatives have attempted suicide. I have had to clean up the vomit of black tar like charcoal that was pumped down a loved one's stomach at the hospital after they attempted suicide with a controlled substance; and had to clean it off their bodies. More than once I have received the terrifying phone call and had to travel across the State to be with a relative that was near death and or dying in the hospital due to substance abuse and addiction. Alcoholism doesn't run in our family-it gallops.

I have over one-hundred cousins. With a family that large, you are exposed to every type of humanity. I see my own family members when I look at defendants.

We had a defendant in the Dallas County Jail on suicide watch, failure to thrive. The judge called meetings with several professionals, all of us in a room desperately trying to find a legal remedy. Our mental health coordinator baked a big batch of her famous chocolate chip cookies, went into the jail, sat down with the man, and looked him in the eye. She told him that she cared about him. He ate the cookie, then slowly began eating other foods, and was well in a few days. She accomplished in one simple, sweet, thoughtful gesture what none of us could accomplish as a group.

What to do if someone you know is contemplating suicide:

1. Listen. Be there. The main thing is that they need someone to listen to them, someone who has empathy for their situation. They can be told and shown that their personal worth is a CONSTANT and that all the garbage the world heaps upon them can't touch that.
2. Assure them that they will get through this. Explain to the person that the suicide would be a painful loss for you. Call a hotline for them.
3. Make them promise to call you before they act (put distance between themselves and the suicidal act).
4. Exercise. Take a walk with them. Have them relax. Take deep breaths and do something that that they enjoy that relaxes them. Take a bath. Listen to some nice music. (See the chapter above on the subject of depression).
5. Try to come to some type of an agreement about what the person will do if he or she is suicidal, and try to get the person to make a commitment that he or she will not die by suicide under any circumstances. Tell them to not confuse ending their pain with ending their life. The two are very different.
6. Tell them: "Make this commitment for all of the people who care for you, and for yourself. Remember that if you try to end your pain by ending your life, you will start a world of pain for the loved ones that you leave behind. And you will deprive yourself of many wonderful things that you have yet to experience."
7. Ask the suicidal person if they have considered the means

to go through with the act. While any threat of suicide must be taken seriously, one where specific means of death have been considered, i.e. gun, overdose, hanging, etc. indicate a more serious intention.

8. Consider entering into a "No Suicide Contract". www.suicide.org

Contacts:

- Call the National Suicide Prevention Lifeline at 1-800-273-8255 (TTY:1-800-799-4TTY) .
- Call 1-800-SUICIDE (1-800-784-2433) or 1-800-273-TALK (1-800-273-8255) to get listings for clinics in your area.
- Teenagers, call Covenant House NineLine, 1-800-999-9999.
- Call a psychotherapist .
- Carefully choose a friend, minister, rabbi, or someone who is likely to listen. http://www.metanoia.org/suicide/samaritans.htm This organization consists of trained volunteers who are available 24 hours a day to listen and providing confidential and non-judgmental emotional support. Short of a psychotherapist, the best source of online help.

CHAPTER FORTY-NINE

COMMUNITY PROSECUTION UNITS

*"Every society gets the kind of criminal it deserves. What is
equally true is that every community gets the kind of law
enforcement it insists on."*
Robert Kennedy, *The Pursuit of Justice*

The definition of Community Prosecution: "Community
prosecution focuses on targeted areas and involves a long-
term, proactive partnership among the prosecutor's office,
law enforcement, the community, and public and private
organizations, whereby the authority of the prosecutor's office is
used to solve problems, improve public safety, and enhance the
quality of life in the community."[309] The number one habit of
highly effective people is being proactive and these units are
proactive.[310]

The purpose of these units in district attorney's offices is to
target problem areas in a community, especially troubled youth,
and work proactively to solve problems before they occur. This is
done by cultivating relationships, keeping statistics, documenting
significant regular activities, maintaining e-mail lists and other
social media, and writing and distributing a newsletter regularly.
Participants in these units must listen carefully to the community's
suggested strategies. Such units are involved in implementing
crime prevention programs such as presentations at neighborhood
watch meetings and schools. As noted in a Wake Forest Law

---

[309] APRI/BJA Community Prosecution Focus Group, 1995.
[310] Steven R. Covey, *The Seven Habits of Highly Effective People* (1990).

Review article:

> Community prosecuting takes prosecutors out of the courthouse and into the community and casts them in a more proactive role. Community prosecutors typically work with members of the community to identify recurring, ongoing criminal justice problems (drug dealing, graffiti, vagrancy) and then work in tandem with community representatives and agencies to address these problems through a project, policy, or strategy, often involving nontraditional methods....[311]

"Under community prosecution, prosecutors serve as active problem solvers, rather than as reactive case processors. The goal is to connect with the community in order to increase awareness of criminal activity, renew faith in the criminal justice system, promote community involvement and accountability, improve the quality of life in communities, and reduce the sense of vulnerability faced by citizens. Instead of relying solely on criminal law to fight crime, prosecutors pursue non-traditional strategies and partnerships...."[312]

The four key factors known to be related to violence are substance abuse, psychopathy or anti-social personality disorder, victimization, and community disorganization.[313] These units can identify the problem areas and work for resolutions before offenses

---

[311] See Bruce A. Green & Alafair S. Burke, *The Community Prosecutor: Questions of Professional Discretion*, 47 Wake Forest L. Rev. 285, 292 (2012);

[312] Catherine Coles, *Community prosecution, problem-solving, and public accountability: The evolving strategy of the American prosecutor*, Working Paper No. 00-02-04 (Program in Criminal Justice Policy and Management), John F. Kennedy School of Government, Harvard University (2000).

[313] Alison MacPhail and Simon Verdun-Jones, *Mental Illness and the Criminal Justice System*, International Centre for Criminal law Reform and Criminal Justice Policy (2013).

occur.

Research indicates that the delivery of swift services and interventions to those who fall into a category of high re-offense risk and those having other risk factors that are indicators of criminal behavior offers the greatest opportunity for public safety. These strategies also provide for the best use of criminal justice resources by investing resources in those who pose the greatest risk to the community.

CHAPTER FIFTY

WHAT FAMILY MEMBERS CAN DO FOR THEIR MENTALLY VULNERABLE LOVED ONE

*"Let us have faith that right makes right, and in that faith let us to the end dare to do our duty
as we understand it."*
Abraham Lincoln

Fight for your family even if you are afraid they will hate you. In reality they will most likely be compliant, and eternally grateful for your help. Psychiatrists will tell you they never had a client angry with them for helping the client get well. Families are the solution to managing mental illness.

Family members must be an advocate for their mentally ill loved one. If the doctor is changing their medicine and it is resulting in new negative side effects, be sure to inform the doctor of the problems the new drugs are causing. If you believe they would be better off on a previous medication and cannot get it changed, see another doctor.

The most important thing for family to do is get their loved one connected - connected with therapists, doctors, etc. Join NAMI.org. Providing resources to a family member can transform their lives. Mental health is improved by knowing that there are others who support you, who you can rely on for protection and sustenance.

Some third world countries do a better job with schizophrenia than the United States because they are better at keeping sick people at home, engaged in the community, and employed (and most important – not incarcerated).

What to do if your loved one finds themselves in the criminal justice system:

- If you must call 9-1-1 for a family member, friend, loved

one or stranger in crisis, do the following:

- o Inform the dispatcher that the nature of the call relates to someone who is suffering from mental illness;
- o Inform the dispatcher of any relevant medical history of the subject, and
- o Request that a Crisis Intervention Team member respond to the scene.

- If the police become involved in your crisis, state strongly and emphatically that the mentally ill person needs to be transported to the hospital and not the jail. Record the arrest if possible via video. Ask the initial officers to put information in their report that you requested that the person be taken to the hospital. If your mentally ill loved one is arrested, notify the jail immediately that the person has a mental illness, what the illness is, and any medication that the person takes.

- If you believe that your mentally ill loved one has been mistreated, notify the chief of that department as soon as possible. Consider putting your complaint in writing; it will go in the officer's permanent file.

- If you do not receive relief from the Chief of Police, go to the City Council and address the council publically about the treatment. Take a written complaint.

- If you still do not believe that you have obtained the relief you requested, go to the media. Make their job easy-draft a press release the media can print as is.

- Make sure your loved one is in the safest place they can be in the jail-the psych ward. Apply for legal guardianship so you can control their treatment regimen. Contact the judge via letter or e-mail explaining your loved one's mental problems.

- Family members should visit their loved ones often in jail. In the largest study of its kind, researchers with the Minnesota Department of Corrections tracked 16,000 prisoners for five years and found inmates who received at least one personal visit while incarcerated were thirteen percent less likely to commit another felony and twenty-five percent less likely to violate parole. The recidivism rates dropped with each visit. Studies have also shown that inmates who receive visitors more frequently are treated better by the staff of those facilities in which they are incarcerated. Attend every court proceeding. Be involved in any release plan.

- Consider a civil commitment.
- Keep a journal, document medications, treatments, relapses, etc. Be prepared to advise doctors and therapists of your loved one's history. Finally, encourage your loved ones to take advantage of any services or therapy offered to them through the courts. Freedom from prison does not mean freedom from addiction.
- Above all, take care of yourself.

CHAPTER FIFTY-ONE

WHAT POLICE CAN DO FOR THEIR COMMUNITIES

"It is not the strongest of the species that survives, nor the most intelligent that survives. It is the one that is the most adaptable to change."
Charles Darwin

What to Do Before Cuffing And Stuffing.

Police time is disproportionately consumed dealing with people living with a mental illness. A significant portion of this is due to noncriminal behavior.

Police should educate their ranks about mental illness. They should receive Crisis Intervention Training (CIT).[314] Departments should offer pay incentive to those officers who take the training (just as many departments do for bilingual officers).

When police determine they are dealing with a mentally ill person, they should allow the mentally ill person to rant and redirect as much as the situation will allow. One should not put their hands on people suffering from mental illness when possible. Verbal judo should be used if necessary.[315] CIT officers must appear nonthreatening and helpful. CIT training should include officers receiving some training in a mental hospital. Such training

---

[314] Miami, Florida police officers receive a 2.5% increase in salary if they've received CIT training.
[315] Verbal judo is designed to train the officers how they can diffuse a situation by engaging a suspect verbally instead of by the use of physical force.

should also include listening to parents speak at police training events about what it's like to be a parent of a mentally ill child. Police must have empathy. Police must be trained to appear to know what the participants are going through.

Training tools taught in police academies are designed to work when dealing with sane, rational individuals; however, yelling, threatening, closing in upon, displaying weapons and using physical force exacerbate the paranoia of the schizophrenic and only serves to confirm what he believes in his mind, namely that people are "out to get him." Officers who undergo Crisis Intervention Team Training are taught how to identify persons with mental illness and then speak to them in calmer tones, allow a safe distance between the subject and the officer (reducing the paranoia), and control these subjects without the use of physical force. In violent situations police should use less than lethal weapons such as Tasers (stun guns) when possible.[316] The benefits are fewer injuries to the officers and the subjects, reduced worker's compensation claims filed by officers injured on duty and fewer lawsuits filed against the law enforcement agencies.

When the family asks a police officer to take a person to the hospital (instead of jail), the police should when possible.

Police need to use the same verbal tricks that psychiatrists use in hospitals to calm psychotic suspects. The police priority should be getting a mentally disturbed suspect to a hospital and not to jail. Police must view mental illness as a disease and not a crime.

Also, if police are at the scene of someone who has been traumatized (e.g. family members who have just discovered a loved one's suicide or other tragic death) and they don't know what to say, it's best to say nothing. Saying the right words to traumatized individuals can be beneficial to their mental health.

---

[316] Conducted Energy Devices (CED) more commonly referred to as Tasers result in 48 to 68 percent decrease in injuries (to officers and suspects) according to a study conducted by the United States Department of Justice.

241

Improper comments to traumatized individuals can be very detrimental and may take months or years of therapy to correct, if ever.

Officers must be trained in science-based procedures, such as, overdose-reversal medications such as naloxone hydrochloride. It can be administered intranasally by nonmedical personnel.[317]

The departments can get the community involved by sending out notices and information to residents with their utility bills. In the event residents are required to call the police for situations involving persons in crisis, residents are instructed to notify the 911 operator so that the information can be included in the dispatch to the police. The goal is to have the officers on notice before they arrive on the scene and increase the likelihood that a CIT member will respond to the call initially.

Call takers (dispatch, communications) must also develop the skills needed to provide the responding officer with critical information prior to arriving on the scene. They must learn techniques on how to de-escalate a caller situation; and assess the stages of suicide, suicidal behaviors and signs in individuals as well as intervention techniques. They must develop effective communication techniques including a greater awareness of the growing statistical information and community resources provided.

Departments should consider developing an app as a reference tool when it is suspected that an individual is mentally ill. The app could show the phone number for a mobile crises team and lists of questions to ask i.e. "do you have mental health issues?", "have you ever been hospitalized? If so, where?"

Aggressive and physical policing is not the final definition of good policing: active listening, compassionate understanding, and human responsiveness are equally important characteristics for officers to possess.

Police should be a mentor for young people in the

---

[317] *Adult Drug Court Best Practice Standards Vol. II* (National Association of Drug Court Professionals 2015) p. 18.

community. They are on the front lines to learn where the problems are. Police can be a lifeline for some disadvantaged children.

Police should take every opportunity to educate people in the community about the dangers of drugs and substance abuse. Using a power point, flyers and pamphlets the police can educate others about the effects of drug abuse. Go to www.drugfreeworld.com to receive free educational material including pamphlets to be distributed.

Use the information in this book to give talks on the subject (see the chapter on "What Citizens Can Do -Top Ten Things to Do".) Talk to children about the dangers of social media, and the consequences of a criminal conviction (see the chapter on "The Solutions-What Every Parent Can Do" above). Explain to citizens and family how to obtain civil commitments. If you do not know this, contact your county or city attorney and ask them (and while you are at it, ask them to conduct training for the police).

The most frequent question I receive from police officers (although it is couched in many different ways) is "Should I file this case?" Of course this question only comes after a lengthy recitation of the facts and my answer is always "Yes, file the case." There needs to be a record of what occurred. If there is a need to call a prosecutor to ask that question, there is a need to file the report with the prosecutor. Prosecutors can take many measures to ensure that justice is served in a particular case.

Investigate the cases involving the mentally ill just as you would any other case. Take statements, even from the defendant if possible. Take photographs. Many times I have begun preparing a case for trial only to discover that almost nothing was done in the way of an investigation and information has been lost forever. Investigators respond with "it was in a mental hospital," or "they were insane," or "they were acting crazy,, or "they were talking gibberish" in an attempt to justify why they did no more work on the case. However, these cases many times still must be tried. Even if the conclusion is not-guilty-by-reason-of-insanity, there still must be a trial. There are still victims and complaining witnesses that deserve answers and our best work.

Police should formulate training classes to take place in the jail. Do not let those people continue to deteriorate and decompensate when they are a captive audience. "First do no harm" is the Hippocratic Oath for doctors. The mantra or creed in the criminal justice system should be, "Make things better."

Under federal law, persons under felony indictment are prohibited from possessing a firearm.[318] Deferred adjudication (a type of probation) is not a final conviction, so a person with a pending deferred adjudication cannot carry a firearm. There are very few cases in the law regarding a mental defective in possession of a firearm. Addicts of controlled substances are prohibited from possessing firearms.[319] A person convicted of a misdemeanor crime of domestic violence is prohibited from possessing a firearm.[320]

Peace officers may hold any firearm found on or about a person who is in a mental health crisis, is determined to be a danger to self or others, and is being detained and transported for an emergency mental health evaluation.[321]

There is general consensus across the state of Texas that law enforcement officers who work in emergency detention situations should have statutory authority and liability protection to secure dangerous weapons presenting a risk of harm to the officers or to the individuals being detained. Until there is a change in State law, officers must rely on the federal law available. Federal law: 18 U.S.C.S § 922(g) prohibits a person that has been adjudicated as a mental defective or who has been committed to a mental institution from possessing any firearm or ammunition.

A person is ineligible for a license to carry a concealed handgun if the person is incapable of exercising sound judgment with respect to the proper use and storage of a handgun, or has a psychiatric disorder, or has entered into a judgment of not-guilty-

---

[318] 18 U.S.C. 922(n).
[319] 18 U.S.C. section 922(g)(2).
[320] 18 U.S.C. 922(g)(9).
[321] Tex. Health and Safety Code, Chap. 573.001 (added 2013), see also Tex. Code Crim. Proc. Article 18.191 (allowing for time to conduct follow-up investigations).

by-reason-of-insanity.[322]

Officers should review the law regarding seizing a weapon in connection with an offense involving use of a weapon.[323] Officers should consider obtaining a warrant based on any offense that has occurred, e.g. the discharge of the firearm.[324] The few federal cases addressing this issue deal with the sale of firearms to a mentally defective person and not the possession of the firearm. The government need not show that the defendant was convicted,[325] was addicted to, or an unlawful user of a controlled substance at the exact moment he purchased firearms, where the government did offer evidence tending to show the defendant was either a user or an addict during the years in question.[326]

On March 12, 2002, the senseless shooting which took the lives of a priest and a parishioner at the Our Lady of Peace Church in Lynbrook, New York, brought attention to the need to improve information-sharing that would enable federal and state law enforcement agencies to conduct a complete background check on a potential firearm purchaser. The man who committed this double murder had a prior disqualifying mental health commitment and a restraining order against him, but passed a Brady background check because the National Instant Criminal Background Check System (known as *NICS*) did not have the necessary information to determine he was ineligible to purchase a firearm under federal or state law.

On April 16, 2007, a student with a history of mental illness at the Virginia Polytechnic Institute and State University shot to death thirty-two students and faculty members, wounded seventeen more, and then took his own life. The shooting (the

---

[322] Tex. Gov. Code § 411.172 (d).

[323] Section 18.19 of the Texas Code of Criminal Procedure.

[324] Deadly Conduct, 22.05 Penal Code and Disorderly Conduct, Penal Code 42.01 [9]) and (2) the federal law (18 U.S.C.S § 922[g] stated above.

[325] Under 18 U.S.C.S. § 922.

[326] *United States v Corona,* (11th Cir.1988) 849 F.2d 562, *cert. den.* 489 U.S. 1084 (1989).

deadliest campus shooting in United States history) renewed the need to improve information-sharing that would enable federal and state law enforcement agencies to conduct complete background checks on potential firearms purchasers. In spite of a proven history of mental illness, the shooter was able to purchase the two firearms used in the shooting. Improved coordination between state and federal authorities could have ensured the shooter's disqualifying mental health information was available to NICS.

Police should educate themselves to provide the most protection for themselves and their partners.

CHAPTER FIFTY-TWO

WHAT DEFENSE ATTORNEYS CAN DO FOR THEIR CLIENTS

"About half the practice of a decent lawyer consist in telling would-be clients that they are damn fools and should stop."
Elihu Root

Those who are seeking legal counsel should read this chapter carefully to determine if they have the right attorney for the case.

Representing criminal defendants may be the highest calling one can do for their country in a time of peace (service in the military being number one). Criminal defense is a noble and honorable calling of the legal profession. Remember the lawyer's creed, "I am entrusted by the people of Texas to preserve and improve our legal system." Criminal defense attorneys owe the administration of justice their personal dignity, integrity, and independence. They must be passionately proud of the profession. Lawyers stand between the abuse of governmental power and the individual, the abuse of corporate power and the individual, and the abuse of judicial power and the individual. The virtuous Atticus Finch, small town lawyer, in the novel *To Kill a Mockingbird* by Harper Lee, was in the midst of deeply flawed sinners during a time of danger and high tension, thereby establishing him as the ultimate role model for the legal profession and the greatest hero ever portrayed in a motion picture, per a 2003 American Film Institute poll.

Strangely, the most rewarding cases in my career as a prosecutor are those involving exonerations-getting people out of prison. To be a cog in the wheel of a machine (The Conviction Integrity Unit) responsible for releasing completely innocent men from prison after lengthy prison terms is exhilarating beyond description.

Melanie, a woman I represented when in private practice, was a very attractive albeit extremely hardheaded and stubborn woman. She was a very frustrating client and difficult to deal with on every level. She was living in her car. We got her an apartment. I loaned her money. And although I never asked for it, she paid back every dime. A defense attorney never expects to see the money given to a client again. A psychiatric evaluation revealed that she was mentally disabled; her I.Q. was less than seventy. The dynamics of our relationship were dramatically altered at that moment. My opinion of her and my approach to the case completely changed. You cannot tell what someone's mental illnesses are just by looking at them (although some professionals claim they can diagnose someone suffering from bipolar disorder a block away because of their exaggerated hand and body movements). Though Melanie was the same, I and my approach to the case were not. The psychiatric report also indicated severe abuse by a former husband. He beat her in the head. So in addition to her mental retardation, she now also suffered from traumatic brain injury. These things could never have been determined just by looking at her. In addition, she was incapable to some extent of advising me about her problems.

There is no cookie-cutter solution to each case. Each case must be evaluated differently. The defense attorney may consider an evaluation to determine whether the defendant is competent to understand the charges filed and is able to assist the attorney in defending the case.

The following is a checklist that can be found on the Dallas District Attorney's website at www.dallasda.com/mental-health along with links to:

- Community Resource Guide (For a list of approximately 300 community resources, and service providers available in the Dallas area.)
- Companies that hire Felons
- Defense Attorney Checklist
- Housing Resource Guide
- Mental Health Resources: websites, phone numbers
- Quick Tips for Families

The use of checklists standardizes human performance and ensures that procedures are followed correctly. It reduces the instances of human error and increases compliance with proper procedures in all disciplines. The multi-disciplinary Safe Surgery checklist invented by WHO (World Health Organization)[327] [328] has been proven to decrease the number of incidents where antibiotics are given at the wrong time before surgical incision is performed. "A systematic review has shown that 1 in 150 patients admitted to a hospital dies as a consequence of an adverse event and that almost two-thirds of in-hospital events are associated with surgical care."[329] Such a checklist has been demonstrated to be the most extensive process measure decreasing such errors. Wouldn't you rather have a lawyer that utilized a checklist? The following is a checklist for criminal defense attorneys representing mentally ill clients.

Mental Health Checklist For Defense Attorneys

MENTAL ILLNESS
1. Ask the client questions to determine the mental illness diagnosis.
    a. Interview the client as soon as possible.
    b. Ask about the facts of the case.
    c. Ask a client whether he or she has been treated for any type of mental illness.

---

[327] The World Health Organization states that up to 25% of patients who had surgeries have had complications and at least half of those cases were preventable. (World Health Organization, 2009).
[328] SURgical Patient Safety System (SURPASS) was developed as a more multidisciplinary checklist, which starts, when the patient is admitted to the hospital and ends when the patient is being discharged.
[329] The Effect of Comprehensive Surgical Safety System On Patient Outcomes, New England Journal of Medicine by Vries et al p. 1 (2010).

       d. Ask if they have ever been prescribed any psychiatric medications.

       e. Review medical records (all of the relevant medical, psychological, and intellectual testing records) if available. You have a right to these.

       f. Ask whether he or she took special classes in school.

       g. Talk to the family.

       h. Interview witnesses.

       i. To the extent possible, explain the law. Inform the client of their legal options regarding disposition of the case and right to a jury trial or a trial before the court, as well as the right to be present at hearings. Review with the client the certificates of current physical, medical, and intellectual examinations. Do they seem to understand this?

2. Is the client competent? (see below)

3. Get the client out of jail on bond, if possible. Review Tex. Code Crim. Proc. art. 16.22 and 17.032 (Early Identification and Release of Mentally Ill).[330]

4. Familiarize yourself with options available in your community. Talk to mental health professionals, public defenders that specialize in mental health, etc.

5. Mentally ill individuals can be placed on probation or

---

[330] "A written assessment of the information collected . . . *shall* be provided to the magistrate not later than the 30th day after the date of any order issued . . . in a felony case and not later than the 10th day after the date of any order issued . . . in a misdemeanor case, and the magistrate shall provide copies of the written assessment to the defense counsel, the prosecuting attorney, and the trial court." Tex. Code Crim. Proc. art. 16.22 (emphasis added). Article 17.032 of the Code of Criminal Procedure provides for release on personal bond of certain mentally ill defendants. "A magistrate *shall* release a defendant on personal bond unless good cause is shown otherwise if the defendant is not charged with and has not been previously convicted of a violent offense". Tex. Code Crim. Proc. art. 17.032 (b)(emphasis added).

promised conditional dismissals with requirements including but not limited to:

    a. Stay on their medications,

    b. Not consume illegal drugs or alcohol (imperative as this exacerbates the mental condition and diminishes and conflicts with the effect of prescribed medications);

    c. See mental health professionals, and

    d. See case managers who can obtain supportive housing, transportation, etc. for the client.

6. An attorney who is appointed or retained to represent a special needs offender or a juvenile with a mental impairment can disclose medical information for the purposes of continuity of care. Tex. Health & Safety Code § 614.017

7. If your client was arrested without a warrant, look at the Texas Health and Safety Code section 573.001 which requires that apprehended persons with mental illness be taken to a mental health facility instead of a jail facility in certain situations. Jail personnel may have the authority to divert the client to a mental health facility. Ask detention personnel if the client can be moved to a medical facility, if appropriate.

8. Familiarize yourself with civil commitments if applicable.

9. Familiarize yourself with "Duties of Attorney" Tex. Health & Safety Code 574.004 (see below).

10. Explain your client's absence to the court at meetings or hearings. Determine if you need an independent psychiatric evaluation.

COMPETENCY

1. Consider an Evaluation for Incompetency. This may be the best way to begin treatment services for the client. Review

46B of the Texas Code of Criminal Procedure.

2. If the client is incompetent, ask the court coordinator to have the client evaluated by a doctor:[331]

When a doctor has determined that an individual is incompetent, the certificates of medical examination are valid for 30 days. Health and Safety Code § 574.066(c). **HAVE A COMPETENCY HEARING WITHIN 30 DAYS OF THE DAY OF THE *EVALUATION*** (not the day of the report). Failure to do so will result in unnecessary delays and incarceration for the client, the wrath of the judge and unnecessary expenses to the taxpayer.

Consider Outpatient Competency Restoration (OCR). "The court *shall* order a defendant released on bail under Subsection (a) to participate in an outpatient treatment program for a period not to exceed 120 days." Tex. Code Crim. Proc. art. 46B.072 (b) (emphasis added).

If appropriate, ask the prosecutor about a Civil Commitment in return for a dismissal. A prosecutor may agree to dismiss the case based on the client's mental health commitment.

Misdemeanor cases shall be dismissed if the defendant is not tried before the second anniversary of the date on which the order of commitment was entered. Tex. Code Crim. Proc. art. 46B.010.

INSANITY

1. Consider an evaluation for insanity. Review 46C of the Texas Code of Criminal Procedure
2. If the client was insane at the time of the offense:

---

[331] If the competency evaluation does not occur within a few days, file a motion suggesting that the defendant may be incompetent and order an evaluation. Failure to do so may result in a claim of ineffective assistance of counsel. *Ake v. Oklahoma*, 470 U.S. 68 (1985).

    a. Give timely Notice of Insanity to the State no less than twenty days prior to the trial. Tex. Code Crim. Proc. art. 46C.051(b)(2).

    b. Advise the client that the court will continue to have jurisdiction over the client. [i]

Consider getting a second medical opinion if necessary.

Conclusion: Familiarize yourself with mental health issues and the many specific deadlines by reading the following suggested articles and/or books:

Mental Illness, Your Client and the Criminal Law , Texas Tech University School of Law (2005). This book is a very valuable resource for defense attorneys and prosecutors and has a helpful guide indicating which medications are prescribed for different mental illnesses (to obtain free copies of this book go to http://www.texasappleseed.net or e-mail info@texasappleseed.net).

Mental Health –Therapeutic Justice, by Cindy Stormer, Advanced Criminal Law, State Bar of Texas 2013 (request from the Dallas District Attorney's Office).

Texas Criminal Procedure and the Offender with Mental Illness by Brian D. Shannon and Daniel H. Benson.

Obtain the book *Texas Small Firm Practice Tools* by James Publishing which devotes two chapters to criminal law. The first chapter has basic information on setting up a law firm and there are over five hundred forms available. It has checklists and forms for how to address a variety of criminal (and civil) problems.

(This is the end of the checklist.)

If it appears to the court that the defendant may be a person with Intellectual Disability (mental retardation), the court shall hold a hearing to determine this in accordance with the law.[332] "The party who filed the application has the burden to prove beyond a reasonable doubt that long-term placement of the proposed resident in a residential care facility is appropriate."[333] While mental illness commitment is for a period not to exceed twelve months, the long term residential care commitment for mental retardation does not specify a time period.[334]

If the state establishes that the person has a severe mental illness or mental retardation and as a result of that mental illness or mental retardation is likely to cause serious bodily injury to another if the person is not provided with treatment and supervision and inpatient treatment or residential care necessary to protect the safety of others, the court *shall* order the person to *inpatient* treatment or residential care.[335]

If the state establishes the person has a severe mental illness or mental retardation and as a result of that mental illness or mental retardation is likely to cause serious bodily injury to another, but the state fails to establish by clear and convincing evidence that inpatient treatment or residential care is necessary to protect the safety of others, the court *shall* order the person to receive *outpatient* or community based treatment and supervision.[336]

A criminal defense lawyer must have a firm command of the facts of the case as well as the governing law before he or she can render reasonably effective assistance of counsel. A natural consequence of this notion is that counsel has the responsibility to seek out and interview potential witnesses. It may not be argued that a given course of conduct was within the realm of trial strategy

---

[332] Tex. Code Crim. Proc. article 46B.103.

[333] Tex. Health and Safety Code § 593.050(d).

[334] Tex. Health and Safety Code §574.035(h) and 593.052.

[335] Tex. Code Crim. Proc. art . 46C.256(a).

[336] Tex. Code Crim. Proc. art . 46C.257(a).

unless and until the trial attorney has conducted the necessary legal and factual investigation which would enable him or her to make an informed rational decision.

The American Bar Association Model Rules of Professional Conduct and the ABA Standards for Criminal Justice provide that a lawyer has a duty to explore disposition without a trial.[337] Whenever the law, nature, and circumstances of the case permit, defense counsel should explore the possibility of an early diversion of the case from the criminal process through the use of other community agencies. Defense counsel must also become familiar with sentencing alternatives available to the court and if community and other facilities may be of assistance in meeting the accused's needs.[338]

Therapeutic Justice Courts or Problem Solving Courts are spreading across the country. These courts are a new vehicle for effecting established rehabilitative objectives. Therapeutic courts should include cases with thefts, most assaults, domestic violence, etc. This improves public safety. They are twice as cost effective when they admit and include people with mental illness because the defendants get more structure and service.

Drug court representation of defendants is non-traditional, more collaborative and less adversarial. These courts are dramatically reducing the high recidivism rate of drug offenders. They require and promote collaboration by courts and judges with other agencies and professionals. Lawyers who do not utilize in all their cases the science and evidence based practices verified in drug courts as being effective are committing malpractice.

The Criminal Defense Attorney representing a person with a diagnosed mental illness has a duty to make reasonable investigations, investigate the defendant's mental health history, speak with at least one member of the defendant's family about his or her mental history, obtain documentation identifying the mental

---

[337] ABA Standard 4-6.1.
[338] ABA Standard 4-8.1.

illness, if none is available, have the defendant evaluated, and advise the prosecutor of the defendant's mental illness as soon as is practicable.

When it is brought to the attorney's attention that the defendant might be incompetent the attorney must familiarize himself or herself with the relevant law[339] and follow those procedures.

When it is brought to the attorney's attention that the defendant might have been insane at the time of the offense the attorney must familiarize himself or herself with that law[340] and seek expert assistance on the issue of insanity.

"The jurisdiction of the court over a person (found not-guilty-by-reason-of-insanity) terminates on the date when the cumulative total period of institutionalization and outpatient community-based treatment and supervision imposed . . . equals the maximum term of imprisonment provided by law for the offense of which the person was acquitted by reason of insanity."[341] A person can be held in a mental hospital for life if the offense committed could have resulted in a life sentence. This is why the man that attempted to assassinate President Ronald Reagan in 1981 has remained under institutional psychiatric care since then after being found not guilty by reason of insanity.

The Texas Code of Criminal Procedure[342] provides for release on personal bond of certain mentally ill defendants.[343] It is

---

[339] 46B of the Texas Code of Criminal Procedure and Tex. Health & Safety Code § 574.004 (Duties of Attorney).

[340] 46C of the Texas Code of Criminal Procedure.

[341] Tex. Code Crim. Proc. art.46C.269.

[342] Article 17.032 of the Texas Code of Criminal Procedure.

[343] "A magistrate shall release a defendant on personal bond unless good cause is shown otherwise if the defendant is not charged with and has not been previously convicted of a violent offense." Tex. Code Crim. Proc. art. 17.032 (b)(emphasis added). Violent offense is defined in the statute. (see attached). The magistrate, unless good cause is shown for not requiring treatment, shall require as a condition of release on personal bond under this article that the defendant submit to outpatient or inpatient mental health or mental retardation

irresponsible for an attorney to allow a mentally ill client to languish in jail when the law has provisions for their release yet it occurs frequently. In Dallas homeless (and possibly other) defendants spend twice as much time in jail as those who have public defenders.

Relevant American Bar Association standards state that "[d]efense counsel should consider all procedural steps which in good faith may be taken, including, obtaining psychiatric examination of the accused when a need appears. . ." [344]

"A person may be suffering from a severe mental disease or defect or he may be highly medicated, but he will be competent to stand trial if he still has the ability to meaningfully consult with his attorney and he had a rational as well as factual understanding of the charged offense and trial proceedings."[345] If there is any reasonable probability that a defendant might be found incompetent, defense counsel must investigate that point.

Defense attorneys must educate their clients and the client's family.

Educate family members on how to help their loved ones. (See the Chapter entitled "What Family Members Can Do".)

Consider giving your client a checklist for what they should know in the event they are arrested (if it is not too late once you become involved):

- Stay calm.
- At the point of arrest do not bring attention to yourself.
- Be sure to tell officers if you or your loved one has a mental illness.

---

treatment as recommended by the local mental health or mental retardation authority, if the condition is chronic or will continue to deteriorate. Tex. Code Crim. Proc. art. 17.032 (c). See also, Tex. Code Crim. Proc. 16.22 regarding release on bond of mentally ill defendants.

[344] ABA Standards for Criminal Justice: Prosecution and Defense Function 4-3.6 (3d ed. 1993).

[345] *Ex parte Thomas*, No. WR-69,859-01, 2009 WL 693606, at *5 (Tex. Crim. App. Mar. 18, 2009) (Cochran, J., concurring) (not designated for publication).

An old man walking down the beach one evening observed a young boy picking up starfish that had washed up on the beach and throwing them back into the water. The man asked "why are you doing this, there are so many, what difference does it make?" The boy looked down at the starfish in his hand and said "it makes a difference to this one" as he tossed it back into the ocean. By educating those with whom the defense attorney comes into contact (and the defense attorney may be the only person in the criminal justice system that has the opportunity and knowledge to make a difference), the defense attorney is saving those souls that would otherwise be lost-one starfish at a time. Before the defense attorney throws that starfish back into the sea, I pray that they will take a moment to redirect a life. A small act of kindness might restore a family or make a significant difference in the life of a child or other affected family member.

Remember that throughout history, citizens have looked to the legal profession for leadership and guidance. In a free society, attorneys keep anarchy and chaos in check. Never forget the noble profession you represent and those lawyers who went before you: Thomas Jefferson, James Madison, Patrick Henry, Theodore Roosevelt, Mahatma Gandhi, Francis Scott Key, Sam Houston, William Barrett Travis, Davey Crockett, Ralph Nader, Abraham Lincoln, William Penn, and so many more.

In the Great Hangings of Gainesville, Texas, in 1862 there was one attorney involved - the prosecuting attorney, William C. Young, who was maintaining law in the prosecution and saw to it that nineteen men were acquitted. When he was assassinated, the killing frenzy began. Acquittals were reversed, nineteen men were immediately hanged and forty-two were eventually wrongfully executed.

"First let's kill all the lawyers." Ironically this rallying cry for lawyer bashers from Shakespeare's quote from *Henry VI* was spoken by an anarchist who Shakespeare describes as "the head of an army of rabble and a demagogue pandering to the ignorant" who sought to overthrow the government. Shakespeare's acknowledgment that the first thing any potential tyrant must do to eliminate freedom is to "kill all the lawyers" is a compliment to the profession. Lawyers are the friends of people who are in trouble.

Adolph Hitler asserted, "I shall not rest until every German sees that it is a shameful thing to be a lawyer." In the entire history of the world, individual rights were never more threatened.

Defense attorneys should think like attorneys (beginning with the conclusion and then convincing others of your hypothesis seeking evidence that supports it and discrediting evidence that doesn't fit your theory). But defense attorneys should remember this is how wrongful convictions occur. Therefore, defense attorneys should also think like scientists (gather evidence and observe it, look for regularities, classify information, make deductions, form theories explaining observations, and test observations). Think outside the comfort zone.

Einstein said if a person studies a subject for just fifteen minutes a day, in a year he will be an expert, and in five years he may be a national expert (I can tell you from personal experience this is not true in the case of classical guitar, but that is the subject for yet another book). Devoting 10,000 hours to any subject will make one an expert. Continuing to practice in a given area increases the mylenization in the brain.[346] Daniel Coyle's bestselling book, *The Talent Code,* stands for the proposition that: greatness isn't born, it is grown. So help yourself, improve your brain, save lives, restore families and become an expert.

---

[346] Daniel Coyle, *The Talent Code* (2009).

CHAPTER FIFTY-THREE

WHAT PROSECUTORS CAN DO

"The duty of the prosecutor is to seek justice, not merely to convict. It is an important function of the prosecutor to seek to reform and improve the administration of criminal justice. When inadequacies or injustices in the substantive or procedural law come to the prosecutor's attention, he or she should stimulate efforts for remedial action."
American Bar Association Standards Standard 3- 1.2 (c) & (d)

"Unlimited power is apt to corrupt the minds of those who possess it; and this I know, my lords, that where laws end, tyranny begins."
William Pitt

Punish bad behavior–treat sick behavior. We must separate those we are just mad at from those of whom we are afraid. Regarding your ability to determine the best sanctions, my fellow prosecutors and learned friends, please do not take this the wrong way-you suck at it. We all suck at it. Rely on the expertise of mental health professionals when possible.

Restoring defendant's health should be a medical matter not a legal issue and there are many things we as prosecutors can do to accomplish this. We must understand that generally, we do not rehabilitate them up to our level, but we do rehabilitate them from where they were. Prosecutors must be willing to make difficult decisions about who is in need of social tolerance rather than incarceration.

After becoming the DNA attorney for the Dallas District Attorney's Office in their internationally famous Conviction Integrity Unit my opinion changed. Having an opportunity to work on exonerations and working with the science, I learned what we could do in the criminal justice system to improve the system. It was not just about working harder and more efficiently, but about working smarter using science and evidence based principles and protocols. Remember it is just as much your job to insure that no one stays in jail one day longer than necessary as it is to seek appropriate sentences.

When I first became a prosecutor I had ten years of experience of police work behind me, but I still found the most difficult part of the job was determining what sentence to offer in my plea negotiations. Determining the length of the sentence was not something I was trained to do. Also, a prosecutor does not typically have access to information about the defendant. After assessments are made by professionals in the mental health field, the prosecutor can then take the circumstances of the crime into consideration along with the background and needs of the defendant before determining a proper plea offer or sentence. This is how defendants can be treated and recidivism reduced. The prosecutor takes the circumstances of the crime into consideration along with the background and the needs of the defendant before determining a proper plea offer or sentence.

Having been an attorney for decades (including private practice for fifteen years), I can say there are few cases outside of prosecution that will ever bring the same level of satisfaction as the cases worked on as a prosecutor. If you ever leave prosecution, you will always look back on those years as the most satisfying of your career and want to go back. I did.

We are blessed to be doing this work. Being assigned an old, difficult case and ensuring a murderer of a small child goes to prison for life when the parents of the child had been falsely accused of the murder of that child for years (an exoneration of sorts) was incredibly gratifying. And resolving issues on cases with mentally ill defendants that were overcharged because someone did not want them around (again, mini-exonerations) is very satisfying. To hook people/families up with the services they so desperately need and assist people who have suffered so much, giving them the compassion they need in their most difficult times, showing mercy for those deserving it—is an honor.

The prosecutor is an essential element for therapeutic justice. The prosecutor has the power to plea bargain, dismiss a case, or proceed to trial. The prosecutor decides whether a particular person is released from jail, whether and which services the defendant will be required to participate in, etc. (of course the judge can decide this also but the judge will not be familiar with the facts until after a trial or other hearing and therefore judges only make such decisions in a small percentage of cases). The prosecutor is the one who contacts the complaining witnesses, police, and other stakeholders in the case. The prosecutor must make sure that medical records, records of prior incarcerations, and other evidence is obtained. And most importantly it is the prosecutor who ensures defendants receive consistent treatment regardless of who the defense attorney is. The defense attorney must convince the prosecutor to go along with the suggestions. Prosecutors fight to get treatment. Defense attorneys fight to get the defendant released. Occasionally a specially trained public defender has the same goal as the prosecutor. This results in a symbiotic, synergistic relationship.

Using a non-adversarial approach, prosecution and defense counsel promote public safety while protecting participants' due process rights. As a prosecutor on mental health cases one becomes acutely aware of the gravity and enormity of each decision made regarding other people's lives. Jail can be a death sentence to some mentally ill people and is life altering to anyone.

As a prosecutor, you are the only one who can instigate this change. Judges can implement change on a smaller scale, but only on those cases which have been properly presented and brought before them. It is only a small fraction of cases which go to trial. It is the prosecutor (and judge in rarer cases) that holds the carrot (therapy/programs, etc.) and the stick (jail, probation, other sanctions). The prosecutor has the power to restore lives and save families.

Find those who need your help. It is probably one for the mental health caseload if they are naked, dancing and throwing feces in the jail, while thinking alternately that they are the President, a vampire, Batman, Satan, a prophet, and bearing God's child. They want to boil water to neutralize the chemicals the government uses to spread obesity. And they don't want to take psychotropic medications because they believe the medicines are shrinking their penis and causing their bowels to back up into their head causing them to have bad breath. All of this is being broadcast live on the internet via a CIA planted chip in their head for the purpose of manipulating the defendant's finances, and exploiting them sexually.[347]

The prosecutor, like the Grand Jury has to decide what is in the best interest of:

- The public/society,
- The victim (which is frequently the family), and finally,
- The defendant.

Mentally ill defendants can be college educated, extremely intelligent, and from a good family. In a murder case I handled, the mentally ill babysitter had murdered the child she was keeping. She convinced the police and the previous District Attorney that she was innocent and the parents had in fact murdered the child (in spite of forensic evidence that demonstrated the contrary).

They don't all look crazy. One perfectly normal young man I prosecuted digs up graves, steals body parts and carries them around in his back pack. He further had homicidal ideations and wanted to immolate (kill and ritually sacrifice) his own mother. She has had to change her identity and move away for her own safety. He was interested in cannibalism, necrophilia, and animal torture.

Another handsome young man I prosecuted liked to throw people from his vehicle at high speeds. He did this until he murdered an innocent car salesman. And remember how non-threatening Jeffrey Dahmer appeared.

Before the Texas Tower incident in 1966 (University of Texas at Austin) the shooter went to a psychiatrist stating, "I'm

---

[347] "Mental illness" means an illness, disease, or condition, other than epilepsy, senility, alcoholism, or mental deficiency, that:
(A) substantially impairs a person's thought, perception of reality, emotional process, or judgment; or
(B) grossly impairs behavior as demonstrated by recent disturbed behavior.
Texas Health and Safety Code 571.003

having thoughts of going up in the Texas tower with a long rifle and shooting people at random." This was ignored because he did not look like a sociopath. He killed thirteen and wounded thirty-three. He had an I.Q. of 138 (top 0.1 percentile). An autopsy revealed a nickel size tumor pressing on his hypothalamus and amygdala (empathy).

When you think you have seen everything, something different and new occurs, such as the man who was masturbating during his confession on video each time the detective left the room. Or the one who testified in his trial for police retaliation that "The police arrested me, stood on my head, then held me in the police car for five hours while they drew stick figures and taunted me saying 'this is your mama, she only has one leg'."

Throughout one trial the witnesses referred to a certain witness as "BFI." I would ask each witness "What does BFI stand for?" Each refused to answer. When BFI, a stoic looking American Indian with chiseled features, six foot five inches, over two hundred pounds of muscle, shining black hair flowing down his back, took the stand-he answered the question of what BFI stood for: "Big F***ing Indian." Apparently he would follow the mentally ill defendant around and always make sure she took her psychotropic medicines. People with mental illness all need a BFI to make sure they take their meds, but it's not a perfect world.

Most people who suffer from bipolar or schizophrenia disorders get diagnosed in their late teens or early twenties. Mental illness and drug abuse not only changes the way the brain looks and functions, it changes the outer appearance. I have seen people that look completely different in a few years (or even months) only because they are now on psychotropic meds (or stopped taking them). This is why they don't like to take their medicine. Medicine makes them feel dead inside, and makes them tired a great deal of the time. It causes them to gain weight. Risperdal (medication for bipolar disorder) causes men to grow breasts.

The empty Dawson State Jail in Dallas is a monument to how difficult these medications and withdrawal can be. It is shut down in large part because they failed to give a woman incarcerated there her methadone, which is treatment for heroin addiction. She died. Methadone withdrawal is worse than heroin withdrawal.

Natural rewards are food, water, sex, nurturing. Food and water feel good right?

Sex feels good right? (I don't hear anything? You don't get out much do you?) Addictive drugs stimulate the reward center of the brain: dopamine. If food were rated on a scale of 100 regarding the stimulation of the reward center, sex would be 200, morphine would be 200, nicotine would be 250, alcohol would be 300, cocaine would be 350, and methamphetamine would soar above the others at 1000.

On the count of three, cross your arms. Now put them down. Now do it again the other way. Feel uncomfortable? Awkward? Behavior pathways become routine. The longer one uses drugs, the more difficult it is to break the habit.

Sometimes the prosecutor discovers the defendant is the victim. An example of one was when I discovered a defendant had been falsely and wrongfully accused by a neighbor of throwing a knife at the neighbor. According to other neighbors at the event, the accusing neighbor made up the story to get the mentally ill neighbor out of the neighborhood (and into jail). The accusing neighbor was nowhere to be found at the time of trial. The defendant spent time in jail unnecessarily. We have a clinical term for people who lie to get mentally ill people out of their lives. We call them *lying little stinker pants* (and a few other choice words).

In another case a stepfather falsely reported that the step-daughter assaulted him. He did this to get her out of the house for a few months (and in jail).

In yet another case a mentally ill man was wrongfully accused of stealing a Metrocare worker's gun from her car. At trial it was revealed the worker had a sexual relationship with the mentally ill man and was trying to protect her job.

An angry girlfriend called the probation officer pretending to be the complaining witness in a case for which a mentally ill defendant was on probation and falsely reported he was harassing her. Criminals get the mentally ill to cash forged checks or knock on doors of houses they want to burglarize. The list is endless.

Always remember-change is possible. Just look up the plethora of mug shots of celebrities and famous people on the internet. To just name a few, Tim Allen–actor comedian, worth eighty million dollars today, had a 1978 drug dealing charge and a

1997 drunk driving charge. Robert Downey, Jr., actor in the movie *Iron Man* had a 1999 drug conviction. Frank Sinatra also had scrapes with the law.

There have been great success stories in Dallas and across the nation. A mentally ill woman charged money on her employer's credit card. All the complaining witness wanted was restitution. She had no criminal history. We placed her on a conditional dismissal (written terms with which she must comply including treatment in order to have the charges dismissed) and after she successfully completed the programs we requested of her, she became a nanny for her family members, and paid back the six-thousand dollars restitution in full.

Another charged with possession of methamphetamine took classes, and completed an Intensive Outpatient Program. She is off methamphetamine now. Her fifteen-year-old son has his mom back.

A grandmother was arrested seventeen times for prostitution and low level drug offenses. She successfully completed the programs offered, reunited with her family, and is now raising a grandson. She says the programs "woke her up" and she finally had someone in her corner, a sense of value.

As a prosecutor, if you get the defendants the needed services and you don't see them again—you have succeeded.

And perhaps one day you will be blessed to receive a phone message like this on your phone, "Hi, Cindy Stormer, I don't know if you remember us but my name is S.M. and I have a brother named G.M.. And I always call you with bad news but I want to call you with some good news. Because all those classes that you put on him, the anger management, the substance abuse-all those classes that you made him attend, has really turned his life around. He's been staying clean and sober. He has his own apartment. He hasn't bothered my Dad, who will be ninety-one next month. At first I said 'Oh my God, he won't be able to do all those classes', but he has been able to do them. They are drug testing him. He has stabilized on his mental illness, he's taking his medication, and he is just doing great. I just want you to know. Thank you so much. We love you. Keep on doing the great job. I know sometimes it is hard to make those decisions but thank you so much, Cindy, for caring enough to put all those stipulations on my brother because it has made his life totally different. Thank you again. Bye Bye."

I received this call just days after my own brother died of a brain aneurism at age sixty after a forty-year struggle with alcoholism.

Prosecutors keep doing that voodoo that you do so well

Solutions

"Everything on earth has a purpose, every disease an herb to cure it, and every person a mission. This is the Indian theory of existence."
Morning Dove (1888 to 1930) Salish Tribe

Incarceration is not a level of care. Jail is not treatment. Criminal justice professionals can:

Number One: Brainstorm. Form a collaborative, multi-disciplinary group that meets regularly and shares information. Prepare a mission statement. The judge should ask team members to brainstorm about whom to use in an advisory capacity to bring the knowledge and skills of the community to the court.

In Dallas we formed the Behavioral Health Steering Committee (BHSC). This committee met once a week for many years. We meet once a month now-for one hour on Thursdays. The group consists of doctors, prosecutors, defense attorneys, judges, probation officers, police officers, deputies, jailers, service providers, psychologists...everyone that is a stakeholder in the mental health field or a representative of their group. Dallas also has the Behavioral Health Leadership Team (BHLT) which consists of many of the same types of players, but those with more authority in their respective fields including County Commissioners. That group is instrumental in encouraging appropriate legislation.

Designate a head of the committee or organization. It can be a social worker, a doctor, an attorney, a judge, anyone who is passionate about the mission.

Brainstorming allows people from all levels to contribute to what is seen as the problem and various solutions, allowing all staff to voice their ideas in a non-threatening environment and producing a balanced picture in one place to come to a consensus on the best decision. Get educated. Share information. Engage in intelligence driven prosecution by analyzing the evidence and identifying the worst offenders and sources of serial criminal activity, as Dallas did with the DNA Auto Theft Unit. Have smarter prosecutions by focusing resources on those individuals most responsible for driving crime. In Dallas we discovered that one hundred individuals were costing the County seven million dollars a year. We built fifty cottages to impact this issue. A place where they can have to live and receive the medical attention they need to prevent their problems from landing them in the jail or hospital.

Number Two: Get mental health professionals involved in your evaluations of the defendants-EARLY. Have psychologists (or at least counselors) interview the defendants. Obtain releases or waivers from the defendants so this information can be shared with the judge and prosecutor. If every other avenue fails due to lack of funding (e.g. very rural areas), have your probation officers well trained in risk assessment, and intense evaluations. The presentence investigation reports should have far more detail about the person's past, trauma, environment, family, support system, etc. Such a report should list all mental institutions and hospitals were the person has been treated. This will give the attorneys involved an opportunity to obtain those records to learn more about the best way to proceed with this defendant.

Number Three: Get as many law enforcement officers trained in Crisis Intervention Training (C.I.T.) as possible[348]. At the very least have one officer trained in this course that is

---

[348] There are 4,000 law enforcement officers in Dallas County trained in CIT; the Dallas Police Department alone has 1400.

passionate enough to educate other officers in your area. This training should include learning how to screen at the scene and divert the mentally ill on the front end to the hospitals instead of jail.

Number Four: Agree on a mission statement and memorialize it in a written project. A sample mission statement might contain the following:

The mission is to make things better. To prosecute the most violent offenders and habitual offenders, but also use the justice system to help those who cannot help themselves. Intervene promptly in cases where defendants have a diagnosis of a mental illness (with a priority as resources permit on less violent offenders) with diversionary programs aimed at preventing or reducing recidivism. To reduce the incarceration of the mentally ill in the jail and decrease utilization of higher levels of care (hospitals, emergency care, etc.). There is a commitment to a data driven, science and evidence based process with a focus on data supported outcomes.

Number Five: Specify policies and procedures concerning incentives and sanctions in a written program handbook or manual, and ensure that all staff members and participants are familiarized with the procedures. Those in the criminal justice system must begin to utilize business process modeling (BPM) tools (found for free on the internet) to map the information flow between criminal justice partners, eliminate duplicative processes and procedures, and identify opportunities for automation or re-engineering. Adapt technologies to advance solutions to your business needs.

Number Six: Use science and evidence based protocols. If you don't have them, get them. The most effective scientific method for influencing behavior is rewarding good behavior.[349]

---

[349] David D. Burns, M. D., *Feeling Good* (1980) page 178.

This has been proved via research on rats, plants, and bacteria. A reward system giving copious attention results in the most effective behavioral conditioning. Punishing bad behavior results in resentment and brings about avoidance.

The American Association of Prosecuting Attorneys recommends:[350]

1. Use science to investigate, solve, and prosecute crimes while recognizing the strengths and limits of the technique(s) applied. DNA, CODIS, fingerprints, shoeprints, tire tracks, tool marks, ballistics, hair, fiber, bite marks, bloodstain patterns, and features of documents (such as the ink used or the presence of additions or deletions), etc.

2. Familiarize yourself with scientific concepts. Prosecutors should be familiar with the statistical terms associated with forensic evidence. Prosecutors can build their knowledge of science by: reviewing the National Academy of Sciences report, attending training, etc.

3. Use reliable experts. Confirm that experts who testify in court are certified by an appropriate, nationally recognized organization.

4. Take a fresh look at cold cases and preserve testable evidence for the long term. Prosecutors should also encourage or help police and sheriff's departments that lack written policies regarding collection and preservation of biological evidence to create a formal Evidence Preservation Protocol.

5. Create a conviction integrity unit and forensic teams.[351]

---

[350] *Smart Prosecution Practices: Seven Recommendations to Integrate Science and Justice,* by Steven Jansen, Vice-President, COO, Association of Prosecuting Attorneys (2014).

[351] The Dallas District Attorney's Office was the first to establish a Conviction Integrity Unit. This Unit, created in 2007, investigates both "legitimate post-conviction claims of innocence" as well as old cases, both DNA and non-DNA

6. Be on the lookout for new technologies and better ways to apply old ones. For example, in Boston, surveillance video in public areas was used in the investigation of the 2013 marathon bombings that led to the identification of the suspects. Also, use of social media, fencing of stolen items and sale of illegal drugs on the internet, etc. can be traded using technology.

7. Use technology to engage communities. Let the public know what is going on.

Remember that it costs three times as much to keep a mentally ill defendant in jail (medicine, doctors, hospital visits, etc). Try to divert mentally ill defendants out of the jail and into services.

Number Seven: Be patient. People with psychotic disorders are: easily manipulated and not as likely to be the instigator of criminal activity.

Don't be too harsh when a mentally ill defendant with a substance abuse problem is unable to comply with a condition of probation. Think about all those New Year's resolutions you have not been able to keep over the years-exercise, lose weight, etc. Have some compassion when mentally ill, drug addicts, with lower intellectual functioning than you and taking psychotropic medications are not able to comply with the terms of their probation.

Number Eight: Engage the community. Get the complaining witness (victim) on board. Traditionally, the

---

related, "where evidence identifies different or additional perpetrators." See the Dallas County District Attorney's web site at www.dallasda.com More conviction integrity units have been developed in other district attorney's offices around the nation, modeled after Dallas' Conviction Integrity Unit.

prosecutor evaluates the case and determines a plea recommendation before contacting witnesses. It is the better practice for the prosecutor to get as much information as possible about the defendant before contacting the complaining witness. Have the defendant evaluated when possible. Review your checklists (provided herein). When the complaining witness is contacted by the prosecutor, they should:

- Start the conversation by introducing yourself and immediately asking how the complaining witness is doing.
- Next, the conversation must be directed to any restitution they are owed. This will assist in evaluating the severity of the case and the witness will respect the fact that the prosecutor's office cares.
- Wait until the end of the conversation to propose solutions.

These witnesses are also more likely to agree when they think this is what others are doing socially. And they are more likely to agree with solutions if there is consistency-consistency in your empathy for them and consistency with their empathy for the defendant.[352] This method is usually not appropriate in violent cases. Sometime only prison will do, and that subject is addressed later.

Every person in every level of the criminal justice system must reach out to those they come into contact with in the community to create outreach programs.

Number Nine: Streamline your criminal justice system so that treatment is delivered early. Social workers should be involved pre-trial, assessing non-dangerous individuals and assessing their needs. The initial magistrates should be looking for mental health issues and requiring risk assessments. A holistic sense of the

---

[352] Robert Cialdini, *Influence* (1984). This is one of the premier psychological classics on negotiations.

person must be obtained early. Ensure that programs or services are available to which to refer the mentally vulnerable.

Number Ten: State and local governmental officials, in conjunction with the persons, agencies and entities involved in mental health issues, must work collaboratively and expeditiously to construct a facility that can be used to house, treat and provide social services in one location to mentally ill inmates who are in custody awaiting trial.

Number Eleven: Create a good public relations machine to get your message out, create community buy-in, and garner more available resources.

Mental Health Checklist For Prosecutors

I. COMPETENCY AND INSANITY - ALWAYS contact the competency attorney immediately when someone has been found incompetent (there are deadlines). Be sure and contact a mental health attorney anytime competency or insanity is an issue in a case

II. If you have a mentally ill defendant that you might consider for probation:

1. What is the diagnosed mental illness?
2. Who is the Attorney?
   a. Public Defender's office. If it is a public defender, bring the mental illness to the defense attorney's attention. They have their own mental health case-managers and attorneys. Getting these specially trained public defenders involved as early as possible is the single most important factor in preventing a mentally ill person from languishing in jail and decompensating when they should be in another program or facility, and it avoids liability.
   b. Private attorney. Ask the attorney if representatives

of ADAPT[353] can speak with the defendant to determine available services. ADAPT will conduct an assessment, develop an exit plan, and provide to both parties. This is similar to a CATS evaluation but shorter and received much sooner. The assessment should provide information on programs, conditions, exit plans, referrals for housing, monitoring, transportation, etc.

3. Probation. Tell probation you would like the defendant on the mental health caseload. Consider sending a plea recommendation to probation indicating you need a CATS evaluation and the plea is "open" (that way you won't have to put a recommendation on a case in which you still need more facts).

4. The Plea. Be sure the Judge's docket reads "hold for Adapt or Transicare". It is very difficult to get the client the treatment, care, and medicine that they need if this is not done.

This is the end of the checklist.

A provider must determine the diagnosis, investigate family history, service history, medical records, and assess the necessity of services. Defendants (referred to as "clients" by the medical professionals) must be assessed to determine which level in the continuum of care is appropriate i.e.

- Early intervention (education alone may be sufficient).
- Outpatient.
- Intensive outpatient.
- Day treatment.
- Residential.

---

[353] ADAPT is a local service provider of mental health services. You may have ADAPT or some other provider in your area.

- Inpatient.

Other conditions can be put in place: Transicare-case management, peer support, behavioral-health transportation services, Qualified Mental Health Professionals, 24/7 access, housing, employment if capable, a Metrocare case manager assigned, attend Metrocare classes as appropriate (e.g. a class entitled *Understanding Schizophrenia*), insure medication compliance and supply before release from jail.

Residential housing is treatment; it is not housing. Residential costs approximately ninety dollars per day. Halfway houses are twenty dollars per day.

When you see a criminal history with numerous criminal trespass cases, be aware you are most likely dealing with a severely mentally ill individual. Selling these programs is part of the prosecutor's job and duty to victims, society, and future victims. If the defendants don't successfully complete the programs, try not to penalize them, just back up, brainstorm, and try another solution if possible.

The Texas Code of Criminal Procedure[354] provides for release on personal bond of certain mentally ill defendants.[355] It is irresponsible for an attorney to allow a mentally ill client to languish in jail when the law has provisions for their release yet it occurs frequently. In Dallas, homeless (and possibly other) defendants spend twice as much time in jail as those who have public defenders.

Relevant American Bar Association standards state that "[d]efense counsel should consider all procedural steps which in good faith may be taken, including, obtaining psychiatric examination of the accused when a need appears. . ." [356]

"A person may be suffering from a severe mental disease or defect or he may be highly medicated, but he will be competent to stand trial if he still has the ability to meaningfully consult with his attorney and he had a rational as well as factual understanding of the charged offense and trial proceedings."[357] If there is any reasonable probability that a defendant might be found incompetent, defense counsel must investigate that point.

Defense attorneys must educate their clients and the client's family.

---

[354] Article 17.032 of the Texas Code of Criminal Procedure.

[355] "A magistrate shall release a defendant on personal bond unless good cause is shown otherwise if the defendant is not charged with and has not been previously convicted of a violent offense." Tex. Code Crim. Proc. art. 17.032 (b)(emphasis added). Violent offense is defined in the statute. (see attached). The magistrate, unless good cause is shown for not requiring treatment, shall require as a condition of release on personal bond under this article that the defendant submit to outpatient or inpatient mental health or mental retardation treatment as recommended by the local mental health or mental retardation authority, if the condition is chronic or will continue to deteriorate. Tex. Code Crim. Proc. art. 17.032 (c). See also, Tex. Code Crim. Proc. 16.22 regarding release on bond of mentally ill defendants.

[356] ABA Standards for Criminal Justice: Prosecution and Defense Function 4-3.6 (3d ed. 1993).

[357] *Ex parte Thomas*, No. WR-69,859-01, 2009 WL 693606, at *5 (Tex. Crim. App. Mar. 18, 2009) (Cochran, J., concurring) (not designated for publication).

Educate family members on how to help their loved ones. (See the Chapter entitled "What Family Members Can Do.")

Consider giving your client a checklist for what they should know in the event they are arrested (if it is not too late once you become involved):

- Stay calm.
- At the point of arrest, do not bring attention to yourself.
- Be sure to tell officers if you or your loved one has a mental illness.

An old man walking down the beach one evening observed a young boy picking up starfish that had washed up on the beach and throwing them back into the water. The man asked "why are you doing this, there are so many, what difference does it make?" The boy looked down at the starfish in his hand and said "it makes a difference to this one" as he tossed it back into the ocean. By educating those with whom the defense attorney comes into contact (and the defense attorney may be the only person in the criminal justice system that has the opportunity and knowledge to make a difference), the defense attorney is saving those souls that would otherwise be lost-one starfish at a time. Before the defense attorney throws that starfish back into the sea, I pray that they will take a moment to redirect a life. A small act of kindness might restore a family or make a significant difference in the life of a child or other affected family member.

Remember that throughout history, citizens have looked to the legal profession for leadership and guidance. In a free society, attorneys keep anarchy and chaos in check. Never forget the noble profession you represent and those lawyers who went before you: Thomas Jefferson, James Madison, Patrick Henry, Theodore Roosevelt, Mahatma Gandhi, Francis Scott Key, Sam Houston, William Barrett Travis, Davey Crockett, Ralph Nader, Abraham Lincoln, William Penn, and so many more.

In the Great Hangings of Gainesville, Texas, in 1862 there was one attorney involved - the prosecuting attorney, William C. Young, who was maintaining law in the prosecution and saw to it that nineteen men were acquitted. When he was assassinated, the killing frenzy began. Acquittals were reversed, nineteen men were immediately hanged and forty-two were eventually wrongfully executed.

"First let's kill all the lawyers." Ironically this rallying cry for lawyer bashers from Shakespeare's quote from *Henry VI* was spoken by an anarchist who Shakespeare describes as "the head of an army of rabble and a demagogue pandering to the ignorant" who sought to overthrow the government. Shakespeare's acknowledgment that the first thing any potential tyrant must do to eliminate freedom is to "kill all the lawyers" is a compliment to the profession. Lawyers are the friends of people who are in trouble.

Adolph Hitler asserted, "I shall not rest until every German sees that it is a shameful thing to be a lawyer." In the entire history of the world, individual rights were never more threatened.

Defense attorneys should think like attorneys (beginning with the conclusion and then convincing others of your hypothesis seeking evidence that supports it and discrediting evidence that doesn't fit your theory). But defense attorneys should remember this is how wrongful convictions occur. Therefore, defense attorneys should also think like scientists (gather evidence and observe it, look for regularities, classify information, make deductions, form theories explaining observations, and test observations). Think outside the comfort zone.

Einstein said if a person studies a subject for just fifteen minutes a day, in a year he will be an expert, and in five years he may be a national expert (I can tell you from personal experience this is not true in the case of classical guitar, but that is the subject for yet another book). Devoting 10,000 hours to any subject will make one an expert. Continuing to practice in a given area increases the mylenization in the brain.[358] Daniel Coyle's bestselling book, *The Talent Code,* stands for the proposition that: greatness isn't born, it is grown. So help yourself, improve your brain, save lives, restore families and become an expert.

---

[358] Daniel Coyle, *The Talent Code* (2009).

CHAPTER FIFTY-FOUR

SANCTIONS

"We shall pass through this world but once. Any good that we can do, or any kindness that we can show another human being, let us do it now and not defer it. For we shall not pass this way again. And remember each person that we genuinely love makes our own survival easier. The greatest gift we can give is rapt attention to one another's existence. We are all one."
Stephen Grellet, also attributed to William Penn, Mahatma Gandhi and Ralph Waldo Emerson.

We lawyers have those degrees. We waited years for gratification because we are all neurotics. We lawyers suffer from lawbotomies. Normal people live in the present. To prevent mass shooting tragedies committed by the mentally ill like those of Newtown, Conn; Tuscan, Az (Gabrielle Gifford); Columbine High School; Aurora, Colorado (theater); Virginia Tech . . . there must be early mental health intervention, now, in the present.

Sanctions that are too low make people worse. Like a frog in the boiling water that does not jump out if the water is heated slowly, people get used to the sanctions.[366] Punishment should be customized to fit the defendant and the crime. For some it would be punishment to sit through nine innings of a baseball game (not that anyone is advocating for such a sanction.). The following is a list of conditions to consider for probation, conditional dismissals,

---

[366] For a list of incentives and sanctions: www.Ndcrc.org/content/list-incentives-and-sanctions.

or bonds.

Conditions of Probation or Conditional Dismissals

The Mental Health Coordinator or the Mental Health Case Managers in the Public Defender's office prepare the defendant and make sure the defendant understands the conditions.

Participate in psychiatric services including:

- Taking all psychiatric medication as prescribed;
- Meeting with a psychiatrist for all scheduled appointments;
- Complying with all instructions of the medical care provider (treatment and therapy, etc.) and of the caseworker, including participating in all programs as recommend or directed; and
- Meet with the case managers in the public defender's office or the Mental Health Coordinator on a monthly basis according to appointment and schedule set by same; and
- Defendant will not consume or take any non-prescribed drugs or alcohol.

The Mental Health Coordinator can see if the defendant has been a client of some service providers (i.e. has a mental illness) and give the defendant a referral to insure that the person has a place to stay and medication, if and when they are released.

Other mental health programs and treatment include but are not limited to the following:

- If there has been trauma, there must be counseling before substance abuse treatment. Maslow's Hierarchy of Needs teaches us that basic needs must be met first.

For substance abuse treatment:

- NEXUS-(lowest level) 45 days (Contract residential treatment in the community, women only). These defendants will not be around violent people. Community Supervision and Corrections Department (CSCD) (also known as probation) pays for this.

- ATLAS[367] (second level).
- Wilmer (third level, if eligible) (note: many treatment centers such as this do not take violent offenders and have many other restrictions.)
- DDC Wilmer–Dual Diagnosis Court – ninety day program.[368]
- JTC Wilmer–Judicial Treatment Center – six month program.
- SAFPF[369]–six months plus three months of aftercare. Special Needs SAFPF is nine months.

MORE CONDITIONS

- Restitution.
- Stay Away from (a specific person)
- No further contact with (a specific person).
- No harassing contact with (a specific person).
- No telephone calls to ___ .
- Defendant will participate in an anger management class and provide proof of such participation to the Mental Health Coordinator.
- Housing.
- Participate in a Twelve-step program–Alcoholics Anonymous (AA), Narcotics Anonymous (NA) (a once-a-week program).
- Drug Offender Education Program (DOEP), twenty-four weeks, one-hour classes
- Safe neighborhood – a one-hour, one-time class.

---

[367] ATLAS Achieving True Liberty and Success mental health court in Dallas where defendants are monitored regularly by the courts.
[368] At DDC the defendant's stay at the facility in Wilmer, Texas, is for sixty days and they receive aftercare through a Dallas District Court. They need to be on their medicine. They will need a CATS evaluation before acceptance.
[369] Substance Abuse Felony Punishment Facility.

- ELM–Electronic Leg Monitoring–can notify the complaining witness when the defendant is in the vicinity (aka Alternative Incarceration Program).
- SOP–Supportive Outpatient.
- IOP–Intensive Outpatient.
- IPS–Integrated Psychotherapeutic Services, which is a step up for those continuing to use (they meet two to three times per week, and it is a very intense program. Twice as much as IOP).
- ACT–Assertive Community Treatment, intensive mental health services for the most severely impaired (ACT–if they have had three hospitalizations in the last year).
- Reporting to Dallas Metrocare Services.
- Continue services with LifeNet.
- Sleep at home.
- Wilkinson Center or DARS (Dallas Area Rehabilitation Services) for employment assistance–occupational therapy.
- Cenikor – twenty-four month substance abuse program where they work to pay for the servies.
- Solace Counseling (geared toward Spanish speakers – to determine need for psychotropic meds).

SPECIFIC OFFENSES

Attend and complete and present verification of completion to case manager:

- PRIDE (misdemeanor), Strengthening Transition and Recovery STAR (Felony) for those charged with prostitution.
- New Friends/New Life (NFNL).[370]

---

[370] Preston Road Church of Christ in Dallas offers financial assistance and access to other services for women who want to leave the sex trafficking industry and have assisted more than 1,000 women and their children.

- NLO–New Life Opportunities (twice a month)
- Anthem Strong Families-Tyro (means warrior and beginner in learning) program. see www.BeTheChampion.org
- BIPP–Batterer's Intervention Prevention Program (a more intense, twenty-four week program) both anger management and BIPP can be required.
- DVVIP–Domestic Violence Victim Impact Panel (a onetime program)

If violence is involved, the required misdemeanor conditions are:

- AFFV (Affirmative Finding of Family Violence),
- DVVIP,
- BIPP if married/intimate, anger if siblings.
- Anti-theft class .
- DWI education.
- No driving.
- Suspend or revoke their driver's license.
- Interlock.
- In Home.
- SCRAM Secure Continuous Remote Alcohol Monitor.
- Soberlink.
- Metrocare sex offender class or Outburst class–is for low functioning individuals, (e.g. indecent exposure.)
- ISF Burnet–Intermediate Sanction Facility (90 days).
- Thinking for a Change Class–might be considered for people engaging in indecent behavior.
- Attend and complete the *Understanding Schizophrenia* class at Dallas Metrocare Services and present verification.
- *Living with Bipolar* class at Dallas Metrocare.
- Refrain from the possession of a weapon of any kind, including but not limited to firearms, knives and other types of sharp objects.
- Mental Health Maintenance Plan and Conditions of Bond– may want to consider this when the defendant is not on probation but is entering a plea that will result in a release

from jail (e.g. being released from a mental hospital, credit for time served)

REHABILITATION

- TORI–Texas Offender Re-entry Initiative, one-year long program at the Potter's House, faith based.
- Resolana (with Volunteers of America)–transitioning incarcerated women back into the community (these classes occur in the jail).
- www.MilesOfFreedom.com[371]–transitioning from prison.
- Misdemeanor mental health court–lasts six months, report weekly to the court.
- SNOP–Special Needs Offender Program (forensic psychiatric division of Metrocare), a psychiatric clinic that offers outpatient mental health services.
- Peer support.

Remember to take care of your own health.

---

[371] Established by Dallas exoneree Richard Miles.

CHAPTER FIFTY-FIVE

WHEN ONLY PRISON WILL DO

". . .each one then had a heart regardless of social duty and a
mind fatally bent on mischief."
Janecka v. State, 739 S.W.2d 813, 835 (Tex. Crim. App.
1987)(Teague's dissent). Pre-1974 definition of malice in the
murder law.

One last thought before you decide that prison is the only option for your mentally ill defendant–Prison Rape Elimination Act of 2003 (PREA). Experts conservatively estimate that during incarceration, twenty percent of males and twenty-five percent of females are raped. One in ten youth in juvenile detention are raped by staff. Inmates with mental illness are at increased risk of sexual victimization. Sexual predators in the prison know the mentally ill will not make good witnesses later and they are more easily manipulated. Often sexual victimization occurs within the first forty-eight hours of incarceration. At Miami-Dade jail (one of the largest in the United States) an inmate was once raped for three days before he was rescued.[372]

Severe physical and psychological effects of sexual assault hinder the mentally ill person's ability to integrate into the community and maintain stable employment upon such victim's release from prison: PTSD, depression, suicide, and the exacerbation of existing mental illness. Prison rape fosters an HIV epidemic.

---

[372] Pete Earley, *Crazy, A Father's Search through America's Mental Health Madness* (2006).

Incarceration and isolation increase the negative symptoms of schizophrenia, anxiety, depression and other mental illnesses.

Remember-if we are just mad at them, we should make an attempt to rehabilitate them. Some of them have never been *habilitated* in the first place. But if we are scared of them . . . prosecute vigorously.

Mental illness is by no means a free pass. Perpetrators are free and responsible people who have made decisions leading them to where they are. The reality of their guilt must be acknowledged.

Sometimes a prosecutor will receive a case with the mentally ill defendant and there is no choice but to proceed and get the maximum sentence possible. An example of such as case is when a mentally ill man burst into a woman's home and tried to sexually assault her in front of her two young children. The children in desperation grabbed kitchen knives to try to protect their mother, but the assailant was too strong. They then ran next-door and convinced a hero of a neighbor to come to their apartment to rescue their mother. The neighbor/hero wrestled with the perpetrator and held him until the police arrived. The jurors told me after this trial "we failed him." They were right. We must help those people that need our help before these events. However, with defendants at this point, we cannot take the risk they are out in the community in the future. While mental illness is not contagious, many times mentally ill defendants do seem to tend to spread mental illness: posttraumatic stress syndrome, paranoia, borderline personality disorder, traumatic brain injury, exposure in utero to drugs and alcohol, etc. and there is a tipping point where society can only benefit if the defendant is put away for a long time. Sex offender's recidivism is reduced significantly after serving a prison sentence.[373]

In those violent cases, it is very important to point out to

---

[373] Council of State Governments Justice Center *County Uniform Recidivism Measure Project: First Year Results for Dallas County* by Dr. Tony Fabelo and Dr. Rebecca Cohen (2015) p.32

juries that the defendant had a choice. Because the defendant had these diagnosed mental illnesses, the defendant has a duty to himself and the rest of society to stay on that medication. Point this out in voir dire (jury selection), opening statements, closing statements, and other opportunities.

The prosecutor must prepare the jurors before they are seated in a case. In the jury selection process, *voir dire*, potential jurors should be asked or informed of the following:

- How many of you have been diagnosed with a mental illness or have a close family member or friend who has?
- Remember, you can ask to come up and speak privately if you wish.
- Mental illness is not to be confused with insanity.[374]
- Mental illness is not a defense.
- Some people are insane at the time of the offense, and that is a defense.
- Insanity is not an issue in this trial.
- Does everyone understand that being bipolar or schizophrenic is not a defense to the commission of a crime?
- Should a person take their medications if they are required to take it?
- Because the defendant had these diagnosed mental illnesses, do you agree the defendant has the duty to himself and the rest of society to stay on that medication?
- Mental illness might be considered in punishment but not guilt/innocence.

---

[374] Texas Penal Code § 8.01. Insanity
(a) It is an affirmative defense to prosecution that, at the time of the conduct charged, the actor, as a result of severe mental disease or defect, did not know that his conduct was wrong.
(b) The term "mental disease or defect" does not include an abnormality manifested only by repeated criminal or otherwise antisocial conduct.

- Mental illness is not an excuse to a commission of a crime.
- Mental illness does not give them a free pass.
- Would the fact that they have a mental illness cause you to be more lenient?
- Would it make you unable to follow the law?

Jurors confuse competency[375] (current ability to understand what is going on) and insanity (ability to understand the nature of one's actions at the time of the offense). Generally, mental illness goes to mitigation (lessens the punishment), not culpability (degree of guilt).

A prosecutor may want to address mental health issues in a Motion in Limine (to limit evidence to that which is relevant at trial) pretrial. After the prosecutor argues the Motion in Limine at court, they will know if the defense just plans to use the mental health evidence as mitigation in punishment or as some type of defense in the case-in-chief (guilt/innocence portion of the trial). To use such evidence in the case-in-chief: "Expert psychiatric testimony concerning mental illness might be relevant, reliable, and admissible to rebut proof of the defendant's *mens rea* (guilty mind)."[376]

---

[375] "No plea of guilty or plea of *nolo contendere* shall be accepted by the court unless it appears that the defendant is mentally competent and the plea is free and voluntary." Tex. Code Crim. Proc. art. 26.13(b).
"A person is incompetent to stand trial if the person does not have: (1) Sufficient present ability to consult with the person's lawyer with a reasonable degree of rational understanding; or (2) A rational as well as factual understanding of the proceedings against the person. A defendant is presumed competent to stand trial and shall be found competent to stand trial unless proved incompetent by a preponderance of the evidence." Tex. Code Crim. Proc. art. 46B.003(a)&(b).
[376] *Ruffin v. State*, 270 S.W.3d 586, 591 (Tex. Crim. App. 2008). A prosecutor might argue that evidence of mental illness should be excluded under Tex. R. Evid. 403 or Tex. R. Evid. 703-705, if the probative value of the proffered evidence is substantially outweighed by the danger of unfair prejudice, if the expert is insufficiently qualified, or the testimony is insufficiently relevant or reliable under Texas guidelines for expert testimony. Such evidence may also be

While a mental illness such as bipolar disorder or schizophrenia is not a defense to the commission of a crime, some people are insane at the time of the offense and insanity is a defense. If a person is found Not-Guilty-by-Reason-of-Insanity, the court will then make a determination of that person's dangerousness to determine which facility they will be sent to in the state mental hospital system. In Texas, persons found "Not Guilty by Reason of Insanity" tend to serve more time incarcerated in mental institutions than they would have had they been sentenced to prison.

"Insanity is the only diminished responsibility or diminished capacity defense to criminal responsibility in Texas."[377] In the seminal Texas case on the subject *Ruffin v. State*, the defendant (and others) testified the defendant suffered from both auditory and visual delusions. Ruffin testified that when he shot at the police officers, he thought he was shooting at "Muslims." Ruffin literally saw and heard Muslims. Under those circumstances, the Court held that the defendant might be entitled to offer expert psychiatric testimony that some people who suffer from serious mental diseases and delusions really can and do "see" and "hear" Muslims (or other figments of their imagination) even though they do not exist. This evidence was relevant to rebut the element that Ruffin intended to shoot police officers and would, if believed, lessen the crime from a first-degree aggravated assault of a police officer to a second-degree aggravated assault (an intentional shooting at "Muslims").

However, in another case, the insanity defense was unsuccessful where the defendant offered no evidence to suggest that he intended to shoot anything or anyone other than the police officers that he killed, the defendant offered no evidence he did not intend to shoot a person, and to the contrary, all of his mental-illness evidence showed why he intentionally and knowingly killed

---

excluded if it does not truly negate the required *mens rea* (guilty mind).
[377] *Ruffin v. State*, 270 S.W.3d 586, 593 (Tex. Crim. App. 2008.).

the deputies: He was paranoid and thought they had mistreated him.[378] Such mental-illness testimony may be relevant for mitigation purposes during the punishment phase, but "expert testimony that does not directly rebut the culpable mental state usually may be excluded at the guilt stage.

If a person who has previously been found Not-Guilty-by-Reason-of-Insanity is to be released from the hospital because the doctors at the facility have determined the person is no longer a threat to public safety, a hearing will be held in the originating court to determine the disposition. The hearing will help educate the families. The community will understand everything has been done that could be done. When a person found not-guilty-by-reason-of-insanity is finally released from custody, the prosecutor should include a provision in the release order (among other things) that the defendant is not to be around weapons under any circumstances. The prosecutor should take a list of conditions to that hearing.

The mentally ill may be sentenced to death.[379] However, the execution of an incompetent person is prohibited.[380]

---

[378] *Mays v. State*, 318 S.W.3d 368, 381 (Tex. Crim. App. 2010.
[379] *Mays v. State*, 318 S.W.3d 368, 379 (Tex. Crim. App. 2010).
[380]See *Ford v. Wainwright*, 106 S.Ct. 2595 (1986), and Tex. Code Crim. Proc. art. 46.05.

CHAPTER FIFTY-SIX

WHAT JUDGES CAN DO

"Four things belong to a judge: to hear courteously, to answer wisely, to consider soberly, and to decide impartially."
Socrates

B e patient. Be kind. Have empathy. If you do not – who will?

Judges are in a unique position to build partnerships between the stakeholders. Judges can take the leadership role and get programs started. Judges can bring together other judges; law enforcement officials; elected officials; jail administrators; mental health, health and other service providers; prosecutors; defense attorneys; probation officials foundation program officers; housing and social service providers; consumers; family members; victim advocates Veterans Health Administration's coordinators, benefits specialists, etc. And it is the court that can hold these entities to a higher standard of care.

Judges can influence oversight of social service agencies, i.e. a call from a judge to a government supported service provider will receive top priority from that organization.

Judges can hold defendants accountable for participating in programs that address their mental health and substance use treatment needs.

Judges can establish formal agreements. Memoranda of understanding (MOUs) are formal agreements between public service agencies that can facilitate service delivery through cooperative efforts.

Prioritize scarce resources. Review resources to avoid duplications. Judges can encourage mentors to volunteer for the programs for the much needed peer support for participants. Offer rewards and positive reinforcement. Use progressive sanctions: consider requiring the participant/defendant to write an essay (if the crime would merit such a mild sanction). If they fail, then consider community service. Use jail as a last resort.

Information is your ally, so share it. Develop information-sharing protocols and flow charts mapping participants. Consequences should be clearly stated in written court policies, manuals, and handbooks.

Study the work of the drug courts and adapt that science to as many of your cases as you can.[381] Develop the workforce. Ensure that participants conducting specialty courts have received the appropriate training. Staff participation in continuing education workshops is the greatest predictor of a program's effectiveness.[382] It takes time and effort for judges to do their jobs most effectively.

Secure new resources on the local, State, federal and private level (SAMHSA, Bureau of Justice BJA).

Judges can ensure that best practices are being followed. Understand that basic needs must be met first, i.e. housing before counseling, trauma based counseling before substance abuse counseling; treatment of the mental or substance abuse issue before employment or dental care.

Do too little and they get worse. Don't do enough and they get worse. Demand too much and they get worse. Expect too little and they get worse (habituation). If this sounds too overwhelming, just remember to have them evaluated by a mental health professional. To avoid damaging individuals, have the mental health professionals give you (1) a risk/needs assessment and (2) distinguish proximal and distal goals.

Understand that proximal goals are those that the participants are already capable of performing and necessary for long-term goals to be accomplished. Distal goals are ultimately

----

[381] Obtain Douglas B. Marlowe, J.D., Ph.D, and Judge William Meyer *The Drug Court Judicial Benchbook* National Drug Court Institute's (2011) and learn the science to apply to all cases where applicable.
[382] *Adult Drug Court Best Practice Standards Vol. II* (National Association of Drug Court Professionals 2015) p. 47.

desired but will take time to accomplish.

Cases must be appropriate analyzed by asking the following:

Who is the person in terms of risk (prognosis) and need (diagnosis)?

Where is the participant (phase of the program)?

Which behavior are we responding to (proximal or distal)?

What is the response choice and magnitude?

How do we explain and deliver the response?

Judges can monitor that individuals are placed in the appropriate categories (or quadrants of high risk, low risk, high needs, low needs). Don't mix individuals with high risk with those of high needs. You will permanently make low risk people worse. High risk people prey on those with high needs (sexually abuse them, sell or provide them drugs, etc.).

With low risk/low needs individuals you can threaten to put them in jail for their first abuse of drugs. They need zero tolerance and drug education. They are most like us. Individuals in the other three categories need a different approach.

With proximal goals you must sanction high, and reward low (remember they are capable of performing now). With distal goals you must sanction low and reward high.

Treatments must be in the correct order or you make things worse. Then you are engaged in malpractice. Treat in this order of needs:

- Clinical disorders - medications
- Responsive - treatments
- Maintenance - housing, hygiene, family support, nutrition, medical, dental, social services, and then employment . If you try to put them in jobs before treatment, you are just adding one more job to their list of lost jobs.

While those with substance abuse and unresolved trauma must have their trauma treated before they receive substance abuse treatment (or you are wasting your time and money on the substance abuse treatment), mental illness and substance abusers must be treated concurrently and not consecutively.[383]

Three indicators of substance abuse addiction (you just need one)

- Triggered binge pattern
- Cravings or compulsions
- Withdrawal symptoms

Ask the people who know them if these are the issues in that person's life.

Turn tax burdens into tax payers. Spend at least three minutes in each court proceeding looking the defendant in the eye and sincerely asking them how they are doing. Do not respond angrily to participants. This can be damaging to those who have suffered trauma, childhood abuse or neglect or those who suffer from PTSD. Ask them how they are doing. Ask questions like: are you having any problems with medicine/treatment/probation/etc. Listen to what the participants have to say. Avoid downward communication.

Catch the participant/defendant doing something good. Recognize and reward good behavior. Commend good behavior. Verbal praise and reduced supervisory obligations can have a positive effect. Building confidence and self-esteem are critical to treatment. Check the status of the participants (with status hearings if possible, as is done in successful drug courts). It is best if this is done electronically in order that automated summary reports may be generated. Data must be timely entered, and when the events occur. Medicare, for instance, requires physicians to document services within twenty-four to forty-eight hours. For a low cost evaluation, consider asking a local college or university to conduct an evaluation of your court. A student might do this as a thesis or

---

[383] *Adult Drug Court Best Practice Standards Vol. II* (National Association of Drug Court Professionals 2015) p. 13.

dissertation. Encourage law schools and police academies to teach the information contained herein.

Above all-care. Treat the participants in your court with dignity and respect. Many of these individuals before you have never had someone to care for them. The chance to be a hero for most people may only happen once in a lifetime, a Judge however may have several opportunities. Witness a miracle.

CHAPTER FIFTY-SEVEN

HOW TO READ PSYCHIATRIC REPORTS

*"There is a wonderful mythical law of nature that the three things
we crave most in life -- happiness, freedom, and peace of mind --
are always attained by giving them to someone else."*
Peyton Conway March

DSM-V

The Diagnostic and Statistical Manual of Mental Disorders
(DSM-V)[384] sets out the diagnostic criteria for clinicians to
diagnose a mental illness. The DSM-V is the most comprehensive
and highly regarded reference for mental health professionals. It is
used by insurance companies, psychiatrists, psychologists, courts,
etc. Competency evaluations, insanity evaluations, pre-sentence
investigation report, all types of psychological evaluations, etc.
will frequently have references to terms found in this book. It is
updated about every fifteen years.

There is more about Neuroscience, DNA, and family
relationships in the DSM-V than the previous edition.

Global Assessment of Functioning (GAF)

The GAF Scale is useful in tracking the clinical progress of
individuals in global terms, using a single measure. The GAF Scale
is to be rated with respect only to psychological, social and

---

[384] The American Psychiatric Association Diagnostic and Statistical Manual of
Mental Disorders, Fifth Edition (May 2013).

occupational functioning. These scores are in psychiatric reports and evaluations, pre-sentence investigations (PSI's) conducted by probation departments, etc. GAF scores below fifty indicate it would be difficult for the individual to comply with the terms of probation because of mental limitations.

With a GAF score below thirty, the individual may not be eligible for some programs, (e.g. in Dallas they are ineligible for the ATLAS[385] Court [a mental health program]). A GAF score below forty-five renders a person ineligible for the STAR court (rehabilitation of persons charged with prostitution).

GAF scores below ten indicate the person is in a persistent danger of hurting self or others. These scores can fluctuate from time to time with the same individual. I have seen scores of sixty-five and then same individual has decompensated and the score becomes thirty and they are hospitalized and the score becomes forty-five–all within a twelve month period (it could happen in less time). One defendant I prosecuted had a GAF of Zero. They carried her into court. She collapsed on the floor wailing incoherently.

Health Insurance Portability and Accountability Act [hereinafter HIPAA]

To improve the efficiency and effectiveness of the health care system, the Health Insurance Portability and Accountability Act of 1996 (HIPAA), required the Department of Health and Human Services to adopt national standards for electronic health care transactions and code sets, unique health identifiers, and security. Congress incorporated into HIPAA provisions mandating the adoption of federal privacy protections for individually identifiable health information.[386]

HIPAA prohibits the disclosure of a person's

---

[385] Achieving True Liberty and Success
[386] The HIPAA rules are found at 45 C.F.R. 160, 162, and 164.

medical/mental health history. There are three types of covered entities: health plans, health care clearinghouses, and health care providers who conduct the standard health care transactions electronically.[387] The state law includes "a governmental unit."[388]

HIPAA allows admission of a defendant's medical records, including statements made to medical staff contained in the records, for law enforcement purposes.[389]

HIPAA regulations can be found at: http://www.dhhs.gov[390]

"A person commits an offense if the person releases or discloses confidential information obtained under this section *for purposes other than continuity of care* and services, except as authorized by other law or by the consent of the person to whom the information relates. An offense under the State law is a Class B misdemeanor."[391] On the state level, enforcement is by the Attorney General's Office. The Department of Health and Human Services, Office for Civil Rights (OCR) is responsible for administering and enforcing the federal standards and may conduct complaint investigations and compliance reviews. There are civil and criminal penalties for violations of the federal law, which could be up to ten years imprisonment.[392] There is proposed legislation in Texas that mental illness be designated on criminal history for the purpose of the continuity of care.

A defense attorney can disclose medical or psychiatric

---

[387] 45 C.R.R. Section 160.
[388] Tex. Health & Safety Code § 181.001(b)(1)(B).
[389] 45 C.F.R. 164.512 (f) and *Gibson v. State*, 225 S.W.3d 824 (Tex. App.-Beaumont 2007, pet ref'd) (defendant's admission that he sexually abused victim admissible).
[390] The Texas District and County Attorneys Association has a publication available, *HIPAA for Prosecutors*, by Markus Kypreos available through their website www.tdcaa.com See also, *Mental Defenses*, by Jane Starnes, for another source by TDCAA for prosecutors.
[391] Tex. Health & Safety Code § 614.017 (e).
[392] Health Insurance Portability and Accountability Act of 1996, Pub. L. No. 104-191, Section 1176, 110 Stat.1936.

information to a prosecutor based on the necessity for continuity of care.

CHAPTER FIFTY-EIGHT

AM I MAKING THINGS BETTER-FUTURE OF CRIMINAL JUSTICE

"It's when you know you're licked before you begin but you begin anyway and you see it through no matter what. You rarely win, but sometimes you do."
Atticus Finch in *To Kill a Mockingbird* by Harper Lee

We have come so far in such a short time. Decades ago when I was a police officer, if I wanted crime scene photos, I would have to call a professional photographer to the scene (getting them out of bed in the middle of the night at times, this was especially true in more rural areas), wait for the film to be developed, and hope they remembered to put film in their camera. Today, as a prosecutor, I go to a crime scene, take my own photographs with my phone and text them to the tech department, and the 8 X 10 glossies for trial are on my desk by the time I get back to the office. When I first started police work, the first night on the job, police officers were given a shotgun and a badge and put out on the streets with no training. Even in the 1970's, training came later.

A Chief of Police I once worked for in rural Bridgeport, Texas, reminisced about the early days of police work (at least in the rural area he patrolled). Before police radios (and the first ones took up the entire front seat of the patrol car leaving only room for the officer to sit), everyone in town knew to call Buella Gregg when there was trouble. Buella would take the call and then flip a switch in her house which illuminated a light at the top of a tower. Chief Dale would see the light and then drive to Buella's house and determine what the emergency was and take care of it.

Yes, technology has taken us very far in a short time. Today we can solve decades old cases with DNA and technology. We have the capability of retracing a criminals actions through

GPS tracking. Blood spatters can be determined regardless of attempts to obliterate them.

But true success is and always has been in the details. On the exonerations of wrongfully convicted men that I worked on, it was the smallest detail that was the tipping point in a case. Each successful exoneration was brought about by many players, many cogs in the wheel of justice. Defense attorneys, prosecutors, scientists, investigators, judges and more, all working together towards the same goal. Exonerations would not have occurred but for all the work of everyone involved. We must carry that spirit of camaraderie forward in our quest to improve the lives of those less fortunate. We accomplish this by brainstorming together. No problems as big as the ones that we are facing are solved by only a few individuals. It takes entire communities working together.

In the future, government will be run with the same science and evidence based methods as the most successful of businesses. Successful businesses are the ones that study the market and give people what they need. Our government must be run like a successful business. Our law enforcement and courts must not waste resources. Sick people will not languish in jail instead of being assisted to assimilate back into the community as soon as possible-saving resources on many levels. Methods will be generated to divert individuals with mental illness from returning to county jails and prisons, or, from ever entering into a jail. Law enforcement and those in the courts will be the thought leaders on addressing core issues that cause crime, such as mental illness and drug abuse. Significant challenges to the criminal justice system will be addressed.

Each entity in the system will have a mission statement addressing the core issues that cause crime, such as mental illness and drug abuse. Each entity will contribute to making our communities safer and stronger and help those who cannot help themselves. Each entity would strive to serve *all* communities equally.

Law enforcement officers, the warriors on the front lines of social change, will ask themselves every day and in each encounter "Am I making things better?" Patrol cars will have a mission statement painted on them "Making things better while protecting and serving". Law enforcement officers-from patrol officers to jailers-will have academy curricula, orientation programs, continuing education training, and other programs that teach how to identify and respond to incidents involving persons with mental health disorders or co-occurring mental health and substance abuse disorders. Officers will know how to evaluate people in the field and deal effectively with sick individuals, taking those that need to go to the hospital to treatment rather than jail.

Social workers, case-managers and service providers will get involved promptly and stay with those sick individuals and report their progress to the courts. Aftercare will be guaranteed. Social workers will proactively ensure clients are complying with an exit plan by texting clients to communicate with them and monitor their progress, check their status, and let the clients know the social workers care. The clients will be informed about possible job opportunities. The social workers will be available if the client needs anything. Therapists could become a part of their lives. Not just writing prescriptions but giving individualized care, and one-on-one therapy would make the difference.

Defense attorneys will ask themselves every day and in each encounter "Am I making things better?" They will contact their client early and thoroughly investigate the cases. Defense attorneys will be knowledgeable about mental illnesses and services available and promptly respond to the needs of the defendant and their families. They will insure that the chronically mentally ill be assigned a social worker who would befriend them, bring them coffee and a meal, ask them each day how they were doing, and try to encourage them to take their medications and receive treatment. This alternative is cheaper than a mental institution.

A computerized monitoring system could keep track of the chronically mentally ill. It could alert the attorney, the court, the social workers, and an administrative case manager when a person stopped attending day-treatment programs or failed to pick up their supply of antipsychotic medication. We already have the ability to track offenders via their cell phones. The cost is less than a GPS monitor. Voiceprints verify the presence of the defendant. Curfew could be monitored. They could be reminded of court dates.

Prosecutors will ask themselves every day and in each encounter "Am I making things better?" Prosecutors would accept the challenge these cases present. Prosecutors would know to take the more difficult and time consuming path of returning people to the community after their mental health is restored. Prosecutors would not judge their success on a conviction rate and winning or losing cases. Prosecutors would say "no" to the easy plea bargain and instead take on the harder job of helping someone get back on track. Prosecutors would do what is best for a community by keeping someone out of prison instead of growing the population of ex-convicts simply because it's the easier path. What prosecutors have been is protectors of society (by locking away those outliers), but what prosecutors can be is a catalyst for change.

Judges will ask themselves every day and in each encounter, "Am I making things better?" They will make sure mentally ill participants in the court process understand they are not forgotten. They will ensure sick defendants do not languish in jail when they might be receiving services. They will congratulate, and praise those who are successful in the programs. Judicial demeanor will always be respectful and caring. Judges will recognize when they can assist mentally ill individuals and have empathy for their situation and commend them for their progress.

Every cog in the wheel will be a trained professional. All those individuals in the legal system will be distinguishable in that they possess the ability to be creative at every moment. They will be proactive and move the cases along. They will possess distinct qualities. They will not fit neatly into any rolls, job descriptions or statistics. They will waste no time complaining or wishing circumstances were otherwise. They will be enthusiastic about their task. There will be no mumbling or groaning. They will be eager to get the job done. They will delight in the reality they are making things better for the community and for individuals they serve. If situations need to be eradicated, they will work at eradicating them. And they will enjoy the work. They will be aggressively curious. They will channel their energy in positive manners. They won't wait for information, they will go after it. They will work at changing situations they do not like. They will not argue, they will simply state their views.

They will take the data provided, filter it through their own values, and use it for improvement. They embrace the best possibilities. They turn the complex and undecipherable to the clear and understandable. They observe and except the world the way it is and work to change that which they can for the better. They do not strive to bring importance to themselves. They are engaged in work that will make other people's lives more pleasant or tolerable. They are creative. They attack problems. They are active and have exceptionally high energy levels. They are never bored. They understand if something is not impossible, there must be a way of doing it.

They will be role models for the communities. They know they are building strong, healthy, communities. They are caring persons especially with children. They are healthy, happy, fulfilled people. They take care of themselves with good exercise and nutrition. They never complain about things that will not change. They are honest and trustworthy. They do not blame others. They serve others because they like it. They are motivated by a desire to grow and improve. They allow others to make their own decisions. They are so busy with their own lives; there is no time for petty matters. They are truth seekers always looking to improve and learn more. They are learners. They are proactive. They are synergistic in their creative cooperation. Like world class athletes, they visualize the end product. They know that the chronically mentally ill, many times, can recover with support.

They are non-worriers. They are not threatened by the unknown. They seek out experiences that are new and unfamiliar to them. They are doers. They are deliberate in their pursuits. If a mistake is made, no time is wasted worrying about it, they just pick up and correct it the best way possible and move on. They learn from their past. They live in the present to reinforce their positive self-image. They are strikingly independent. And they strive to make others independent. "Problems" are not viewed as problems at all, but are instead viewed as "management opportunities". They understand that as in the game of life, it is not the strongest or the fastest who wins, but the most adaptable.

They are incapable of stereotyping. They rarely even notice physical differences in people: sexual, ethnic, racial. They do not judge others by their looks. They see themselves as part of all of humanity. They need not wait for someone else's expression of love before giving it. They understand that by living with these values, the next generation and the following generations will live in a world far better than today's.

They respect everyone. They know life is not fair and that they may fail often, but they take some risks, step up when the times are toughest, face down the bullies, lift up the downtrodden, and never, ever give up. They strive to change the world, making it a better place one case at a time.

And they ask, "Am I making things better?"

CHAPTER FIFTY-NINE

CONCLUSION

"With a good conscience our only sure reward, with history the final judge of our deeds, let us go forth to lead the land we love asking His blessing and with His help but knowing that here on earth God's work must truly be our own."
J. F. Kennedy's Inaugural Address

We must stop criminalizing mental illness. The humanity we all share is more important than the mental illness we do not share. The mentally ill are the most alone and the most isolated. They are the weakest among us. We each have the power to say "this is not how this is going to end." If we are not here to help others, then what are we here for?

Just as the causes and reasons for mental illness are not simple (genetics, drug abuse, environment, etc.), solutions to our society are also complex and require intensive collaboration and brainstorming with all the interested parties in order to solve issues.

Lawyers are trained in the IRAC style: define the issue, identify the rule, analyze the problem, and draw a conclusion. This does not include a business model of implementation of change. Brainstorming and collaboration are what make the business model work. Lawyers (i.e. those in charge of the criminal justice system) see the problems but make few efforts to change. Even when jails are run as a business they meet with failure. Private jails are constantly going out of business-usually for ignoring the needs of the defendants, who are probably not viewed to be the consumers as they are not paying the bill, the government is. Managers of these privately run facilities tend to look at the immediate concerns, not long term solutions. Long term solutions would put them out of business. Professionals in the legal system must be a catalyst for change.

Jail space is a resource paid for by the citizens. It is the single biggest budget item for Dallas County and other jurisdictions as well. We have to be accountable and use that resource wisely. We shouldn't be locking up mentally ill with hardened criminals. Jails do not have sufficient manpower, training or resources to effectively deal with all those suffering from mental illness.

It is estimated that two million people with serious mental illnesses are booked into jail each year, or that prevalence rates of serious mental illnesses in jails are three to six times higher than for the general population.[393] Almost three-quarters of these have co-occurring substance use disorders.[394] Once incarcerated, they tend to stay longer in jail and upon release are at a higher risk of recidivism than individuals without these disorders. Criminogenic needs among offenders (e.g. severe mental illness, lack of job skills, substance dependence, housing, etc.) are not easy to solve.

Putting defendants into programs to help them reduces recidivism, so in the long run, it is keeping the community safer.

Involuntary civil commitments are rare and sometimes difficult to obtain with the current law. Intervention in a criminal setting may be the only help these people will ever get.

One out of four families experience mental illness. Helping those with a mental illness also helps the families and other lives they touch.

There is no shame in having a mental illness. The shame is in not helping someone who does. We need to strive to not criminalize mental illness any more than we already have. There is no better way to be smart on crime than getting people out of jail that do not need to be there, and reducing recidivism at the same

---

[393] Steadman, Henry, et al., "Prevalence of Serious Mental Illness among Jail Inmates" *Psychiatric Services* 60, no. 6 (2009) p. 761–765.
[394] Abram, Karen M., and Linda A. Teplin, "Co-occurring Disorders Among Mentally Ill Jail Detainees," *American Psychologist* 46, no. 10 (1991) p. 1036–1045.

time.

Many defendants I have prosecuted were just like you and me-until they were in a car accident or had some other disabling injury (plunging down an elevator shaft, work injuries, sports injuries, etc.). Traumatic brain injury or addiction to pain killers changed their lives dramatically for the worse.

Detour from Normal by Ken Dickson (2013) should be required reading for all medical students, law students, and police academies and anyone who might come into contact with the mentally ill. Given the wrong medication during surgery, the author spiraled into mania and lost many months (if not years) of his life. The story is a testament to how the mentally ill cannot help themselves and need an advocate, and a multidisciplinary team to assist in recovery. They are grateful to be rescued. It was heartbreaking to read how unprofessionally the mental health staff members were in dealing with the author and how they suffered from "confirmation bias" (the tendency to select favorable information that confirms a hypothesis while ignoring everything else). Confirmation bias was also common in wrongful convictions resulting in decades spent in prison by innocent victims.

Some mentally ill are so desperate for survival they are willing to perform sex acts on strangers for ten or twenty dollars or even just cigarettes. Some mentally ill are so sick they self-medicate with illegal drugs, many of whom were raised in environments where this was considered normal behavior. We can correct their behavior and help heal our communities. We can and must start now. Creativity and problem solving flow from within us. This is why brainstorming with others is so beneficial. The positive energy flowing from all, results in a symphony of solutions.

It is everyone's birthright to achieve their full potential in life. Maslow's famous "Hierarchy of needs" begins with oxygen and water and ends with the need for spiritual and psychological fulfillment. We should be trying as a society to produce more people who have achieved a blend of psychological health and devotion to their work that results in them being highly effective.[395]

Change your mind about mental illness and you can change many lives. You can change many, many lives. Justice is that mysterious phenomenon which corrects the wrongs of mankind. Justice is mercy for those who deserve it and justice is swift and uncompromising punishment for those who do not.

Perhaps in that perfect future world, we will all have Sim cards/flash drive-like devices with intelligence from all of our ancestors and more, at least the basic knowledge all humans should know how to live comfortably together. Until then we will brainstorm together to make a better world. Brainstorming is most effective when there is a diversity of ideas. Brainstorming can be done on an individual basis. Brainstorming for a better tomorrow. . . Until then, we are all doing time together. John Donne wrote "Ask not for whom the bell tolls, it tolls for thee."

If everything were fair, humans would not eat meat or destroy plants. Birds could not eat worms. Cats could not eat mice. Life as we know it would cease to exist in just a matter of days. While in reality a totally fair system of complete justice for all has never existed, we still strive for it, and by working together we can live in a better world. Until we reach that perfect, futuristic world- remember that too many people in a program reduces its effectiveness. If you dilute the penicillin-everyone dies. Until we reach that Utopia, save the ones you can. Do not waste the medicine.

We must all work together to make the ideas contained in this work herein so commonplace as to be obsolete. And we must strive for a day when we marvel that any ideas contained here were novel.

The main thing is to make the main thing, the main thing.

---

[395] Abraham Maslow *The Farther Reaches of Human Nature* (1971).

And the main thing here is to reduce recidivism, inject humanity into the corrections system, and save money by infusing the system with proven science and evidence based procedures. As with many of the world's problems, the solution lies in love, respect, empathy and understanding. In the high calling of our daily work, do we want to be prisoners of the past or pioneers of the future? The best way to predict the future is to create it. History will show we were right. Make history. We can do it through collaboration, brainstorming, WORK-whatever you want to call it. Begin . . . the rest is easy.

"Our task now is not to fix the blame for the past, but to fix the course for the future."
John F. Kennedy

"The future belongs to those who believe in the beauty of their dreams."
Eleanor Roosevelt

ACKNOWLEDGMENTS

After years of drafting outlines for speeches, protocols, news releases, budgets, lectures etc. it made sense to put the information in one source. The book began to take shape. As there was no book on the best way to manage mentally ill defendants, this one was started for my own use. Thanks to Clara Hodge, Steve Hodge, Debra Lay, Stacy Blake, Michael Dailey, Larry Mayfield, Dr. Dave Bunger J.D., PhD., Rev. Bob Massey, Judge Dominique Collins, Rev. Karla Akins, Martin Peterson, Betty Marshall, Bob Jones, Dr. Pat Ledbetter, Angela Chaparro, Ken, Craig Hodge, Malena Calderon, Kristen, Michael Ware, Terri Moore, Craig Watkins, Russell Wilson, Susanna Cord, Andrea, Robert Fuller, Jennifer Savage, Alex Cord, Wendy Risinger, Margie Bienstock, Tyler Boaz, Dave Bunger, Roger Johnson, Denise Campbell, Dr. Christian Carr, Dr, Neil Rosen, Nick Wale Angie Croucher, Doris Studer, Agnes, Dr. Margie York, Barbara Jones, Karen Stewart, Debbie Sicking, Dr. Mehmet Oz, Dr. Daniel Amen, Taylor, Wayne Zatopek, Thomas Bernstein, Lisa McMinn, Doug Sword, Lee Pierson, Lisa Tanner, Missy Wolfe, Judge Brent Carr, Courtney Young, Ron Stretcher, John Carlough, Kendall McKimmey, Bryan Smith, Michael Cole, David Stokes, Judge Don Jones, Dr. William Lawrence, Alan Nash, Kelly Puls, Lynn Richardson, Matthew Perry, Martin Sheen, Kristen Johnston, Douglas Marlowe, Steve Hanson, Robert Stutman, Antonio Banderas, Jimmy Fallon; all those dedicated professionals operating drug, mental health and specialty courts, and many more.

APPENDIX

RESOURCES FOR MENTAL HEALTH / websites, phone numbers

NAMI.org National Alliance on Mental Illness 1-800-950-NAMI (6264)
Drugfreeworld.org (how to talk to children)
samhsa.gov/recovery/ or http://recoverymonth.gov/ (Peer recovery resources in your community)

Dial 211 for 60,0000 services available in Texas through Health and Human Resources.

Others:
A careful mind.org
AA alternatives, Alternatives to AA/NA: non religious community based alternative to AA
     Smartrecovery.org
     Unhooked.com
     Cfiwest.org
ADAPT Mental Health and Mobile Crisis Team for mental health or substance abuse crisis (also known as the NorthStar Mobile Crisis Team) 866-260-8000 or 972 -233-8336
ADHL.org Alcohol and Drug abuse Hot Line (sources, videos, contacts . . .)
Aftermath 800 -366 -9923
Adult and Child Adult Protective 214 252 5400
     Txabusehotline.org
Lib.ada.washington.edu/instruments/ Alcohol and Drug Abuse Institute Library (complementary needs assessments)
Alzheimer's Helpline 800 -272272 -39003900
AuthenticHappiness.org
Boardinghome.org - (for licensed boarding homes for the homeless)
     homeforbasehousing.org
Dallasda.com/mental-health/
     community resources;

      companies that hire felons;
      housing resource guide
      defense attorney checklist;
      resources for mental health/websites

Enterhealth.com 800 388 4601 treatment for alcohol and drug addiction, one of the better websites, get on their list and they will send you information on occasion)

www.ipsyc.com (Educational programs for a number of behavioral health issues can be played on a patient's iPod).

Gainscenter.samhsa.gov/pdfs/disorders/screeningAndAssessment.pdf (complementary needs assessments)

gaincc.org/products-services/instruments-reports/
      Global Appraisal of Individual Needs

Mentalhealthamerica.org

http://www.mentalhealthamerica.net/ has on-line screening for mental health

Mentalhealthfirstaid.org

Mental Health Information Resource Center 1-888-826-9438

MetroCareServices.org (MHMR for Dallas) 214 -283-2121

MOB - Mothers Opposing Bullying

1 800 national hotline, especially as it regards social media (#1 portal for human trafficking) Suicide is not an option Follows up with counseling

Nami.org National Alliance on Mental Illness or specifically NAMIDALLAS.ORG

National Center for Victims of Crime 202 467 8716 (for attorney referrals)

Ncpc.org National Crime Prevention Council (public awareness, best practices, etc.)

NADCP.org
      National Association of Drug Court Professionals
      TADCP.org

NCADD.org/for-youth/233 National Council on Alcohol and Drug Dependence NCSTL.org National Clearinghouse for Science, Technology and the Law
      (Have DVD of lectures available for free)

Ncadi.samsha.gov (has prevention programs)

NCADI – National Clearinghouse of Alcohol and Drug Information

1 800 829 6686

NDCRC.org – National Drug Court Resource Center (free webinars, drug court research, forms, policies, contracts, Research articles, etc)

NewFriendsNewLife.org – gets women out of the sex trade. They need career women mentors. Joyce Shupe

Niaaa.nih.gov -National Institute on Alcohol Abuse and Alcoholism (has prevention programs)

Nih.gov - National Institute of Health (Has prevention programs)

Nida.nih.gov - National Institute on Drug Abuse (has prevention programs)

NorthTexashelp.com; HereForYouth.com;

NRCC-pad.org national Resource Center on Psychiatric Advance Directives

MilesOfFreedom.com (resources after prison)

PeaceOfMind.com; For OCD Dr Elizabeth McIngvale; Iocdf.org

Rape, Abuse, and Incest National Network 1-800 -656 -4673

SAMHSA - Substance Abuse and Mental Health Services Administration.

> http://www.samhsa.gov/find-help/national-helpline - to find a therapist in your area
> Or call 1-800-662-HELP (4357)
> This site has literature on:
> *What Is Substance Abuse Treatment? A Booklet for Families*
> Created for family members of people with alcohol abuse or drug abuse problems. Answers questions about substance abuse, its symptoms, different types of treatment, and recovery. Addresses concerns of children of parents with substance use/abuse problems.
> *Alcohol and Drug Addiction Happens in the Best of Families*
> Describes how alcohol and drug addiction affect the whole family. Explains how substance abuse treatment works, how family interventions can be a first step to recovery, and how to help children in families affected by alcohol abuse and drug abuse.
> *It's Not Your Fault (NACoA)*
> Assures teens with parents who abuse alcohol or drugs that,

"It's not your fault!" and that they are not alone. Encourages teens to seek emotional support from other adults, school counselors, and youth support groups such as Alateen, and provides a resource list.

It Feels So Bad: It Doesn't Have To

Provides information about alcohol and drug addiction to children whose parents or friends' parents might have substance abuse problems. Advises kids to take care of themselves by communicating about the problem and joining support groups such as Alateen.

After an Attempt: A Guide for Taking Care of Your Family Member After Treatment in the Emergency Department

Aids family members in coping with the aftermath of a relative's suicide attempt. Describes the emergency department treatment process, lists questions to ask about follow-up treatment, and describes how to reduce risk and ensure safety at home.

Family Therapy Can Help: For People in Recovery From Mental Illness or Addiction

Explores the role of family therapy in recovery from mental illness or substance abuse. Explains how family therapy sessions are run and who conducts them, describes a typical session, and provides information on its effectiveness in recovery.

StepUpTogether.org a National Initiative to reduce the number of people with mental illness in jails

Stoprxdrugabuse.org (Developmental Model of Recovery)

Suicide and Crisis Center Hot Line 214 -828 -1000

TexasSuicidePrevention.org

Transicareinc.com (A private, for profit provider of non-emergency behavioral-health transportation services Telephone: 214.342.5800)

Web therapy:

     PrettyPaddedRoom.com

     Breakthrough.com

WeHelpOurselves.org (teaching children how to avoid victimization)

Nrepp.samhsa.gov
Ev based practices.

Mindtools.com teaches leadership, problem solving, decision making etc
U.S. Substance Abuse and Mental Health Services Administration (SAMHSA)

For criminal justice professionals:
AllRISE.org (drug courts)
Learning.csgjustice.org (To develop a mental health court)

About 100 system websites, for HHSC for example:
HHSC — "Your Texas Benefits": www.yourtexasbenefits.com
DADS — "Long Term Care Quality Reporting System": http://facilityquality.dads.state.tx.us
DFPS — "Help for Parents, Hope for Kids": www.helpandhope.org
DSHS — "Speak Your Mind": www.speakyourmindtexas.org and

"Healthy Texas Babies": www.healthytexasbabies.com

About 28 system hotlines, for example:
DADS — consumer rights and services
DFPS — statewide intake for abuse, neglect, or exploitation
DSHS — numerous public health hotlines such as partnership for a drug free America, vaccine questions, and helplines for health services programs like women's health
HHSC — many hotlines for services

The Family Place - Domestic Violence 214 -941 -1991 1991

NDCI.org (drug testing)

Erowid.com (information about drugs)

myconsumerTeam.com

National Center for PTSD

Ptsd.va.gov
Istss.org
Isst-d.org
Ptsd.va.gov/professional/ptsd101/course-modules.asp

Rachelschallenge.org to equip elementary, middle and highschools with tools to extend kindness
Choosekind.tumblr.com – to prevent bullying

RESOURCES FOR PROSECUTORS

American Society of Crime Laboratory Directors / Laboratory Accreditation Board
The American Society of Crime Laboratory Directors/Laboratory Accreditation Board is a not-for-profit organization specializing in the accreditation of public and private crime laboratories.
http://www.ascld-lab.org/

Arizona Forensic Science Academy
The Academy is the first of its kind in the United States and has been hailed as a model for other states to follow. The Basic Academy offers instruction on topics that include DNA, toxicology, controlled substances, crime scene analysis, fingerprints, ballistics, digital evidence, and death investigations. The Advanced Academy offers more in-depth training in the areas of DNA, ballistics, and fingerprints.
https://www.azag.gov/azfsac/academy

Association of Prosecuting Attorneys
The Association of Prosecuting Attorneys is a non-profit organization and a "think tank" for prosecutors. They have recently published a framework for the "high performance" prosecutor that includes "integrating the progression of forensic science and technology into criminal investigations and trial courtrooms."
www.APAinc.org

National Forensic Science Technology Center
A resource for non-scientists, the website covers the core concepts, capabilities, and limitations of key forensic science disciplines.
www.ForensicScienceSimplified.org

Scientific Working Groups
Since the early 1990s, American and international forensic science laboratories and practitioners have collaborated in Scientific Working Groups (SWGs) to improve discipline practices and build

consensus standards. For a list of working group web sites, visit: https://www.fiswg.org/about_swgs

Strengthening Forensic Science in the United States: A Path Forward
This report published by the National Academies Press in 2009 provides an overview of the forensic sciences and recommendations for improvement.
www.ncjrs.gov/pdffiles1/nij/grants/228091.pdf.

Resources
Educational programs for a number of behavioral health issues can be played on a patient's iPod (see www.ipsyc.com). As Ron Paul suggests in his book *The School Revolution: A New Answer for Our Broken Education System* (2013) about how to improve education in America, training should be videotaped and then made a part of the core curriculum for police academies, prosecution courses, judicial training, etc. Such classes should be available on the web. This is the most efficient and practical way to deliver this message and education.

Numerous sites around the country are using telepsychiatry, in which a psychiatrist uses remote computer technology to interview and assess patients directly and either directly provides treatment or provides consultation to the patient's primary care physician.

The Health Buddy System is a primary care practice serves a large indigent population that struggles with adherence to treatment and attendance at follow-up appointments. The system gives patients a mini-computer like apparatus that connects to their telephone at home. Each day, the Health Buddy displays questions about the patient's condition. The patient inputs his or her responses, which are monitored by the primary care office via the Internet. The Health Buddy can remind patients to take medication and suggest self-management techniques. Programs have been developed for a number of behavioral health issues (see www.healthbuddy.com).

Cindy Stormer

INSANITY RELEASE ORDER

Resolution

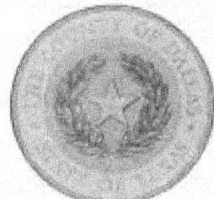

ORDER NO. 2015-0932

DATE: July 7, 2015

STATE OF TEXAS §

COUNTY OF DALLAS §

"Stepping Up Initiative to Reduce the Number of People with Mental Illnesses in Jails"

BE IT REMEMBERED, at a regular meeting of the Commissioners Court of Dallas County, Texas, held on the 7th day of July, 2015 on motion made by ___Dr. Elba Garcia, Commissioner of District 4___ and seconded by ___Dr. Theresa Daniel, Commissioner of District 1___ the following resolution was adopted:

WHEREAS, Counties routinely provide treatment services to the estimated 2 million people with serious mental illnesses booked into jail each year. Prevalence rates of serious mental illnesses in jails are three to six times higher than for the general population; and

WHEREAS, Almost three-quarters of adults with serious mental illnesses in jails have co-occurring substance use disorder. Adults with mental illnesses tend to stay longer in jail and upon release are at a higher risk of recidivism than people without these disorders; and

WHEREAS, County jails spend two to three times more on adults with mental illnesses who require interventions compared to those without these treatment needs. Without the appropriate treatment and services, people with mental illnesses continue to cycle through the criminal justice system, often resulting in tragic outcomes for these individuals and their families; and

WHEREAS, Dallas County values the integration of physical and behavioral healthcare while recognizing the social determinants of health and takes pride in their responsibility to protect and enhance the health, welfare and safety of its residents in efficient and cost-effective ways; and

WHEREAS, Dallas County has several collaborative policy and planning groups designed to reduce and divert the mentally ill in jail such as the Behavioral Health Leadership Team, the Behavioral Health Steering Committee, the Behavioral Health Housing Work Group, the Criminal Justice Advisory Board, and Jail Population Committee; and

WHEREAS, Dallas County has various initiatives that include Mental Health and Substance Abuse Specialty/Diversion Courts, designated Public Defender/District Attorney Mental Health Teams, Pre Book-in Diversion programs, Crisis Intervention and Mobile Crisis Teams, as well as the Crisis Services/1115 Waiver Project, the Competency Restoration Units, Parkland Correctional Health Program, Jail Instant Messaging which provides real-time data matching book-in and behavioral health utilization, the Serial Inebriate Program, and the Forensic Mental Health Diversion Program; and

WHEREAS, Dallas County embraces the national initiative Stepping Up, created by the National Association of Counties, the Council of State Governments Justice Center and the American Psychiatric Foundation, designed to encourage public, private and nonprofit partners to reduce the number of people with mental illnesses in jails.

NOW, THEREFORE BE IT RESOLVED THAT the Dallas County Commissioners Court does hereby sign on to the Call to Action to reduce the number of people with mental illnesses in our county jail, commit to sharing lessons learned with other counties in Texas and across the country to support a national initiative and encourage all county officials, employees and residents to participate in Stepping Up. Dallas County resolves to utilize the comprehensive resources available through Stepping Up to support:

- A diverse team of leaders and decision makers from multiple agencies committed to safely reducing the number of people with mental illnesses in jails.
- Collecting and reviewing prevalence numbers and assessing individuals' needs to better identify adults entering jails with mental illnesses and their recidivism risk, and use that baseline information to guide decision making at the system, program, and case levels.
- Examining the treatment and service capacity to determine which programs and services are available in the county for people with mental illnesses and co-occurring substance use disorders, and identifying state and local policy and funding barriers to minimizing contact with the justice system and providing treatment and supports in the community.
- Developing a plan with measurable outcomes that draws on the jail assessment and prevalence data and the examination of available treatment and service capacity, while considering identified barriers.
- Implementing research-based approaches to develop best practices and alternative programs that advance the goal of reducing the number of mentally ill and substance abuse inmates in the jail and the criminal justice system.
- Creating a process to track progress using data and information systems, and to report on successes.

DONE IN OPEN COURT, this 7th day of July, 2015.

Clay Lewis Jenkins, County Judge   Dr. Theresa M. Daniel, District 1   Mike Cantrell, District 2

John Wiley Price, District 3   Dr. Elba Garcia, District 4

(Form for an Insanity Release Order – to monitor a defendant after they are being released from a mental institution)

The Defendant thinks alternately that the Defendant is the President, a vampire, Batman, Satan, and bearing God's child. And that someone is putting drugs in the Defendant's medication that is causing the Defendant's bowels to back up into their head causing them to have bad breath. Defendant claims the Defendant is a prophet and goes by the alias of "Sweet Peaches", chips have has been implanted in the Defendant's head resulting in the monitoring of the defendant's thoughts and theft of the Defendant's original music, the CIA is manipulating the defendant's finances, and exploiting the defendant sexually. All of this is being broadcast live on the internet. Defendant has frequently been found dancing naked in the jail. The defendant has a lengthy history of mental illness, including a self-reported "Schizodefective disorder", and has been committed to various mental health facilities in the past).

II. No Weapons

There shall be no weapons in the residence where [Defendant] resides; and [Defendant] is not to be around weapons under any circumstances per the Texas Government Code (ineligible to carry a weapon due to a psychiatric disorder or has entered into a judgment of not guilty by reason of insanity). Tex. Gov. Code § 411.172. (d)

III. Further Conditions
Further Conditions Of Release For [Defendant] are:

- Live at _____ house;
- Follow the rules of that residence;
- Not consume or possess alcohol or illegal drugs;
- Take his medicine as directed by a doctor;
- Report to the Mental Health Coordinator, once per month;
- Follow the directions of the assigned Metrocare case manager;
- Continue psychiatric medication and treatment as prescribed by Dallas Metrocare Services;

- Keeping all scheduled appointments with Metrocare Services of Dallas County;
- Meet with the case manager and the ACT team as scheduled by Dallas Metrocare Services;
- Have [Defendant]'s medication regimen supervised by _____;
- Have no contact with _____ until further order of this court;
- Have no contact with the children of _____ until further order of this court;
- No unsupervised visits with any children until further order of this court;
- Attend alcoholics anonymous and narcotics anonymous programs ___ per week until further order of this court;
- Obtain and maintain employment;
- No associations with persons who deal illegal narcotics or who engage in criminal activity;
- Report to the court monthly; and
- [Defendant] shall have periodic alcohol and drug screening to ensure abstinence.

[Defendant] is advised that "The jurisdiction of the court over a person (found not guilty by reason of insanity) terminates on the date when the cumulative total period of institutionalization and outpatient community-based treatment and supervision imposed . . . equals the maximum term of imprisonment provided by law for the offense of which the person was acquitted by reason of insanity." 46C.269 CCP In this case that would be LIFE.

Tex. Code Crim. Proc. art. 16 and 17

Art. 16.22. EARLY IDENTIFICATION OF DEFENDANT SUSPECTED OF HAVING MENTAL ILLNESS OR MENTAL RETARDATION.

(a)   (1) Not later than 72 hours after receiving credible information that may establish reasonable cause to believe that a defendant committed to the sheriff's custody has a mental illness or is a person with mental retardation, including observation of the defendant's behavior immediately before, during, and after the defendant's arrest and the results of any previous assessment of the defendant, *the sheriff shall provide* written or electronic notice of the information to the magistrate. On a determination that there is reasonable cause to believe that the defendant has a mental illness or is a person with mental retardation, the magistrate, except as provided by Subdivision (2), shall order the local mental health or mental retardation authority or another qualified mental health or mental retardation expert to:

> (A) collect information regarding whether the defendant has a mental illness as defined by Section 571.003, Health and Safety Code, or is a person with mental retardation as defined by Section 591.003, Health and Safety Code, including information obtained from any previous assessment of the defendant; and
>
> (B) provide to the magistrate a written assessment of the information collected under Paragraph (A).

(2) The magistrate is not required to order the collection of information under Subdivision (1) if the defendant in the year preceding the defendant's applicable date of arrest has been determined to have a mental illness or to be a person with mental retardation by the local mental health or mental retardation authority or another mental health or mental retardation expert described by Subdivision (1). A court that elects to use the results of that previous determination may proceed under Subsection (c).

(3) If the defendant fails or refuses to submit to the collection of information regarding the defendant as required under Subdivision (1), the magistrate may order the defendant to submit to an examination in a mental health facility determined to be appropriate by the local mental health or mental retardation authority for a reasonable period not to exceed 21 days. The magistrate may order a defendant to a facility operated by the Department of State Health Services or the Department of Aging and Disability Services for examination only on request of the local mental health or mental retardation authority and with the consent of the head of the facility. If a defendant who has been ordered to a facility operated by the Department of State Health Services or the Department of Aging and Disability Services for examination remains in the facility for a period exceeding 21 days, the head of that facility shall cause the defendant to be immediately transported to the committing court and placed in the custody of the sheriff of the county in which the committing court is located. That county shall reimburse the facility for the mileage and per diem expenses of the personnel required to transport the defendant calculated in accordance with the state travel regulations in effect at the time.

(b) A written assessment of the information collected under Subsection (a)(1)(A) shall be provided to the magistrate not later than the 30th day after the date of any order issued under Subsection (a) in a felony case and not later than the 10th day after the date of any order issued under that subsection in a misdemeanor case, and the magistrate shall provide copies of the written assessment to the defense counsel, the prosecuting attorney, and the trial court. The written assessment must include a description of the procedures used in the collection of information under Subsection (a)(1)(A) and the applicable expert's observations and findings pertaining to:

(1) whether the defendant is a person who has a mental illness or is a person with mental retardation;

(2) whether there is clinical evidence to support a belief that the defendant may be incompetent to stand trial and

should undergo a complete competency examination under Subchapter B, Chapter 46B; and

(3) recommended treatment.

(c) After the trial court receives the applicable expert's written assessment relating to the defendant under Subsection (b) or elects to use the results of a previous determination as described by Subsection (a)(2), the trial court may, as applicable:

> (1) resume criminal proceedings against the defendant, including any appropriate proceedings related to the defendant's release on personal bond under Article 17.032;
>
> (2) resume or initiate competency proceedings, if required, as provided by Chapter 46B or other proceedings affecting the defendant's receipt of appropriate court-ordered mental health or mental retardation services, including proceedings related to the defendant's receipt of outpatient mental health services under Section 574.034, Health and Safety Code; or
>
> (3) consider the written assessment during the punishment phase after a conviction of the offense for which the defendant was arrested, as part of a presentence investigation report, or in connection with the impositions of conditions following placement on community supervision, including deferred adjudication community supervision.

(d) This article does not prevent the applicable court from, before, during, or after the collection of information regarding the defendant as described by this article:

> (1) releasing a mentally ill or mentally retarded defendant from custody on personal or surety bond; or
>
> (2) ordering an examination regarding the defendant's competency to stand trial.

(emphasis added)

Art. 17.032. RELEASE ON PERSONAL BOND OF CERTAIN MENTALLY ILL DEFENDANTS.

(a) In this article, "violent offense" means an offense under the following sections of the Penal Code:

(1) Section 19.02 (murder);

(2) Section 19.03 (capital murder);

(3) Section 20.03 (kidnapping);

(4) Section 20.04 (aggravated kidnapping);

(5) Section 21.11 (indecency with a child);

(6) Section 22.01(a)(1) (assault);

(7) Section 22.011 (sexual assault);

(8) Section 22.02 (aggravated assault);

(9) Section 22.021 (aggravated sexual assault);

(10) Section 22.04 (injury to a child, elderly individual, or disabled individual);

(11) Section 29.03 (aggravated robbery);

(12) Section 21.02 (continuous sexual abuse of young child or children); or

(13) Section 20A.03 (continuous trafficking of persons).

(b) A magistrate shall release a defendant on personal bond unless good cause is shown otherwise if the:

(1) defendant is not charged with and has not been previously convicted of a violent offense;

(2) defendant is examined by the local mental health or mental retardation authority or another mental health expert under Article 16.22 of this code;

(3) applicable expert, in a written assessment submitted to the magistrate under Article 16.22:

(A) concludes that the defendant has a mental illness or is a person with mental retardation and is nonetheless competent to stand trial; and

(B) recommends mental health treatment for the defendant; and

(4) magistrate determines, in consultation with the local mental health or mental retardation authority, that appropriate community-based mental health or mental

retardation services for the defendant are available through the Texas Department of Mental Health and Mental Retardation under Section 534.053, Health and Safety Code, or through another mental health or mental retardation services provider.

(c) The magistrate, unless good cause is shown for not requiring treatment, shall require as a condition of release on personal bond under this article that the defendant submit to outpatient or inpatient mental health or mental retardation treatment as recommended by the local mental health or mental retardation authority if the defendant's:

(1) mental illness or mental retardation is chronic in nature; or

(2) ability to function independently will continue to deteriorate if the defendant is not treated.

(d) In addition to a condition of release imposed under Subsection (c) of this article, the magistrate may require the defendant to comply with other conditions that are reasonably necessary to protect the community.

(e) In this article, a person is considered to have been convicted of an offense if:

(1) a sentence is imposed;

(2) the person is placed on community supervision or receives deferred adjudication; or

(3) the court defers final disposition of the case.

Tex. Code Crim. Proc. art. 46C.253. Hearing on Disposition

(a) The hearing on disposition shall be conducted in the same manner as a hearing on an application for involuntary commitment under Subtitle C or D, Title 7, Health and Safety Code, except that the use of a jury is governed by Article 46C.255.

(b) At the hearing, the court shall address:

(1) whether the person acquitted by reason of insanity has a severe mental illness or mental retardation;

(2) whether as a result of any mental illness or mental retardation the person is likely to cause serious harm to another; and

(3) whether appropriate treatment and supervision for any mental illness or mental retardation rendering the person dangerous to another can be safely and effectively provided as outpatient or community-based treatment and supervision.

(c) The court shall order the acquitted person committed for inpatient treatment or residential care under Article 46C.256 if the grounds required for that order are established.

(d) The court shall order the acquitted person to receive outpatient or community-based treatment and supervision under Article 46C.257 if the grounds required for that order are established.

(e) The court shall order the acquitted person transferred to an appropriate court for proceedings under Subtitle C or D, Title 7, Health and Safety Code, if the state fails to establish the grounds required for an order under Article 46C.256 or 46C.257 but the evidence provides a reasonable basis for believing the acquitted person is a proper subject for those proceedings.

(f) The court shall order the acquitted person discharged and immediately released if the evidence fails to establish that disposition under Subsection (c), (d), or (e) is appropriate.

OUTPATIENT COMPETENCY RESTORATION

Art. 46B.071. OPTIONS ON DETERMINATION OF INCOMPETENCY.

(a) Except as provided by Subsection (b), on a determination that a defendant is incompetent to stand trial, the court shall:
> (1) commit the defendant to a facility under Article 46B.073; or
> (2) release the defendant on bail under Article 46B.072.

(b) On a determination that a defendant is incompetent to stand trial and is unlikely to be restored to competency in the foreseeable future, the court shall:
> (1) proceed under Subchapter E (Civil Commitment charges Pending) or F (Civil Commitment Dismissal); or
> (2) release the defendant on bail as permitted under Chapter 17.

Art. 46B.072. Release on Bail

(a) Subject to conditions reasonably related to assuring public safety and the effectiveness of the defendant's treatment, if the court determines that a defendant found incompetent to stand trial is not a danger to others and may be safely treated on an outpatient basis with the specific objective of attaining competency to stand trial and if an appropriate outpatient treatment program is available for the defendant, the court:
> (1) may release on bail a defendant found incompetent to stand trial with respect to a felony or may continue the defendant's release on bail; and
> (2) shall release on bail a defendant found incompetent to stand trial with respect to a misdemeanor or shall continue the defendant's release on bail.

(b) The court shall order a defendant released on bail under Subsection (a) to participate in an outpatient treatment program for a period not to exceed 120 days.

(c) Notwithstanding Subsection (a), the court may order a defendant to participate in an outpatient treatment program under this article only if:

> (1) the court receives and approves a comprehensive plan that:
>
>> (A) provides for the treatment of the defendant for purposes of competency restoration; and
>> (B) identifies the person who will be responsible for providing that treatment to the defendant; and
>
> (2) the court finds that the treatment proposed by the plan will be available to and will be provided to the defendant.

(d) An order issued under this article may require the defendant to participate in:

> (1) as appropriate, an outpatient treatment program administered by a community center or an outpatient treatment program administered by any other entity that provides outpatient competency restoration services; and
> (2) an appropriate prescribed regimen of medical, psychiatric, or psychological care or treatment, including care or treatment involving the administration of psychoactive medication, including those required under Article 46B.086.

WEAPONS AND THE MENTALLY ILL

411.172 Government Code
§ 411.172. Eligibility
(a) A person is eligible for a license to carry a concealed handgun if the person:

. . .

(d) For purposes of Subsection (a)(7), a person is incapable of exercising sound judgment with respect to the proper use and storage of a handgun if the person:
b) For the purposes of this section, an offense under the laws of this state, another state, or the United States is:

> (1) except as provided by Subsection (b-1), a felony if the offense, at the time the offense is committed:
>
>> (A) is designated by a law of this state as a felony;
>> (B) contains all the elements of an offense designated by a law of this state as a felony; or
>> (C) is punishable by confinement for one year or more in a penitentiary; and
>
> (2) a Class A misdemeanor if the offense is not a felony and confinement in a jail other than a state jail felony facility is affixed as a possible punishment.

(b-1) An offense is not considered a felony for purposes of Subsection (b) if, at the time of a person's application for a license to carry a concealed handgun, the offense:

> (1) is not designated by a law of this state as a felony; and
> (2) does not contain all the elements of any offense designated by a law of this state as a felony.

. . .

> (1) has been diagnosed by a licensed physician as suffering from a psychiatric disorder or condition that causes or is likely to cause substantial impairment in judgment, mood, perception, impulse control, or intellectual ability;
> (2) suffers from a psychiatric disorder or condition described by Subdivision (1) that:
>
>> (A) is in remission but is reasonably likely to redevelop at a future time; or
>> (B) requires continuous medical treatment to avoid

redevelopment;

(3) has been diagnosed by a licensed physician, determined by a review board or similar authority, or declared by a court to be incompetent to manage the person's own affairs; or

(4) has entered in a criminal proceeding a plea of not guilty by reason of insanity.

(e) The following constitutes evidence that a person has a psychiatric disorder or condition described by Subsection (d)(1):

(1) involuntary psychiatric hospitalization;

(2) psychiatric hospitalization;

(3) inpatient or residential substance abuse treatment in the preceding five-year period;

(4) diagnosis in the preceding five-year period by a licensed physician that the person is dependent on alcohol, a controlled substance, or a similar substance; or

(5) diagnosis at any time by a licensed physician that the person suffers or has suffered from a psychiatric disorder or condition consisting of or relating to:

(A) schizophrenia or delusional disorder;

(B) bipolar disorder;

(C) chronic dementia, whether caused by illness, brain defect, or brain injury;

(D) dissociative identity disorder;

(E) intermittent explosive disorder; or

(F) antisocial personality disorder.

(f) Notwithstanding Subsection (d), a person who has previously been diagnosed as suffering from a psychiatric disorder or condition described by Subsection (d) or listed in Subsection (e) is not because of that disorder or condition incapable of exercising sound judgment with respect to the proper use and storage of a handgun if the person provides the department with a certificate from a licensed physician whose primary practice is in the field of psychiatry stating that the psychiatric disorder or condition is in remission and is not reasonably likely to develop at a future time.

Brady Handgun Violence Prevention Act 18 USC 922 (effective 1986), federally, someone with a diminished mental capacity (mentally ill) can have his/her firearms taken

Title VII of the Omnibus Crime Control and Safe Streets Act of 1968, 18 U.S.C. App. § 1202(a)(1) (1968), amended by Firearms Owners' Protection Act of 1986, Pub. L. No. 99-308, § 104(b), 100 Stat. 449, 459 (current version at 18 U.S.C. § 922(a)(1)(A)).
Title VII of the Omnibus Crime Control and Safe Streets Act of 1968, 18 U.S.C. App. § 1202(a)(1) (1968), amended by Firearms Owners' Protection Act of 1986, Pub. L. No. 99-308, § 104(b), 100 Stat. 449, 459 (current version at 18 U.S.C. § 922(a)(1)(A)).

18 U.S.C.S § 922(d) and 27 C.F.R. § 178.99(c) prohibit licensed dealers from selling firearms or ammunition to a person whom the dealer knows or has reasonable cause to believe has been adjudicated mentally defective or has been committed to any mental institution.

Forfeiture Statute 59.01 CCP Subsection 2 defines contraband – does not address mere possession
18.19 – disposition of prohibited weapons

Health & Safety Code § 614.017. Exchange of Information

(a) An agency shall:

(1) accept information relating to a special needs offender or a juvenile with a mental impairment that is sent to the agency to serve the purposes of continuity of care and services regardless of whether other state law makes that information confidential; and

(2) disclose information relating to a special needs offender or a juvenile with a mental impairment, including information about the offender's or juvenile's identity, needs, treatment, social, criminal, and vocational history, supervision status and compliance with conditions of supervision, and medical and mental health history, if the disclosure serves the purposes of continuity of care and services.

(b) Information obtained under this section may not be used as evidence in any juvenile or criminal proceeding, unless obtained and introduced by other lawful evidentiary means.

(c) In this section:

(1) "Agency" includes any of the following entities and individuals, a person with an agency relationship with one of the following entities or individuals, and a person who contracts with one or more of the following entities or individuals:

(A) the Texas Department of Criminal Justice and the Correctional Managed Health Care Committee;

(B) the Board of Pardons and Paroles;

(C) the Department of State Health Services;

(D) the Texas Juvenile Justice Department;

(E) the Department of Assistive and Rehabilitative Services;

(F) the Texas Education Agency;

(G) the Commission on Jail Standards;

(H) the Department of Aging and Disability Services;

(I) the Texas School for the Blind and Visually Impaired;

(J) community supervision and corrections departments and local juvenile probation departments;

(K) personal bond pretrial release offices established under Article 17.42, Code of Criminal Procedure;

(L) local jails regulated by the Commission on Jail Standards;

(M) a municipal or county health department;

(N) a hospital district;

(O) a judge of this state with jurisdiction over juvenile or criminal cases;

(P) an attorney who is appointed or retained to represent a special needs offender or a juvenile with a mental impairment;

(Q) the Health and Human Services Commission;

(R) the Department of Information Resources;

(S) the bureau of identification and records of the Department of Public Safety, for the sole purpose of providing real-time, contemporaneous identification of individuals in the Department of State Health Services client data base; and

(T) the Department of Family and Protective Services.

(2) "Special needs offender" includes an individual for whom criminal charges are pending or who after conviction or adjudication is in custody or under any form of criminal justice supervision.

(3) "Juvenile with a mental impairment" means a juvenile with a mental impairment in the juvenile justice system.

(d) An agency shall manage confidential information accepted or disclosed under this section prudently so as to maintain, to the extent possible, the confidentiality of that information.

(e) A person commits an offense if the person releases or discloses confidential information obtained under this section for purposes other than continuity of care and services, except as authorized by other law or by the consent of the person to whom the information relates. An offense under this subsection is a Class B misdemeanor.

ABBREVIATIONS MENTAL HEALTH

1115 Waiver —This is a plan which allows the federal government to match NorthSTAR funding for
      MH programs.

ABC —ABC Behavioral Healthcare (ABC is just put on the front of the name and is not an
      acronym for anything) (Kim Carson doesn't know what this stands for but it is like
      LIFENET) in Mesquite

ADAPT —(acronym stands for nothing) provides services. See above for more detailed
      description.

ACS —Adapt Community Solutions

ACT —Assertive Community Team, intensive MH services for the most severely impaired
      They must have been to the hospital to qualify for this.

ALF —Assisted living facility

AOT —Assisted Outpatient Treatment

APAA —Association of Persons affected by Addiction, 3116 Martin Luther King Blvd Dallas,
      Texas 75215 Phone: 214 -6342722 Fax: 214-6342721
      Email: www.apaarecovery.org

ASP —Alternate Sentencing Program

ATLAS —Achieving True Liberty and Success - Defendants on felony probation that have
      violated the terms of probation are eligible for this program.

BHHWG —Behavioral Health Housing Work Group

BHO —Behavioral Health Organization (Value Options)

BIPP —Batterer's Intervention Program. A more intense program than the Anger
      Management program. It lasts 24 weeks.

BNO —Book in number
BO status —Behavior observation
BOT —A computer program system that automatically provides the names of anyone in jail
who has previously been a NorthSTAR client.
CAST-MR —The competence assessment for standing trial for defendants with mental retardation
CATS —Comprehensive Assessment Treatment Services - evaluates defendants for problems
that might interfere with the successful completion of probation
CAT —computerized axial tomography
CBT —Cognitive Behavioral Therapy
CE or CME —Certificate of Medical Examination
CD —Conditional dismissal
CD —Chemical dependency
CSH —Corporation for Supportive Housing
CIT —Crisis Intervention Team. Officers and non-officers specially trained for
intervention. Ron Cowart, Asst Manager 214 671 3496 DPD
CM —Contingency Management
COPSD —Co-occurring Psychiatric and Substance Use Disorders
CSP —Crisis Services Project
CRCG —Community Resource Coordination Group – The Bridge and includes ABC
Behavioral Health, Turtle Creek Recovery Center, Adult Protective Services, Value
Options, Metrocare, Lifenet Texas, Parkland Homes, Veteran's Administration, City
of Dallas Crisis Intervention Team, Reach of Dallas, Salvation Army, City Square,
Adapt Community Solutions, and Stewpot. All other entities in Dallas County that
provide services for adults experiencing homelessness are invited to participate and
present appropriate guests. Every 4th Wednesday of the month at 9:30 am Location:

The Bridge, 1818 Corsicana Street, Dallas, TX 75201, Services Building, Room 108

DADS   –Department on Aging and Disability Services

DAR   –Department of Assistive Rehabilitation

DARS   –Dallas Area Rehabilitation Services

DBT   –Dialectical Behavior Therapy

DD   –Developmental disabilities (mental retardation)

DDC   –Dual diagnostic court; 265th Judicial District Court- defendant's stay at DDC for 60 days or 90 days and receive 6 months of after-care through this court. They need to be on their meds. They will need a CATS evaluation before acceptance. It is run out of Wilmer. The waiting list is not as long.

DDG   –Dual Diagnosis Groups

DMR   –Determination of Mental Retardation

DSM 4   –Diagnostic and Statistical Manual

ECT   –Electroconvulsive therapy (treatment for depression)

ELM   –Electronic leg monitor

F2f   –Face to face

FACT   –Family Adolescent and Child Team

FDU   –Forensic Diversion Unit for clients with an extensive history of frequent arrests and incarcerations; at SNOPS clinic at Metrocare. Intensive case management. Like ACT but clients have an extensive history of incarcerations. Casemanagers work to reduce future incarcerations.

FDU   –Forensic Diversion Unit is a program centralized at Dallas Metrocare SNOPS. Please contact Angela Heggins at Angela.Heggins@metrocareservcies.org or 214-554-5593 to make a referral.

GAD   –Generalized Anxiety Disorder

GAF   –Global Assessment Function (GAF scores below 50 – probably unable to comply with probation; GAF scores below 30 – ineligible for ATLAS)

GCDF —Global Career Development Facilitator. CCE promotes country-specific certification

as a valid index of quality. The countries listed at left have established GCDF

certification programs - each with customized knowledge to assure competence in

that particular country.

ICM —Intensive Case Management; the defendant must be on deferred to be eligible for

this. A "CATS evaluation" and "ICM at Metrocare" are basically the same thing

(except the prosecutor gets the information with a CATS eval.)

IIG —Intensive Intervention Group (the outpatient version of ISP)

IDT —Inner Disiplinary Team

IOP —Intensive Outpatient Treatment (Metrocare drug classes are most common)

(see IOP providers below)

IPAT —Electronic Integrated Practice Assessment Tool (IPAT)©. ValueOptions own,

Andrea Auxier, participated in the development of this evaluation tool designed to

help health care providers more accurately determine their integration level. Data

collected will enable providers, researchers and payors to better measure integration

both within and across health care settings.

IPS —Integrated Psychothreapuetic Services, a step up for those continuing to use ; meet

2-3 times per week . Very intense. Twice as much as IOP.

ISF —Intermediate Sanction Facility (This is quicker to get into than SAFPF but less

organized.) 282nd does not like to use this. ISF will only accept those with 4 meds

or less

IST-MR —Incompetent to stand trial, mentally retarded

JDIM —Jail Data Instant Messaging. Real time

identification and linkage for existing SPN
(Service Provider Network) clients presenting in
the jail
JTC Wilmer –Judicial Treatment Center
LCTR –Lifenet Crisis Transitional Residence-- for people
coming out of the hospital. Helpe
with mental health, homelessness, unemployment
and addiction, 9708 Skillman
Street, Dallas, Tx 75243-5150
MAP –Medical Assesssment Program
MET –Motivational Enhancement Therapy
MIMR –Mental Illness/Mental Retardation
MOU –Memorandum of Understanding
MR –Mental retardation, now called developmental
disabilities, will be called intellectual
disability when the new DSM- V comes out
2/10/10
MRI –Magnetic resonance imaging
MRT –Moral Reconation Thearpy – substance abuse
NAMI –National Alliance on Mental Illness
N* –NorthSTAR
NLO –New Life Opportunities (2014) prostitution
initiative
NOS –No other symptoms
OCD –Obsessive compulsive disorder (also Organized
Crime Division)
OCR –Outpatient Competency restoration (no if more
than 3 felonies)
OPC –Order of Protective Custody
OTC –Over the Counter
PATS –Post Acute Transitional Services
Psychotropic drugs –Prescribed medications that affect a person's
behavior and thought processes.
RAISE –Recovery after initial schizophrenic episode
R&R –Reasoning and rehabilitation
RPT –Relapse prevention therapy
SAFERR –Screening and Assessment for Family
Engagement, Retention and Recovery
SABC –Southern Area Behavorial Health Care (67 and I

20); after hours care

SAMHSA —Substance Abuse and Mental Health Services Administration

SBRIT —National Drug Control Policy have implemented Screening, Brief Intervention,

Referral and Treatment programs.

SIP —Serial Inebriate Program

SOP —Supportive Outpatient (substance abuse)

SPN —Service provider network, AKA "Spin", Act, ocr, fdu, ddrtc (in patient at wilmer),

Tcoomi, etc.

SNOP —Special Needs Offender Program (forensic psychiatric division of Metrocare), a

psychiatric clinic that offers outpatient mental health services

T4C —Thinking for a Change (classes)

Talyst —(prounounced Talis) machines in jail, prepacked medicine, 600 order per day,

$285,000 value

TORI —Texas Offender Reentry Initiative, one year long program at the Potter's House

Betty George, TORI program, gave a presentation to BHSC (5/13)outlining what

TORI does, who it serves and how. This is a 12 month faith based program started

by the Potter's House that services anyone who has a criminal background. The

person does not have to be a recent offender but their charges can not be sex

offenses. The program offers hands on assistance from dedicated staff and training

in self sufficiency. An example is they teach clients "you can not be a leader until

you learn how to serve." For understanding of the statement, they allow participants

to go out and be a part of community outreach, community services and mission

trips. They offer various classes such as employment coaching, anger management, parenting classes, drug treatment and if needed, housing. For additional information

on TORI, contact administration at 214-941-1325, ext. 300 or www.medc-tori.org.

Referrals are welcome!

TCOOMMI –Texas Correctional Office on Offenders with Medical or Mental Impairments -

coordinates transitions from prison to community mental health care. There are

three TCOOMMI funded entities in Dallas County: Metrocare, ABC, and LifeNet.

TTC –Transitional Treatment Center

WDDC –Wilmer Dual Diagnosis Court - for defendants who have completed a court ordered

inpatient drug treatment program at Wilmer Dual Diagnosis Treatment Center.

YES –Youth Empowerment Services

YSAB –Youth Services Advisory Board

WRAP –Wellness Recovery Action Plan

NorthSTAR Acronyms & Terminology

340B –A federal drug pricing program

ACO –Accountable Care Organization

ACOT –Adult Clinical Operations Team

ACS –Adapt Community Solutions (Mobile Crisis Provider for NorthSTAR, see MCOT)

ACT –Assertive Community Treatment

AICPA –American Institute of Certified Public Accountants

AOT –Assisted Outpatient Treatment

APAA –Association of Persons Affected by Addiction (an RCO)

APN –Advanced Practice Nurse

APOWW –Apprehension by a Police Officer Without a Warrant

BH –Behavioral Health (includes MH and CD)

BHLT –Behavioral Health Leadership Team

BHO –Behavioral Health Organization (ValueOptions)

BOD –Board of Directors

BPD —Bipolar Disorder
The Bridge —Homeless Assistance Center in Dallas
C&A —Child and Adolescent
CAP —Corrective Action Plan
CBC —Complete Blood Count
CBT —Cognitive Behavioral Therapy
CCART —Collin County Area Regional Transit
CD —Chemical Dependency
CFAC —Consumer and Family Advisory Council
CHIP —Children's Health Insurance Program (aka SCHIP)
CIT —Crisis Intervention Training (40 hour event sponsored by the City of Dallas
Police Dept.)
CMBHS —Clinical Management of Behavioral Health
Services
CMO —Chief Medical Officer
CMP —Comprehensive Metabolic Panel
COC —Continuum Of Care
COMI —Coalition on Mental Illness
CRCG —Consumer Resource Coordination Group
DARS —Texas Department of Assistive and Rehabilitative
Services
DBSA —Depression and Bipolar Support Alliance
DDC —Dual Diagnosis Center
DEA —Drug Enforcement Administration
DHA —Dallas Housing Authority
DOORS —Dallas One-stop Optimized Reentry System
DPS —Department of Public Safety
DSCT —Direct Services Cost Target
DSHS —Texas Department of State Health Services
DSRIP —Delivery System Reform Incentive Payment
EBP —Evidence based Practice
ECHPP —Enhanced Comprehensive HIV Prevention Plan
ED —Executive Director
ER —Emergency Room
FACT —Families Adolescents Children's Team
FMAP —Federal Medical Assistance Percentage for
Medicaid
FPL —Federal Poverty Level

FQHC —Federally Qualified Health Center
FTE —Full-time Employee
GAAP —Generally Accepted Accounting Principles
GASB —Governmental Accounting Standards Board
GOH —Green Oaks Hospital
GR —General Revenue
HCIC —Health Care Innovation Challenge (grant)
HHSC —Health and Human Services Commission
HUD —Housing and Urban Development
ICM —Intensive Case Management
IDD —Intellectual and Developmental Disabilities
IGT —Intergovernmental Transfer
IOP —Intensive Outpatient Treatment
LAR —Legislative Appropriations Request
LBB —Legislative Budget Board
LCDC —Licensed Chemical Dependency Counselor
LCSW —Licensed Clinical Social Worker
LMHA —Local Mental Health Authority
LOC —Level of Care
LOC-A —Level of Care - Authorized (as specified by Service Packages approved by VO
                for a client)
LOC-R —Level of Care – Requested (by the SPN to VO)
LPC —Licensed Professional Counselor
LPHA —Licensed Professional of the Healing Arts (Graduate degrees with specific licenses)
LSAP —Local Service Area Plan
MAC —Medical Advisory Council
MCO —Managed Care Organization
MCOT —Mobile Crisis Outreach Team (In NorthSTAR, ACS is the MCOT, providing phone
                and face-to-face intervention.)
MDD —Major Depressive Disorder
MDHA —Metro Dallas Homeless Alliance
MH —Mental Health
MHA —Mental Health America
MIMR —Mental Illness Mental Retardation (probation officers)
MLR —Medical Loss Ratio

MOE –Maintenance Of Effort
MOU –Memorandum Of Understanding
NAMI –National Alliance on Mental Illness
NARSAD –National Alliance for Research on Schizophrenia and Depression
NIMH –National Institute of Mental Health
NTBHA –North Texas Behavioral Health Authority
NTSPP –North Texas Society of Psychiatric Physicians
OCR –Outpatient Competency Restoration
OIG –Office of Inspector General
OPC –Order of Protective Custody
OSDA –Other Service Delivery Areas
P&Ps –Policies and Procedures
P&T Committee –VO's Pharmacy and Therapeutics Committee
PA –Pre-authorization
PAC –Provider Advisory Council
PAP –Pharmaceutical Assistance Program
PASRR –Pre-Admission Screening and Resident Review
PBM –Pharmacy Benefit Manager
PCG –Public Consulting Group
PCP –Person-Centered Planning (utilized by the SDC program)
PDR –Physician Desk Reference
PE&O –Prevention, Education, and Outreach
PESC –Psychiatric Emergency Service Center (aka 23-Hour Observation)
PIF –Penalty Incentive Funds
PLAG –Psychiatrists Leadership and Advocacy Group [formerly known as NTBHA
              Physician Advisory Panel (PAP)]
PLAN –Planned Living Assistance Network of North Texas, Inc.
PMPM –Per Member Per Month
PSH –Permanent Supportive Housing
QM –Quality Management
QMHP –Qualified Mental Health Professional (Bachelor's degree in specific helping
              field majors)
RCO –Recovery Community Organization

RDM –Resiliency and Disease Management
RFI –Request For Information
RFA –Request For Application
RFP –Request For Proposal
RHP –Regional Healthcare Partnership
ROI –Return On Investment
ROSC –Recovery Oriented System of Care
RR –Recidivism Rate
SA –Substance Abuse
SABH –Southern Area Behavioral Healthcare
SAMHSA –Substance Abuse and Mental Health Services Administration
SCHIP –State Children's Health Insurance Program
SDC –Self-Directed Care
SED –Severe Emotional Disturbances
SFY10, SFY11, SFY12, SFY13, etc. –State Fiscal Years. SFY12 began September 1, 2011 and will
end August 31, 2012.
SGA –Second Generation Atypicals (medication)
SME –Subject Matter Expert
SNF –Skilled Nursing Facility
SNRI –Selective Norepinephrine Reuptake Inhibitor
SOP –Supportive Outpatient Treatment
SP-1, SP-1S, SP-2 SP-3, SP-4 (ACT) –Adult Service Packages associated with LOCs in RDM—the
higher the number, the more intensive the services provided. Similarly, children
have RDM service packages.
SPA –Single Portal Authority
SPMI –Serious and Persistent Mental Illness, alternately, Severe and Persistent
Mental Illness
SPN –Specialty Provider Network
SSRI –Selective Serotonin Reuptake Inhibitor
SUD –Substance Use Disorder
TCADA –Texas Commission on Alcohol and Drug Abuse
TCM –Targeted Case Management (coordination of care with the Collin County Jail)
TCOOMMI –Texas Correctional Office on Offenders with

Medical or Mental Impairments
TDC   –Texas Department of Corrections
TDI   –Texas Department of Insurance
TIMA   –Texas Implementation of Medication Algorithms
TJPC   –Texas Juvenile Probation Commission
TLETS   –Texas Law Enforcement Telecommunications System
TP 55   –Type of Medicaid for medically needy clients whose increased medical bills make
                  them eligible for Medicaid (not currently eligible for NorthSTAR)
TRAG   –Texas Recommended Assessment Guidelines
TRR   –Texas Resilience and Recovery. ACT is a part of TRR
TSH   –Terrell State Hospital
UA   –Uniform Assessment
UC   –Uncompensated Care
UM   –Utilization Management
UPL   –Medicaid Upper Payment Limit funds
UTMB   –University of Texas Medical Branch
UTSW   –University of Texas Southwestern
VA   –Veterans Administration
VO   –ValueOptions (the NorthSTAR BHO)
WBC   –White Blood Cell
WRAP   –Wellness Recovery Action Plan

www.ingramcontent.com/pod-product-compliance
Lightning Source LLC
Chambersburg PA
CBHW051850170526
45168CB00001B/56